Bumper FAMILY Quiz Book

Bumper FAMILY Quiz Book

COSMO BROWN

PaRragon

Bath · New York · Singapore · Hong Kong · Cologne · Delhi
Melbourne · Amsterdam · Johannesburg · Auckland · Shenzhen

First published by Parragon in 2012

Parragon
Queen Street House
4 Queen Street
Bath BA1 1HE, UK
www.parragon.com

Produced and designed by Design Principals
Edited by Cosmo Brown
Cover Design by Talking Design

ISBN 978-1-4454-6171-7
Printed in China

CONTENTS

~~~~~~~~~~

INTRODUCTION

There are over 5000 family-friendly questions in the book, divided into 314 compact quizzes. The mix of questions in each individual quiz covers all ages, from children at primary school to their parents and grandparents.

Questions for younger children are indicated by the symbol ☀, so that you can conveniently go straight to them. Though of course there is nothing to stop young children testing their knowledge on some of the other questions too. You will find all the answers at the back of the book.

The *Bumper Family Quiz Book* is just the thing for holidays, long journeys and other family get-togethers. Entertaining and informative, it will stretch young minds and refresh older ones. And there are plenty of questions to go round – however big the family.

Good luck!

QUIZ 1

1. What is called 'The Old Lady of Threadneedle Street'?

2. In which war was the Battle of Balaclava?

3. Scrooge is a character in which story by Charles Dickens?

4. What is the next prime number after 71?

5. Which bestselling author also wrote as 'Mary Westmacott'?

6. What is England's largest national park?

7. How many hearts does Dr Who have?

8. What colour is carmine?

9. Which grow upwards, stalactites or stalagmites?

10. What blocks the sun's ultra-violet rays?

11. How many legs does an insect have?

12. Which famous riding school is in Vienna?

13. Who did New Zealand beat in the 2011 Rugby World Cup?

14. The island of Zanzibar is part of which country?

15. Which friend of Winnie-the-Pooh has orange and black stripes?

16. How many books are there in the New Testament?

QUIZ 2

① What do 'almost' and 'biopsy' have in common?

② The first-ever TV commercial in the UK was for which product?

③ The island of Malta is situated in which sea?

④ A Turk's Head is a type of what?

⑤ What did the Pope become in 1870?

⑥ Which sense does the kiwi use to hunt for food?

⑦ Who went with Christopher Robin to see the changing of the guard?

⑧ In which ocean is the Gulf Stream?

⑨ What military campaign in World War I gave birth to ANZAC Day?

⑩ Who is the captain of the *Pequod* in *Moby Dick*?

⑪ What is the square root of 16?

⑫ Which football club's ground is Hillsborough?

⑬ A gallivat is a type of what?

⑭ Which Brontë sister wrote the novel *Jane Eyre*?

⑮ What kind of animal is the Australian dingo?

⑯ How many petals are there on a wild orchid?

QUIZ 3

1. Into which sea does the River Jordan flow?

2. Which 1960s England cricket all-rounder died in 2011?

3. Who is the 'Enlightened One'?

4. Which member of the Royal Family is the Earl of Wessex? ☼

5. What was the world's first skyscraper?

6. Which of the Seven Wonders of the World was at Olympia?

7. Who in 1848 wrote *The Communist Manifesto*?

8. Painted Lady, Brimstone and Red Admiral are all types of what? ☼

9. Who succeeded Bobby Robson as England's football manager?

10. Which Greek artist painted the *View of Toledo*?

11. Where in California is Disneyland?

12. Conkers come from which tree? ☼

13. What is a natterjack?

14. Which English monarch gave his name to a potato?

15. Alphabetically, what is the first creature in the dictionary?

16. Who is Farmer Hoggett's prize pig? ☼

QUIZ 4

① What are the robots in *Blade Runner* called?

② What do bees live in?

③ Who made famous the phrase 'The Iron Curtain'?

④ Which garden insect belongs to the locust family?

⑤ Who was the 2010 *X Factor* champion?

⑥ Which prehistoric monument is located on Salisbury Plain?

⑦ What did Anton Drexler found in 1919?

⑧ Which group of islands includes St Martin's and Tresco?

⑨ Who wrote *The Forsyte Saga*?

⑩ What sport takes place at Silverstone?

⑪ Who plays Hawkeye Pierce in the film version of *M.A.S.H*?

⑫ Which number is the current French Republic?

⑬ By what two other names has St Petersburg been known?

⑭ Who is the patron saint of Wales?

⑮ At sea, how long is a dogwatch?

⑯ Which is the sixth of the Ten Commandments?

QUIZ 5

① 'Oranges and lemons, say the bells of . . .' ?

② Coal is composed of what element?

③ What French town gave the bayonet its name?

④ They may be complex, vulgar or mixed – what are they?

⑤ What is a baby swan called?

⑥ Which 20th-century English poet's middle name is Chawner?

⑦ Elijah Wood plays which hobbit in *Lord of the Rings*?

⑧ Into which bay does the US Susquehanna river flow?

⑨ What word can follow pencil, suit or nut?

⑩ Which royal dynasty followed the Tudors?

⑪ What colour is the 'black box' on an aircraft?

⑫ What do the initials stand for in the year AD 2012?

⑬ Who wrote the *Swallows and Amazons* books?

⑭ What is the collective name for toads?

⑮ In snooker, which colour ball is worth four points?

⑯ Which Salman Rushdie novel won the 1981 Booker Prize?

QUIZ 6

① In Beatrix Potter's *Tale of Mr Tod*, what is Mr Tod?

② Where in the human body is the labyrinth?

③ In Ireland, what is the prime minister called?

④ What word both means halo and cloud?

⑤ In what kind of place was Oliver Twist born?

⑥ Who coined the phrase 'What's new, pussycat?'?

⑦ What is UNESCO short for?

⑧ Whose motto is 'Nation Shall Speak Peace Unto Nation'?

⑨ Where is home to Manchester United football club?

⑩ Which poet wrote *The Waste Land*?

⑪ Whose catchphrase is: 'What am I like!'?

⑫ In which country are the Southern Alps?

⑬ How many blackbirds were baked in the pie?

⑭ In which year did the Russian Revolution begin?

⑮ What is the principal ingredient in the Indian dish dahl?

⑯ Which rap star remarried his ex-wife Kimberley in 2006?

QUIZ 7

① What is the war cry of The Daleks?

② With which novel did Aravind Adiga win the 2008 Booker Prize?

③ What part of an animal's body is its carapace?

④ What is the highest mountain in Africa?

⑤ How old was Kate Middleton when she married: 25, 27 or 29?

⑥ When was the Battle of Agincourt: 1415, 1515 or 1615?

⑦ In which sport is 'nose riding' a manoeuvre?

⑧ Which literary family lived at Haworth in Yorkshire?

⑨ What was Pinocchio originally made of?

⑩ What is the capital of Vietnam?

⑪ What Home Guard platoon does Captain Mainwaring command?

⑫ Who did Edward Heath succeed as Conservative Party leader?

⑬ What breed of owl is Harry Potter's Hedwig?

⑭ Where do mice that are proverbially poor live?

⑮ What is the largest organ in the body?

⑯ In which year were the poll tax riots in London?

QUIZ 8

① Which bear raises money for Children in Need? ·ϙ·

② What do the initials stand for in H G Wells?

③ Who wrote the music for the 2008 film *Changeling*?

④ What item of headgear first appeared in London in 1797?

⑤ Who is the lion in *The Lion, the Witch and the Wardrobe*? ·ϙ·

⑥ In which country is the Dolomites mountain range?

⑦ What was George VI before he came to the throne?

⑧ At what time of the year do nails grow fastest?

⑨ Whose motto was 'All for one, one for all'?

⑩ What is the name of Artemis Fowl's bodyguard? ·ϙ·

⑪ Who is the host of *Knowing Me, Knowing You*?

⑫ Where is Charles Darwin buried?

⑬ Whipped cream flavoured with vanilla is called what?

⑭ What instrument does the leader of an orchestra play? ·ϙ·

⑮ What is Gordon Brown's first name?

⑯ Which flag is flown when a ship is about to sail?

QUIZ 9

① Who played the title role in the film *Hans Christian Andersen*?

② What is the centre of an atom called?

③ What is the name of Shrek's wife?

④ Who is the patron saint of Venice?

⑤ What are Norway lobsters called when cooked?

⑥ Which *Room* is a final exit?

⑦ What is a baby kangaroo called?

⑧ Who was prime minister during Edward VIII's abdication?

⑨ What are inflamed if you suffer from nephritis?

⑩ In Greek mythology, which trio represented beauty?

⑪ Which ground is known as the 'Home of Cricket'?

⑫ How many people rule in a triumvirate?

⑬ What is Australia's most northern capital city?

⑭ Which US vice-president couldn't spell 'potato'?

⑮ Cocker, Springer and King Charles are breeds of which dog?

⑯ Name the third part of the *Lord of the Rings* trilogy.

QUIZ 10

① Who is the creator of Discworld?

② What is the name of Roo's mother in *Winnie-the-Pooh*?

③ Which hemisphere of the brain controls the left half of the body?

④ What rope is used for tying up a ship?

⑤ Radio Direction Finding became better known as what?

⑥ In which British city is Holyrood Palace?

⑦ Who painted the ceiling of the Sistine Chapel?

⑧ What name is given to a yacht with two hulls?

⑨ Who was the Egyptian sun god?

⑩ Indiana Jones is a professor of what subject?

⑪ In which country is Mt Ararat?

⑫ How was Henry John Temple better known?

⑬ In which Charles Dickens novel is Mrs Pardiggle a character?

⑭ How many squares are there on a chess board?

⑮ What colour is a ship's quarantine flag?

⑯ Which barrel is larger, a butt or a hogshead?

QUIZ 11

① What was the first bird released from Noah's Ark?

② What expression did style guru Peter York coin in 1975?

③ Where did the 2008 Olympic Games take place?

④ Who composed music for both the 1937 and 1953 Coronations?

⑤ Where is the thyroid gland located?

⑥ What did British Honduras become?

⑦ In tennis, what term is used when the score is 40-40?

⑧ How was Manfred von Richthofen better known?

⑨ Which art movement did Pablo Picasso and Georges Braque begin?

⑨ When was the first London Marathon: 1975, 1981, 1987?

⑩ In the verse, which bells said: 'You owe me five farthings'?

⑪ What colour are motorways on British road maps?

⑬ Which is greater, 2/3rd or 7/10th?

⑭ Logan International Airport serves which US city?

⑮ Which Italian city is famous for its Leaning Tower?

⑯ Whose feline companion at the White House was called Socks?

QUIZ 12

① Where did Chris Evans and Billie Piper get married in 2001?

② What do the letters stand for in the film *E.T.*? ☼

③ Which composer died first, Franz Schubert or Robert Schumann?

④ What shocking world event took place on 6 August 1945?

⑤ In which country is the world's highest railway station?

⑥ How much of the world is covered by water: 30%, 50% or 70%? ☼

⑦ What was a 'first' for England v Spain at Wembley in 1955?

⑧ Which sharp-tongued poet was known as the 'Wasp of Twickenham'?

⑨ In which Western is Gregory Peck a man of the sea?

⑩ What was the name of King Arthur's court? ☼

⑪ What do the stripes on the US flag represent?

⑫ In 1988 singer Sonny Bono became mayor of which city?

⑬ With which family does Paddington Bear live? ☼

⑭ What name is given to a widespread epidemic?

⑮ With what art form do you associate Henri Cartier-Bresson?

⑯ Who wrote the poem 'The Female of the Species'?

QUIZ 13

① What is someone who makes casks called?

② Jan Christian Smuts is a former prime minister of which country?

③ In which battle was General George Custer killed?

④ What is the name of the river that flows through Paris?

⑤ Acid turns litmus paper which colour?

⑥ Which English football team is known as the 'Seasiders'?

⑦ Before becoming a writer Arthur Conan Doyle qualified as a what?

⑧ What can be broad, green or baked?

⑨ Which actor was accidentally shot dead while filming in 1993?

⑩ What does DEFRA stand for?

⑪ Who is in charge of Gerry, Jack and Brian in *New Tricks*?

⑫ In the film *Mary Poppins*, Mr Banks works in a what?

⑬ What is a samovar?

⑭ Which country's flag is a white star against a blue background?

⑮ Who was the first professional to captain England at cricket?

⑯ Who was the first man on the Moon?

QUIZ 14

① Complete the saying: 'The best laid plans of . . .'

② What is a female rabbit called?

③ How many letters are there in the modern German alphabet?

④ What is a bayou?

⑤ In which country did the Impressionist art movement begin?

⑥ Slip, Reef and Granny are all types of what?

⑦ The redpoll is a member of which family of British birds?

⑧ Who was the second Stuart monarch?

⑨ In the TV series, who does Bergerac work for?

⑩ What is the name of the *Kung Fu Panda*?

⑪ Which two nations share the island of Santo Domingo?

⑫ When was the siege of the Alamo: 1836, 1846, 1856?

⑬ What did *The Collector* collect in John Fowles' novel?

⑭ Which dog has black or brown spots?

⑮ What was invented first, the telephone or the light bulb?

⑯ What are leptons and quarks?

QUIZ 15

① What is the capital of Ghana?

② Sugarloaf Mountain overlooks which South American city?

③ Which planet is known as the 'Red Planet'?

④ What is Northern Ireland's parliament building?

⑤ To which playwright was Marilyn Monroe married?

⑥ What is the irregular Pacific Ocean current that affects weather?

⑦ Who do Sheriff Woody Pride and Buzz Lightyear belong to?

⑧ Which European capital gets its hot water from hot springs?

⑨ What geological period did the Jurassic follow?

⑩ Who wrote the 19th-century classic *Daniel Deronda*?

⑪ What is a fox's home called?

⑫ Which Scottish football side is nicknamed 'The Honest Men'?

⑬ Who was the first and third wife of actor Don Johnson?

⑭ When did Pablo Picasso die: 1953, 1963 or 1973?

⑮ Which sea borders the east coast of Great Britain?

⑯ What did Ignatius Loyola found in 1534?

QUIZ 16

1. What is a dhoti?

2. Who is the red engine in *Thomas the Tank Engine*? 💡

3. What colour was the lamp outside British police stations?

4. Where in London was the 18th-century artist William Blake born?

5. What is a millibar?

6. Hollywood is a part of which American city? 💡

7. Who kept an eye on everyone in George Orwell's *1984*?

8. The Victoria Falls are on which African river?

9. Who attempted to steal the English Crown Jewels in 1671?

10. Irons, woods and putters are all types of what? 💡

11. Who, despite living to 120, never reached the Land of Israel?

12. What historical event is the background to *A Tale of Two Cities*?

13. Which West Indian cricketer was knighted in 1964?

14. What is the largest county in England? 💡

15. Which American university is older, Harvard or Yale?

16. In which country did the poet Lord Byron die?

QUIZ 17

1. Which is the commonest element in the universe?

2. What is the hottest planet in the solar system?

3. In the nursery rhyme, which bridge is falling down?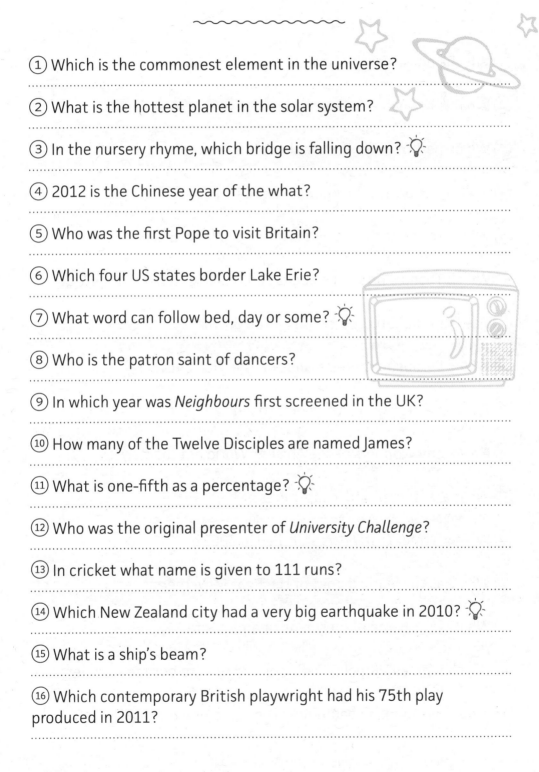

4. 2012 is the Chinese year of the what?

5. Who was the first Pope to visit Britain?

6. Which four US states border Lake Erie?

7. What word can follow bed, day or some?

8. Who is the patron saint of dancers?

9. In which year was *Neighbours* first screened in the UK?

10. How many of the Twelve Disciples are named James?

11. What is one-fifth as a percentage?

12. Who was the original presenter of *University Challenge*?

13. In cricket what name is given to 111 runs?

14. Which New Zealand city had a very big earthquake in 2010?

15. What is a ship's beam?

16. Which contemporary British playwright had his 75th play produced in 2011?

QUIZ 18

① Which English football league club is the most southerly?

② What is the name of Bob the Builder's cat? ☿

③ Which part of Peter Pan was kept in a drawer?

④ In which sport would you wear an obi?

⑤ What are the top universities in the USA known as?

⑥ Which Thames bridge can be raised to allow ships through? ☿

⑦ The Periodic Table is a classification of what?

⑧ Which European capital stands on the Vitava River?

⑨ What is a large group of islands called?

⑩ How many Wonders of the Ancient World are there? ☿

⑪ What are 'spring' and 'neap' types of?

⑫ Which former *EastEnders* star died in 2007?

⑬ Who was the leading poet of the Beat Movement?

⑭ What is the name of President Obama's wife? ☿

⑮ Which famous UK political father and son are both teetotallers?

⑯ Who is Madonna's chauffeur in the video of her song 'Music'?

QUIZ 19

① Complete the proverb: 'Knowledge is . . .'

② What was the capital of Australia before Canberra?

③ Which Beatrix Potter character is a frog? 💡

④ Who was the first Holy Roman Emperor?

⑤ What was the title of the fourth *Harry Potter* film?

⑥ How many times has Paris hosted the Olympic Games?

⑦ Who is the patron saint of England? 💡

⑧ What was Terry Wogan before he became a broadcaster?

⑨ What is the government's emergency committee called?

⑩ In computer speak, what does ALGOL stand for?

⑪ What is the name for a badger's home? 💡

⑫ Which country produced the first two Miss World winners?

⑬ What is an angle of less than 90° called?

⑭ Who was known as the 'Waltz King'?

⑮ How many legs does a spider have? 💡

⑯ Which English football club did Sheikh Mansour bin Zayed Al Nahyan buy in 2008?

QUIZ 20

① What does Mrs Tabitha Twitchit do for a living?

② What is Broadway's theatre district known as?

③ In which sector of Cyprus is Kyrenia, Greek or Turkish?

④ Tweedledum and Tweedledee appear in which famous book?

⑤ What is the first name of the French designer Chanel?

⑥ Which number symphony is Schubert's 'Great C Major'?

⑦ What went up in 1961 and came down in 1989?

⑧ A wooden horse was used in the siege of which city?

⑨ What protects a computer from illegal access?

⑩ Which pop singer's real name is Marvin Lee Aday?

⑪ What is an ulster?

⑫ Who invented the safety lamp for miners?

⑬ Which British prime minister did Gordon Brown come after?

⑭ Sleipnir was the eight-legged horse of which Norse god?

⑮ Which ex-England cricketer was offered the throne of Albania?

⑯ Which has the longer gestation period, a buffalo or polar bear?

QUIZ 21

① What is the Russian parliament called?

② What part of a ship is its prow?

③ Who was president of France from 1974 to 1981?

④ What is the principal constituent of glass?

⑤ Which singer started life as Annie Mae Bullock?

⑥ In which country was Justin Bieber born?

⑦ What was used in the 1973 FA Cup final for the one and only time?

⑧ Where are the highest tides in the world recorded?

⑨ Who was the first Briton to carry out a space walk?

⑩ Whose address is No 10 Downing Street?

⑪ When did cricket last feature as an Olympic sport?

⑫ And which country did 'Great Britain' beat in the final?

⑬ How many piano concertos did Rachmaninov compose?

⑭ Who is the presenter of the Muppet's TV show?

⑮ Which black American leader was assassinated in 1965?

⑯ Which country invaded Switzerland in 1798?

QUIZ 22

① What is another name for ping-pong?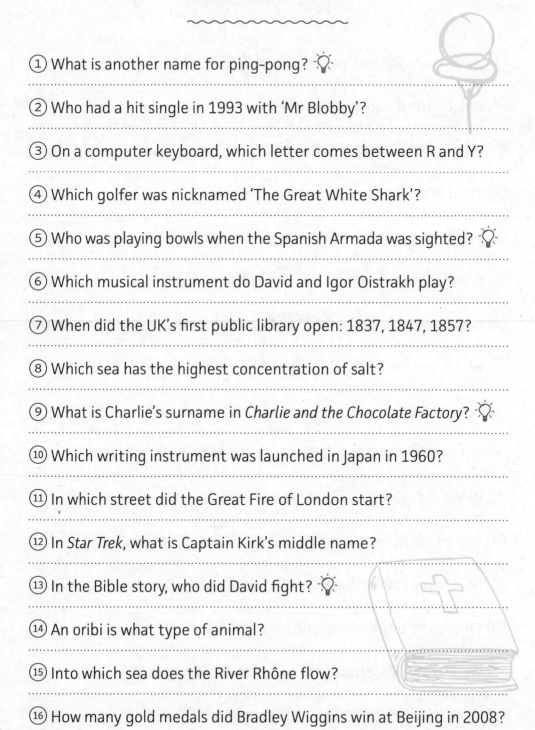

② Who had a hit single in 1993 with 'Mr Blobby'?

③ On a computer keyboard, which letter comes between R and Y?

④ Which golfer was nicknamed 'The Great White Shark'?

⑤ Who was playing bowls when the Spanish Armada was sighted?

⑥ Which musical instrument do David and Igor Oistrakh play?

⑦ When did the UK's first public library open: 1837, 1847, 1857?

⑧ Which sea has the highest concentration of salt?

⑨ What is Charlie's surname in *Charlie and the Chocolate Factory*?

⑩ Which writing instrument was launched in Japan in 1960?

⑪ In which street did the Great Fire of London start?

⑫ In *Star Trek*, what is Captain Kirk's middle name?

⑬ In the Bible story, who did David fight?

⑭ An oribi is what type of animal?

⑮ Into which sea does the River Rhône flow?

⑯ How many gold medals did Bradley Wiggins win at Beijing in 2008?

QUIZ 23

① Which bird walks underwater?

② What is the highest mountain in the UK?

③ Which royal house preceded the Tudors?

④ What is the laryngeal prominence in the neck popularly called?

⑤ How many Spice Girls were there originally?

⑥ Who falls in love with a robot named EVE?

⑦ What does the name Joyce mean?

⑧ Which animal was domesticated first, cat or dog?

⑨ What is the world's smallest ocean?

⑩ In the song, what was given on the 'Sixth Day of Christmas'?

⑪ DZ on a car number plate indicates which country of origin?

⑫ What does ANZAC stand for?

⑬ Which actor starred in the film *School of Rock*?

⑭ What is the most expensive location in *Monopoly*?

⑮ Which American state is bordered by Oregon and Idaho?

⑯ What is a tonsorial artist?

QUIZ 24

① The Owl and the Pusssy-Cat went to sea in a what?

② Which English rugby club is the 'Saints'?

③ Who composed the opera *The Trojans*?

④ What is the world's largest sea?

⑤ What is the name of Postman Pat's black and white cat?

⑥ Which Tongan monarch attended Elizabeth II's coronation in 1953?

⑦ What is the anatomical name for the chest?

⑧ Which ballet dancer defected from Russia in 1961?

⑨ How many in a 'baker's dozen'?

⑩ What does the phrase *in extremis* mean?

⑪ Who was the first US president to visit China?

⑫ What word can come before man, polish and window?

⑬ Which precious stone is hidden in the letters THATMESY?

⑭ What is the plural of mongoose?

⑮ Which English comedian's real name was William White?

⑯ What is the maximum break in a game of snooker?

QUIZ 25

① When Jack and Jill went up the hill, what did Jack break? 💡

② Name the detective agency in the TV series *Moonlighting*.

③ Which nut is the name of a South American country?

④ In which town do Wallace and Gromit reside?

⑤ What separates the North and South Islands of New Zealand?

⑥ What building is the home of Big Ben? 💡

⑦ Which US vice-president was forced to resign in 1973?

⑧ Who wrote the poem 'The Charge of the Light Brigade'?

⑨ And in which battle did the 'charge' take place?

⑩ What can be a fruit or an item on a calendar? 💡

⑪ Paddy Ashdown served in which branch of the military?

⑫ What is the floral emblem of South Africa?

⑬ What are Argentinean cowboys called?

⑭ What is used to propel the ball in the game pelote?

⑮ What are trees that have leaves all year round called? 💡

⑯ In which city was Martin Luther King shot?

QUIZ 26

① Who was the 2010 BBC Sports Personality of the Year?

② What type of letter are A, E, I, O, U?

③ Which animal's droppings are called spraint?

④ Where is the National Library of Wales located?

⑤ The 'Angel of the North' is near which town?

⑥ What breed of dog is used to pull a sledge?

⑦ Which Civil War general became 18th president of the USA?

⑧ The Kalahari Desert spans which two African countries?

⑨ What supplies central Australia with water?

⑩ Who was the chivalrous Muslim leader who fought the Crusaders?

⑪ Koalas feed on the leaves of which tree?

⑫ Which ecclesiastical group made the classical charts in 2008?

⑬ What did Texas Instruments launch in 1971?

⑭ Which leading conductor of classical music is Indian?

⑮ What are the canal boatmen in Venice called?

⑯ Is the crocodile species 2 million, 20 million or 200 million years old?

QUIZ 27

① What is the Roman numeral for 489?

② Which liner sank on its very first voyage in 1912?

③ What is the smallest particle of a chemical element called?

④ Who composed the music for the film *A Fistful of Dollars*?

⑤ Which England bowler took a Test hat-trick in 2011?

⑥ How many children are in the care of Nanny McPhee?

⑦ When was the Shah of Iran overthrown: 1975, 1977, 1979?

⑧ Where in the USA is the National Gallery of Art?

⑨ Which architect designed the original St Pancras station?

⑩ Which English king came first, Charles II or James II?

⑪ The word feline refers to which type of animal?

⑫ Which mountain range divides France and Spain?

⑬ What was Harold Wilson's title when he became a peer?

⑭ Which motor race lasts 24 hours?

⑮ What board game has bishops, knights and castles?

⑯ How many Oscars did the *Lord of the Rings* trilogy win?

QUIZ 28

① How many sides has a cube?

② In *Thomas the Tank Engine*, what colour is Henry?

③ Who was the US Republican vice-presidential candidate in 2008?

④ Ernest Hemingway's *Death in the Afternoon* is about what?

⑤ Flotta is an island in which Scottish group?

⑥ What were the ancient rulers of Egypt called?

⑦ Which mountain overlooks Cape Town?

⑧ What in 1917 stated Britain's policy regarding a Jewish homeland?

⑨ Which Hun died on the night of his marriage in 453 AD?

⑩ Who was the Roman god of the sea?

⑪ What was the world's first Garden City?

⑫ What alcoholic drink is made from honey?

⑬ In which year did Hillary and Tenzing conquer Everest?

⑭ What is a leviathan?

⑮ What word can follow air, hand or paper?

⑯ How did motor racing driver Graham Hill die?

QUIZ 29

① In 'Oranges and Lemons', what do the bells of Shoreditch say?

② Which counting device uses wires and beads?

③ What is Andy Murray's tennis-playing brother's name?

④ Who said: 'A week is a long time in politics'?

⑤ How many miles long is the Channel Tunnel: 21, 31 or 41?

⑥ In which country is The Great Dividing Range?

⑦ Who in the Bible is the only female judge of Israel?

⑧ Where were all roads said to lead to?

⑨ In *The Simpsons*, what is Chief Wiggum's favourite snack?

⑩ Who wrote the play *Endgame*?

⑪ In which London park is there a statue of Peter Pan?

⑫ Who won the 2010 Six Nations rugby championship?

⑬ In which city will you find the Eiffel Tower?

⑭ Who did Britain go to war with in 1839?

⑮ How many railway stations are there in *Monopoly*?

⑯ In Norse mythology, what is the home of the gods?

QUIZ 30

① What is the body's largest artery?

② In Roald Dahl's story, what is Matilda's surname? 🔅

③ What has forests but no trees, rivers but no water?

④ Which one of a famous English jazz duo died in 2010?

⑤ 'Summertime' is an aria from which opera?

⑥ What does CD stand for? 🔅

⑦ Where are a cricket's ears located?

⑧ What is a behemoth?

⑨ Which poem begins: 'If I should die, think only this of me'?

⑩ Where was the Pied Piper from? 🔅

⑪ Who became Israel's first female prime minister in 1969?

⑫ A sentence that contains every letter of the alphabet is a what?

⑬ What do you play faro with?

⑭ How many years are there in a millennium? 🔅

⑮ What kind of gem is the 'Star of India'?

⑯ Which English mathematician won the Nobel Prize in Literature?

QUIZ 31

① What is Margaret Thatcher's middle name?

② Whose tomb at Halicarnassus was a Wonder of the Ancient World?

③ Name the other half: Gilbert and . . .

④ Anne Elliot is the central character in which Jane Austen novel?

⑤ What were the Boyoma Falls in Congo formerly known as?

⑥ Who was England's first football manager?

⑦ Which *Strictly Come Dancing* winner became a judge?

⑧ What was the Soviet Union's state news agency called?

⑨ Which Pope died in 1963 at the age of 81?

⑩ What failed to recreate a big bang in 2008?

⑪ Who picked a peck of pickled peppers?

⑫ What is an animal that visually resembles a plant called?

⑬ Who was presented to Julius Caesar rolled up in a carpet?

⑭ Who became the female face of Burberry in 2009?

⑮ What sport is played at Twickenham?

⑯ What is the difference between a knighthood and a baronetcy?

QUIZ 32

1. What does Las Vegas mean in English?

2. What are the bees that collect pollen called? ☀

3. Which English football team is nicknamed 'The Toffees'?

4. In which county is the Aldeburgh Music Festival staged?

5. And who founded the festival?

6. Whose sisters are Flopsy, Mopsy and Cottontail? ☀

7. GBZ on a car number plate indicates which country of origin?

8. What was Gregory Peck's real first name?

9. Complete the saying: 'To err is human, to forgive . . .'

10. In which US state is the ski resort of Aspen?

11. What can be black, blue or straw? ☀

12. Which seminal space movie was premiered in 1968?

13. What does the abbreviation E&OE stand for?

14. Which Brit won the Girls' Singles title at Wimbledon in 2008?

15. How many horns does a rhinoceros have? ☀

16. What was Thailand's former name?

QUIZ 33

① In which pantomime is Buttons a character? 💡

② A comma with a full point above it is a what?

③ Which US president offered the American people a New Deal?

④ What did France officially adopt in 1799?

⑤ What was the name of King Arthur's sword? 💡

⑥ On which river is Philadelphia?

⑦ Which British newspaper was nicknamed 'The Thunderer'?

⑧ Which country's flag is a solid red circle on a white background?

⑨ When did Christopher Columbus discover America: 1292, 1392, 1492? 💡

⑩ Siddhartha Gautama is better known as who?

⑪ In opera, what is a performer who doesn't sing called?

⑫ What is a French high school?

⑬ Which England cricketer is known as 'KP'? 💡

⑭ Who wrote the novel *The Manchurian Candidate*?

⑮ Which order of knights was founded in 1348?

⑯ What is the capital of Nepal?

QUIZ 34

① Which US sportsman's nickname was 'The Juice'?

② Who is Donald Duck's girlfriend?

③ Which English royal dynasty means 'sprig of broom'?

④ In which UK city is the Royal Mile?

⑤ Kos and Symi are in which group of Greek islands?

⑥ What is a baby meerkat called?

⑦ How was the Spanish republican Dolores Ibárruri better known?

⑧ What can be electric or jellied?

⑨ Who in 1866 invented dynamite?

⑩ Which was the first British motorway?

⑪ How old was Tatum O'Neal when she won an Oscar for *Paper Moon*?

⑫ Who was Yogi Bear's best friend?

⑬ Which word can follow hand, win and whole?

⑭ Who is the patron saint of Ireland?

⑮ What in the high street is BHS?

⑯ Which US state's official song is 'Yankee Doodle'?

QUIZ 35

① What special day is 31st October?

② Who signalled: 'England expects that every man will do his duty'?

③ On which musical instrument would you play a 'pataflafla'?

④ Which 'Tropic' is south of the Equator?

⑤ Who is captain of the *Black Pearl*?

⑥ Which singing duo called their child Chastity?

⑦ When was the MOT test for vehicles introduced in the UK?

⑧ Who was the first Russian ruler to be crowned tsar?

⑨ What type of animal is Ratty in *The Wind in the Willows*?

⑩ Which TV show gave birth to *The Simpsons*?

⑪ What is the official language of the Ivory Coast?

⑫ Who succeeded his mother as prime minister of India?

⑬ In which 60s film is the line: 'They call me *Mister* Tibbs!'?

⑭ What is a musical ensemble of nine players called?

⑮ Which country has over 450 different cheeses?

⑯ What is Victoria Beckham's maiden name?

QUIZ 36

① Who are Donald Duck's three nephews? 💡

② Which US preacher famously had a dream about equal rights?

③ French writer Victor Hugo lived in exile on which Channel Island?

④ Which gas constitutes 78% of atmospheric air?

⑤ What is a female sheep called? 💡

⑥ Which US president launched 'The Great Society'?

⑦ A Fata Morgana is a type of what?

⑧ Whose funeral in 1963 brought Paris to a standstill?

⑨ What are the arms on a windmill called? 💡

⑩ When was the Bolshoi Ballet founded: 1676, 1776, 1876?

⑪ Which league football club's mascot is Roary the Tiger?

⑫ What is the state capital of Alaska?

⑬ Who, in 1954, was the first BBC Sports Personality of the Year?

⑭ What is sound too low for human hearing called?

⑮ Who is Aladdin's brother? 💡

⑯ Who composed 'The Stars and Stripes Forever'?

QUIZ 37

① Which Teletubby is purple?

② Good King Wenceslas looked out on the feast of . . . ? ☼

③ What are the muscles between the ribs called?

④ 'The Impossible Dream' is a song from which musical?

⑤ What is alloyed with steel to make it stainless?

⑥ Whose best friend is Captain Archibald Haddock? ☼

⑦ 'Breeks' is the Scottish name for what?

⑧ How is Haydn's Symphony No 101 better known?

⑨ Whose legislative body is the Tynwald?

⑩ What did Guy Fawkes try to blow up in 1605? ☼

⑪ Who was queen of England in all but name in 1553?

⑫ What is Japan's highest peak?

⑬ On which Caribbean island was the poet Derek Walcott born?

⑭ How do the French say 'Good Morning'? ☼

⑮ Who was the first batsman to score a triple-century at Lord's?

⑯ Which two acting superstars does Michael Jackson thank on the sleeve notes of *Bad*?

QUIZ 38

① Which VIP was born on 21 April 1926?

② What is the name of the dog in *Peter Pan*?

③ How many of the singing Walker Brothers were fraternally linked?

④ What term describes a victory that is no victory at all?

⑤ Who was Jimmy Carter's vice-president?

⑥ What are Hazel, Fiver and Bigwig in *Watership Down*?

⑦ Which Russian tsar was assassinated in 1881?

⑧ What is England's most southerly mainland point?

⑨ 'I coulda been a contender' is a line from which film?

⑩ How many King Williams have sat on the English throne?

⑪ Where does a prawn keep its heart?

⑫ What is Hay-on-Wye most famous for?

⑬ How were the Spice Girls recruited in 1994?

⑭ Which political quartet made up the 'Gang of Four'?

⑮ Who is the youngest of *The Simpsons* children?

⑯ A palomino is a type of what?

QUIZ 39

① Which Scottish islands are further north, Orkneys or Shetlands?

② What interrupted Little Miss Muffet's meal?

③ What is the medical term for the collarbone?

④ What do the crime-busting initials FBI stand for?

⑤ At which sporting event is 'Abide With Me' traditionally sung?

⑥ How many Billy Goats Gruff were there?

⑦ What is the most destructive thing about the Bond villain Oddjob?

⑧ Whose joint autobiography was entitled *Facing the Music*?

⑨ RP on a car number plate indicates which country of origin?

⑩ What was the name of Lord Nelson's most famous ship?

⑪ Which big cat is the largest to be found in the Americas?

⑫ What 1980s dolls were children encouraged to 'adopt'?

⑬ What is the Beastie Boys hometown?

⑭ What is JFK spelled out?

⑮ What do Scotsmen traditionally wear instead of trousers?

⑯ Who wrote *Don Quixote*?

QUIZ 40

① In which country was the world's first motorway built?

② What kind of ship did Noah build?

③ Who was the creator of *Only Fools and Horses* who died in 2011?

④ What is the medical term for inflammation of a nerve?

⑤ Who founded Virgin Records?

⑥ What is the name of the snake in *The Jungle Book*?

⑦ Which Japanese ruler died in 1989?

⑧ What, in the Verdi opera, does *Il Trovatore* mean?

⑨ How many times did Timothy Dalton play James Bond?

⑩ Which wall is more than 5,000 miles long?

⑪ What is the birthstone for November?

⑫ What is the mythological character Paul Bunyan by trade?

⑬ Which poem begins: 'A thing of beauty is a joy forever'?

⑭ Anabolic steroids are used to build or repair what?

⑮ Which range of hills separates Yorkshire and Lancashire?

⑯ Someone born on 29th February will have how many birthdays by the age of 72?

QUIZ 41

① Who did Boris Yeltsin appoint as Russian prime minister in 1999?

② Who is Tintin's dog?

③ What is the square root of one million?

④ How was Sœur Sourire better known?

⑤ The Ashanti tribe is native to which African country?

⑥ Who stole the Queen of Hearts' tarts?

⑦ What colour are hotels in *Monopoly*?

⑧ Who wrote the musical *Blitz*?

⑨ Which scale measures levels of alkalinity and acidity?

⑩ Who was the UK's first female television newsreader?

⑪ What does VIP mean?

⑫ Which book ends: 'After all, tomorrow is another day.'?

⑬ Who was lead vocalist for Led Zeppelin?

⑭ Name the acting brothers, Philip and Robert . . .

⑮ The month of June is named after which Roman goddess?

⑯ What bird is known as a 'laughing jackass'?

QUIZ 42

① Who is Peter Pan's enemy?

② What is the world's largest active volcano?

③ Name the film-making Coen Brothers.

④ In the USA, how many senators are elected for each state?

⑤ Where do Winnie-the-Pooh and his friends live?

⑥ Carl XVI Gustaf is king of which country?

⑦ What is a hen less than a year old called?

⑧ How many animals are there in the Chinese calendar?

⑨ 'Hail to thee, blithe spirit' is the first line of which poem?

⑩ What is the New Zealand rugby team called?

⑪ Who played Rudolph Valentino in the 1977 film *Valentino*?

⑫ What was the speed limit in the UK increased to in 1896?

⑬ Who was knighted first, Elton John or Paul McCartney?

⑭ Which set of fins on a fish enable it to manoeuvre?

⑮ What is President Obama's first name?

⑯ Who became president of Uganda in 1971?

QUIZ 43

① What is the last letter of the bottom row on a computer keyboard?

② What is Wee Willie Winkle wearing when he runs through the town? 💡

③ How is the disease pertussis more commonly known?

④ What commemorative day is 10th January on the Falkland Islands?

⑤ In heraldry, what colour is gules?

⑥ Who is Tom Kitten's mother? 💡

⑦ What song featured in the film *Butch Cassidy and the Sundance Kid*?

⑧ Who in 2002 was appointed Archbishop of Canterbury?

⑨ In Greek mythology, who are the twin sons of Zeus?

⑩ What do you traditionally eat on Shrove Tuesday? 💡

⑪ Queen Anne was the daughter of which English king?

⑫ What is the wife of a marquess?

⑬ In which city is the Topkapi Palace?

⑭ What was the name of John Lennon's cat?

⑮ What did England's cricketers retain in 2010? 💡

⑯ Who kidnapped the US heiress Patricia Hearst in 1974?

QUIZ 44

① What animals guard Nelson's Column in Trafalgar Square?

② Who plays 'Me' in the film *Me and Orson Welles*?

③ What is 0.65 as a fraction?

④ Who is fatter, Laurel or Hardy?

⑤ King and Rockhopper are types of which bird?

⑥ How many spots are there on a standard dice?

⑦ In which event did Sally Gunnell win gold at the 1992 Olymics?

⑧ Louise Brown, born in 1978, was the world's first what?

⑨ What was Johnny Mathis' 1976 Christmas hit?

⑩ Which shade of green did outlaw Robin Hood wear?

⑪ How many passengers would travel in a palanquin?

⑫ Which TV series featured the spaceship *Liberator*?

⑬ What game is played on a diamond?

⑭ Which children's book author was knighted in 2009?

⑮ Which university wears dark blue, Oxford or Cambridge?

⑯ Kishinev is the capital of which European country?

QUIZ 45

① On what part of a ship will you find the Plimsoll line?

② In *Jack and the Beanstalk*, what does Jack swap for some beans?

③ What does the word *ultimo* mean?

④ In which year was Hong Kong handed over to the Chinese?

⑤ What is the state capital of Texas?

⑥ Which member of the royal family had his 90th birthday in 2011?

⑦ How many storeys does the Empire State Building have?

⑧ What does the musical term 'piano' mean?

⑨ Which UK prime minister introduced the three-day working week?

⑩ What word can mean very serious or the back end of a boat?

⑪ Which Shakespeare play was written first, *Hamlet* or *Othello*?

⑫ What do the five Olympic rings represent?

⑬ Where do skylarks nest?

⑭ What is Jeeves the manservant's first name?

⑮ What grow in an arboretum?

⑯ What causes the opposite effect in the weather to El Niño?

QUIZ 46

1. In a Christmas pantomime, who plays the dame? 💡

2. Who were the losing finalists in the 2010 FIFA World Cup?

3. Which pop star dressed down for her role in the film *Precious*?

4. In mythology, who was the father of Romulus and Remus?

5. How many spots has the common ladybird: five, six or seven? 💡

6. Which word can follow bull, chaff and green?

7. What in heraldry is a saltire?

8. Which religion came first: Buddhism or Islam?

9. Who is Wet Wet Wet's lead singer?

10. Who is older, Ant or Dec? 💡

11. Which English county cricket team plays at New Road?

12. Which British comedian starred in the 60s film *The Rebel*?

13. Which female won gold for both the 800m and 1500m in 2004?

14. What sport takes place in a velodrome? 💡

15. Which make of car was the Felicia?

16. Who played Mr Bergstrom in *The Simpsons*?

QUIZ 47

1. What does the Australian word dinkum mean?

2. Who is the greedy boy in *Charlie and the Chocolate Factory*?

3. What is the medical term for a bulge in an artery wall?

4. Which opera singer was called 'The Swedish Nightingale'?

5. What was Che Guevara's first name?

6. In *Shrek*, what are the children of Donkey and Dragon called?

7. What does an Indian *durzi* make?

8. Which European military dictator died in 1975?

9. In which US city did rap originate?

10. Who did Prince William and Kate Middleton become?

11. Which modern city was once Byzantium?

12. In the Discworld books, who or what is Jerakeen?

13. Who wrote the music, Gilbert or Sullivan?

14. In which film was Paul Newman Billy the Kid?

15. Name the other half: Torvill and . . .

16. Which is the most populous state in the USA?

QUIZ 48

① Who is the rabbit in *Bambi*?

② What is the chemical symbol for calcium?

③ Who performed the world's first vaccination?

④ How many people found refuge on Noah's Ark?

⑤ What do most birds do at night?

⑥ In which year was the Japanese attack on Pearl Harbor?

⑦ What is the name of the Duchess of Cambridge's brother?

⑧ Who was Frank Sinatra's second wife?

⑨ Which ex-footballer's nickname is 'Jukebox'?

⑩ What kind of creature is poor Dobby in *Harry Potter*?

⑪ Add the clothing item to the film's title: *The Duke Wore* . . .

⑫ What are the high-speed trains in Japan called?

⑬ What does adulate mean?

⑭ In which Charles Dickens novel is Mr Gradgrind a character?

⑮ What colour are emeralds?

⑯ What are Ant and Dec's real names?

QUIZ 49

① In which subject does Prince William have a university degree?

② What animal looks like a horse but has a horn on its head?

③ Which father and son were Formula One world champions?

④ What would you be eating if you had a 'Scotch woodcock'?

⑤ Who commanded the US Expeditionary Force in World War I?

⑥ How many years in a decade?

⑦ Name the cousin of the Queen killed by the IRA in 1979.

⑧ Who defeated the British at the Battle of Majuba Hill in 1881?

⑨ Going west, which Thames bridge comes after Chelsea Bridge?

⑩ 'The Soldier's Song' is the national anthem of which country?

⑪ What colour are rubies?

⑫ Which French film director was Jane Fonda's first husband?

⑬ What is the main religion in India?

⑭ Who was the Greek god of dreams?

⑮ How many sides has a pentagon?

⑯ What was the first minor planet to be discovered?

QUIZ 50

① What word means 'three times'?

② Where in the USA was the atom bomb developed?

③ What is the capital of Ukraine?

④ How wide is a regulation cricket pitch?

⑤ What came over the hill and blew, blew, blew, blew?

⑥ Who directed the film *The Battleship Potemkin*?

⑦ What instrument did jazz musician Django Reinhardt play?

⑧ Who is the youngest of the Bennet girls in *Pride and Prejudice*?

⑨ Which UK motoring organization was founded in 1905?

⑩ Who was known as the 'Lady with the Lamp'?

⑪ Whose signature tune was 'Moonlight Serenade'?

⑫ How many characters are there in the Braille alphabet?

⑬ Which brass instrument has the lowest pitch?

⑭ What TV programme has the name of a naval flag?

⑮ Who was captain of the ill-fated *Titanic*?

⑯ What was wood engraver Thomas Bewick's signature mark?

QUIZ 51

① How many 'golds' did Rebecca Adlington win at the 2008 Olympics?

② In which century was Jane Austen born?

③ From which tree do acorns come?

④ How many degrees has a right-angled triangle?

⑤ Which Canadian city is across the river from Detroit?

⑥ Who took over from Roger Moore as 'The Saint' on television?

⑦ In which county is the city of Norwich?

⑧ Which jockey won The Derby in 2007 at his fifteenth attempt?

⑨ Who became known as the 'Butcher of the Somme'?

⑩ Where in London is the National Gallery?

⑪ Which member of the Royal Family is Duke of York?

⑫ 'Crucible' was the German code name for bombing which UK city?

⑬ Who shockingly beat England 1-0 in the 1950 FIFA World Cup?

⑭ What number symphony is Beethoven's 'Pastoral'?

⑮ In which mountain range is Mt Everest?

⑯ Which German writer was W H Auden's father-in-law?

QUIZ 52

1. Who succeeded Queen Victoria on the British throne?

2. What turn into frogs? 💡

3. Who wrote the story 'The Curious Case of Benjamin Button'?

4. What was the wartime injunction to the British to grow food?

5. The deadly taipan snake is native to which country?

6. How many people in a musical quintet? 💡

7. When was Londonderry's 'Bloody Sunday'?

8. What are the Hopi?

9. What cut of meat comes between the rump and topside?

10. In aviation jargon, what are 'LO CIGS'?

11. Who are the 'Dynamic Duo'? 💡

12. In which century was the English artist John Constable born?

13. Who won the first rugby Heineken European Cup in 1996?

14. Who was the last UK prime minister born in the 19th century?

15. What is the Scottish word for a lake? 💡

16. Which member of Queen gained a first-class honours degree in electronics?

QUIZ 53

① What southern US city has a dance named after it?

② How many men did the Grand Old Duke of York have?

③ What is the collective name for cats?

④ In which Shakespeare play is Malvolio a character?

⑤ How is the British bird *Troglodytes troglodytes* better known?

⑥ What is secret agent James Bond's code name?

⑦ How many bridges are there over the Amazon river?

⑧ What word can come before window, leaf and rum?

⑨ Which Tracy is the father in *Thunderbirds*?

⑩ What is the capital of Italy?

⑪ Who did Marlon Brando play in *On the Waterfront*?

⑫ How many players in a netball team?

⑬ What called itself the 'Station of the Nation'?

⑭ In boxing, what is someone who leads with their right hand?

⑮ Which New Zealand bird doesn't fly?

⑯ Which of Henry VIII's wives was the mother of Edward VI?

QUIZ 54

① What is the name of Scotland's national football stadium?

② What is the name of the Queen's residence in London?

③ What is clownish comedy called?

④ Which country's flag features a maple leaf?

⑤ When did William Shakespeare die: 1606, 1616, 1626?

⑥ How many holes are there on a full-sized golf course?

⑦ *Ananas* is French for which fruit?

⑧ Which US singer was nicknamed 'The Prince of Wails'?

⑨ Which Greek god's temple was at Delphi?

⑩ Who designed St Paul's Cathedral?

⑪ Which Swiss town holds an annual international TV festival?

⑫ Who composed 'On Hearing the First Cuckoo in Spring'?

⑬ Which two South American countries border Lake Titicaca?

⑭ What name is given to a mock or sham trial?

⑮ Who was the Roman god of war?

⑯ Which European country's national anthem has 158 verses?

QUIZ 55

① How many eyes did the Greek giant Cyclops have?

② Who was appointed the UK's Chief Scout in 2009?

③ Which artist created the Beatles' *Sgt Pepper* album cover?

④ What is a person who studies animals called?

⑤ Which detective lives at 221B Baker Street?

⑥ The Swankers was the former name of which punk group?

⑦ On which river does Boston, Massachusetts stand?

⑧ What was painter Alfred Munnings' favourite subject?

⑨ In which year did London host its first Olympic Games?

⑩ Which famous English writer is known as 'The Bard of Avon'?

⑪ What extinct bird was originally called a Walckvogel?

⑫ What does the singer Björk's name mean?

⑬ Which boy never grew old?

⑭ In which city is the Trevi Fountain?

⑮ What does GPS stand for?

⑯ Who was the first singer to sell a million copies of a record?

QUIZ 56

① Who is Aladdin's nasty uncle?

② In the *Bourne* films, what is the hero's first name?

③ And who wrote the books on which the films are based?

④ What breed of dog is *caniche* in French?

⑤ Name the last serving prime minister to sit in the House of Lords.

⑥ Who are the guards at the Tower of London?

⑦ When did the white ball become legal in football: 1950 or 1960?

⑧ Which English monarch founded the Order of the Garter?

⑨ Who did Adolf Schicklgrüber become?

⑩ Which London football club's ground is Stamford Bridge?

⑪ What was the name of the Queen's first corgi?

⑫ Which American singer made a habit of wearing black?

⑬ Who found himself *Down and Out in Paris and London*?

⑭ Who played the title role in the TV series *Remington Steele*?

⑮ What variety of fruit is a Granny Smith?

⑯ Which leading South African black activist died in police custody in 1977?

QUIZ 57

① Who couldn't put Humpty Dumpty together again? ☀

② Whose home was Neverland Ranch?

③ The Gulf of Carpentaria is off which country's northern coast?

④ Who made a work of art out of an unmade bed?

⑤ How was William Frederick Cody better known?

⑥ Eating which fruit a day is said to keep the doctor away? ☀

⑦ What was the name of the hurricane that hit New Orleans in 2005?

⑧ Which South American country is named after an Italian city?

⑨ What is another name for a castle in chess?

⑩ In the song, what was given on the first day of Christmas? ☀

⑪ What is a computer's memory called?

⑫ What was the title of the Spice Girls' 1997 film?

⑬ Which US novelist created the TV series *ER*?

⑭ What is the Zodiac symbol for Sagittarius?

⑮ In which house does the American president live? ☀

⑯ What colour is traditional Bristol glass?

QUIZ 58

① Who was the Nordic god of thunder?

② In the song, a spoonful of what helps the medicine go down?

③ The word equine refers to which animal?

④ In Dickens' novel, what is the name of Mr Pickwick's manservant?

⑤ John J Rawlings was the inventor of which DIY essential?

⑥ Which is longer, a mile or a kilometre?

⑦ Who was Britain's last Catholic monarch?

⑧ Which British golfer won The US Masters in 1988?

⑨ Who directed the first *Harry Potter* film?

⑩ Which couturier designed the 'A line' and 'H line'?

⑪ What is the tenth letter of the alphabet?

⑫ Which Test cricketer was knighted in 1990?

⑬ Which county name did singer David Cook adopt?

⑭ In which region of France is La Rochelle?

⑮ What do the initials UN stand for?

⑯ Which bird eats with its bill upside down?

QUIZ 59

① Add the showbiz surname: Emilio and Renée . . .

② Which three went with Dorothy to find the Wizard of Oz? ☼

③ What is a squirrel's nest called?

④ How many edges does a cube have?

⑤ Which preacher said: 'I look upon the world as my parish'?

⑥ What was Dick Turpin? ☼

⑦ In which year did Eurostar begin its service?

⑧ Who is the patron saint of carpenters?

⑨ Which shopping chain once advertised 'Nothing over sixpence'?

⑩ What is a sobriquet?

⑪ Which king was a merry old soul? ☼

⑫ The film *Strictly Ballroom* is set in which country?

⑬ What does the word *sekt* on a German wine label mean?

⑭ What nationality was the artist Edvard Munch?

⑮ Which bird lays its eggs in other bird's nests? ☼

⑯ Arsenal manager Arsène Wenger has university degrees in which two subjects?

QUIZ 60

1. Mars, Venus and Earth are all what?

2. Which cricketer was nicknamed 'Big Bird'?

3. How many degrees in a semicircle?

4. Which Greek hero was the subject of a 1997 Disney animated film?

5. What is the capital of Ireland?

6. In which country was the Monteverdi car manufactured?

7. Who wrote the novel *I, Claudius*?

8. And who played Claudius in the TV adaptation?

9. The Bosphorus Strait separates which two continents?

10. What is the name of the dog in the *Famous Five* books?

11. In which sport do you 'catch a crab'?

12. What was the former currency of The Netherlands?

13. Which supermodel was Richard Gere married to?

14. What wild species of animal is a mouflon?

15. Who is the Queen's youngest child?

16. What turned out the lights in 18th-century houses?

QUIZ 61

① What is 'Happy Feet's' name?

② The musical *West Side Story* is based on which Shakespeare play?

③ Who was the first goalie to save a penalty in an FA Cup final?

④ What is the debris of a glacier called?

⑤ Who does Ewan McGregor play in the *Star Wars* films?

⑥ Which classic novel is subtitled 'The History of a Foundling'?

⑦ What was Gladys Knight's backing group?

⑧ Which actor died during the filming of *Gladiator* in 1999?

⑨ What is a doctor who looks after animals called?

⑩ When was Thomas Becket murdered: 1170, 1270, 1370?

⑪ Which song-writing duo wrote 'Ol' Man River'?

⑫ The film *Schindler's List* is based on which book?

⑬ And who wrote it?

⑭ How is the Boeing 747 aeroplane better known?

⑮ Which US miler was nicknamed the 'Stork in Shorts'?

⑯ What triangle has two sides of equal length?

QUIZ 62

① Which aunt do you throw things at? 💡

② What are Blue Vinney and Lanark Blue?

③ Who was the Roman equivalent of Zeus?

④ In which war was the Battle of Trenton?

⑤ What does Little Tommy Tucker have for his supper? 💡

⑥ Which Noel Coward play was the basis for *Brief Encounter*?

⑦ What is a tika dot?

⑧ What is the capital of Uzbekistan?

⑨ Which Smith was an 18th-century economist?

⑩ What is dancing Billy Elliot's father's job? 💡

⑪ In which sport would you need a foil or an *épée*?

⑫ What does a BCG vaccination protect you against?

⑬ What did Wee Johnny Hayes & the Bluecats change their name to?

⑭ Who plays Sue Sylvester in *Glee*?

⑮ Which canal separates North and South America? 💡

⑯ What iconic UK pictorial publication was launched in 1938?

QUIZ 63

1. What is the fifteenth letter of the alphabet?

2. How many tasks did Hercules have to perform?

3. What does ASBO stand for?

4. Who was head of the German SS?

5. How many arms does an octopus have?

6. Ulundi was the final battle in which Anglo-colonial war?

7. Which part of a flower produces pollen?

8. Which actor, playwright and composer was known as 'The Master'?

9. What type of bird are falcons, hawks and eagles?

10. Heavy water is used in the development of what?

11. Which US singer shaved her head in 2007?

12. In which century did Samuel Pepys write his diary?

13. What do winners of the US Masters golf tournament get to wear?

14. Who dined on mince and slices of quince?

15. In the Shakespeare play, Cymbeline is king of where?

16. Which English motorway is also known as the Ross Spur?

QUIZ 64

1. Who went to the cupboard and found it bare?

2. What is the first letter of the Greek alphabet?

3. Ag is the chemical symbol for what metal?

4. Who plays Mrs Hudson in the 2009 film *Sherlock Holmes*?

5. Which ocean is larger, Atlantic or Pacific?

6. The cor anglais belongs to which section of an orchestra?

7. Which US state is known as the 'Evergreen State'?

8. How is the mountain Chomolongma better known?

9. Which female received the 1979 Nobel Peace Prize?

10. In *Treasure Island*, whose parrot says 'Pieces of eight!'?

11. What geological feature is a monticule?

12. Cricket umpire Billy Bowden is from which country?

13. Which major geological fault runs through California?

14. Who wrote the novel *A Suitable Boy*?

15. How many legs has a quadruped?

16. Which Shakespeare play begins: 'O for a muse of fire'?

QUIZ 65

① Great Aunt Greta thinks Horrid Henry is a what? ·ᣟ·

② How many ounces are there in a pound?

③ Who played runner Harold Abrahams in *Chariots of Fire*?

④ Ben Nevis is in which Scottish mountain range?

⑤ Which golfer is nicknamed 'Double D'?

⑥ Where did Tom Brown spend his schooldays?

⑦ YAR on a car number plate indicates which country of origin?

⑧ What were the labour camps in Soviet Russia called?

⑨ Which planet do the satellites Deimos and Phobos orbit?

⑩ What precious stone is hidden in the letters MADNODI? ·ᣟ·

⑪ Who did Angela Merkel succeed as German chancellor in 2005?

⑫ Who comes from Darkest Peru and loves marmalade? ·ᣟ·

⑬ What is the eighth of the Ten Commandments?

⑭ St Anne is the 'capital' of which Channel Island?

⑮ What Australian team is called The Wallabies – cricket or rugby? ·ᣟ·

⑯ What colour is St Elmo's fire?

QUIZ 66

① Who is Mother Goose's criminal son in *Pet Squad*?

② 'The Best of Both Worlds' is the theme to which TV series?

③ Which artist painted the *Mona Lisa*?

④ And by what other name is the painting known?

⑤ How many sporting events in a triathlon?

⑥ What was the symbol of the Free French forces in World War II?

⑦ Cardiff lies at the mouth of which river?

⑧ What was the original name for the bicycle?

⑨ Which US president made the Gettysburg Address?

⑩ In the film *Finding Nemo*, where does Nemo get lost?

⑪ How do the Spanish say 'goodbye'?

⑫ What is the layman's term for nitrous oxide?

⑬ Which US city is the headquarters of the Mormon Church?

⑭ What is the Queen's Scottish home?

⑮ In which game is there a 'Doubling Cube'?

⑯ Which film includes the line: 'This is Mrs Norman Maine . . .'?

QUIZ 67

① What does the F stand for in F Scott Fitzgerald?

② Who are Lily Kettle's sisters in *Tracy Beaker*? ☿

③ What date is St George's Day?

④ Indira Gandhi was the daughter of which Indian leader?

⑤ What is a butterfly pupa called?

⑥ Which word can come before hop, tower and push?

⑦ What tree is weeping but never crying? ☿

⑧ Which Olympic 'discipline' began in 1968?

⑨ What did the Romans call a marketplace or public square?

⑩ 'Tickety boo' is the bingo call for which number?

⑪ What is the wizard's name in *The Legend of Dick and Dom*? ☿

⑫ What type of bird is a booby?

⑬ In which year was Saddam Hussein captured?

⑭ Which peninsula do Spain and Portugal occupy?

⑮ What is the name of the US president's official plane? ☿

⑯ In which Bond film does 'Margaret Thatcher' appear?

QUIZ 68

1. How is the disease rubella more commonly known?

2. What are the large black birds that live at the Tower of London? 💡

3. Who wrote the play *Caesar and Cleopatra*?

4. What is an Indian deep-fried pastry?

5. Which Latin-American dance is Portuguese for 'new style'?

6. Why does the Caterpillar in the story never stop eating? 💡

7. On how many hills is Rome built?

8. In which year did Argentina invade the Falkland Islands?

9. What can be a recorder-like instrument or a bean?

10. Who is Arthur the Aardvark's little sister? 💡

11. Which element has the atomic number '1'?

12. Who compete for rugby's Calcutta Cup?

13. What is the iridescent inner layer of an oyster shell called?

14. What is French for snail? 💡

15. Whose music accompanied the film *Amadeus*?

16. Who wrote the dramatic monologues *Talking Heads*?

QUIZ 69

① Which great English playwright died on St George's Day?

② Renfield is the faithful family retainer in which TV series? ☼

③ What musical instrument is on Ireland's coat of arms? ☆

④ Which film star's real name was Bernard Schwartz?

⑤ In *Horrid Henry*, whose baby is Vomiting Vera? ☼

⑥ Whose *Spycatcher* memoirs were banned in the UK?

⑦ Where did the St Valentine Day's massacre take place?

⑧ Which is the largest of the Channel Islands? ☼

⑨ Which ex-England cricketer is known as 'Freddie'?

⑩ Who commanded the Royalist cavalry in the English Civil War?

⑪ What chemical element is represented by the letter F?

⑫ How many players are there in a rugby league team? ☼

⑬ Mozzarella cheese is made from what?

⑭ What is Canada's highest mountain?

⑮ Which of the cricketing Morkels is older, Albie or Morné?

⑯ Stratfield Saye is the stately home of which duke?

QUIZ 70

① Which of Gandalf's three rings has a red stone?

② What colour is a West Highland Terrier?

③ Which major war took place between 1950 and 1953?

④ Spell the name of the US state of which Boston is the capital?

⑤ Who was the inventor of the C5 pedal-powered tricycle?

⑥ 'Traveller' was which American Civil War general's horse?

⑦ Which two letters in front of ICE make a fruit drink?

⑧ When was the crossbar introduced in soccer: 1865, 1875, 1885?

⑨ Which breed of dog is traditionally used to hunt hares?

⑩ What is the last thing of the Cheshire Cat to disappear?

⑪ Which novel by Salman Rushdie prompted a fatwa?

⑫ What did Prince Charles do without at his wedding in 2005?

⑬ In which century was the Taj Mahal built?

⑭ For which film did Barbra Streisand win an Oscar in 1968?

⑮ What is Britain's only poisonous snake?

⑯ Which elephant has the biggest ears, African or Indian?

QUIZ 71

1 Who is the 'eating machine' in *Shaun the Sheep*?

2 What is the world's largest bird of prey?

3 Spell the word for someone who owns a restaurant?

4 Which Michael Haneke film won the Palme d'Or at Cannes in 2009?

5 What two rivers merge to become the Shatt-al-Arab?

6 How many pence in £2?

7 Who composed the opera *Rigoletto*?

8 Which two famous American writers died in 1916?

9 Who is the commanding officer in *Battlestar Galactica*?

10 What is the opposite of sharp?

11 John Flamsteed became the first what in 1675?

12 What is 'picking oakum'?

13 Who hosted the first football World Cup in 1930?

14 How many degrees in a circle?

15 What is the capital of Switzerland?

16 Who is the only English pope to date?

QUIZ 72

① How much was a florin worth in the old currency?

② Who is Bob the Builder's business partner? 💡

③ Who played Batman in the TV series?

④ Which Calvin became US president in 1923?

⑤ In which novel did teenage spy Alex Rider first appear?

⑥ Add the fraternal sporting surname: Michael and Ralf . . .

⑦ What is the plural of ox? 💡

⑧ What is an eagle's nest called?

⑨ What were once known as 'iron horses'?

⑩ Excluding Antarctica, which continent stretches furthest south?

⑪ What is the world's largest mammal?

⑫ How many yards long is a standard cricket pitch? 💡

⑬ What was the first battle of the English Civil War?

⑭ To which writer was actor Clive Swift once married?

⑮ What is the capital of Egypt? 💡

⑯ What type of garment is a banyan?

QUIZ 73

① Was Abraham Lincoln a Republican or a Democrat?

② Who is the trainee fairy in *Sesame Street*?

③ Who was the first *Blue Peter* pet?

④ What is the world's smallest breed of cat?

⑤ Which European explorer served the Mongol emperor Kublai Khan?

⑥ *Manhattan Transfer* is a novel by which American writer?

⑦ Change one letter and turn RUMBLE into a fall?

⑧ Who plays Bernado O'Reilly in *The Magnificent Seven*?

⑨ Which female athlete made her name running barefoot?

⑩ What relation is the wicked queen to Snow White?

⑪ When was the National Trust formed: 1894, 1904, 1914?

⑫ What was Jackie Kennedy's maiden name?

⑬ In which Canadian province is Ottawa?

⑭ What is the 'mother of invention'?

⑮ How many gold medals did Chris Hoy win at the Beijing Olympics?

⑯ Bernadotte is the family name of which country's royal house?

QUIZ 74

① What flying machine can you make out of CHEER PILOT? 💡

② Who were rugby's Six Nations champions in 2011?

③ 'Good morning Starshine' comes from which musical?

④ Which insect is the longest in the world?

⑤ Put two letters in front of ANT and turn it into something huge. 💡

⑥ On which river does the Hoover Dam stand?

⑦ What is the cube root of 512?

⑧ Which former motor-racing driver set up his own airline?

⑨ Who is Asterix's best friend? 💡

⑩ Who hung up his boots with LA Galaxy in 2011?

⑪ Albuquerque is in which US state?

⑫ Which sport featured in the film *The Final Test*?

⑬ Who was 'Papa Doc'?

⑭ What does Toad disguise himself as in *The Wind in the Willows*? 💡

⑮ Who was the first American woman to travel in space?

⑯ What is Boxing Day also known as?

QUIZ 75

① What does a pluviometer measure?

② How many days are there in a leap year?

③ What were the poets Wordsworth, Coleridge and Southey called?

④ How do you convert miles into kilometres?

⑤ Who composed the opera *Don Giovanni*?

⑥ Is a dolphin a fish or a mammal?

⑦ Name the Royal Navy frogman who mysteriously disappeared in 1956.

⑧ Which US president famously had a dog named Checkers?

⑨ What party was a prelude to the American War of Independence?

⑩ What does Bella Cullen become in *Twilight*?

⑪ Which US state comes between Illinois and Ohio?

⑫ What is the collective name for budgerigars?

⑬ Which one of these is not a pasta: Cavatelli, Ditalini, Salatini?

⑭ The TV series *ER* is set in which hospital?

⑮ Who was known as 'The Virgin Queen'?

⑯ What unlikely material does artist Chris Ofili use in his work?

QUIZ 76

① What did Miss Muffett sit down to eat? 🔅

② How many psalms in the Book of Psalms?

③ What is the French national anthem?

④ In folklore, what will be the result of rain on St Swithin's Day?

⑤ What word can go in front of drop, flake and man? 🔅

⑥ Which UK chancellor introduced the 1909 'People's Budget'?

⑦ In the operetta, who is the son of the Mikado?

⑧ Which Western star's last film was *Ride the High Country*?

⑨ What was England's last territorial possession in France?

⑩ Who founded the Boy Scouts movement in 1908? 🔅

⑪ How did Manchester United goalie Alex Stepney dislocate his jaw?

⑫ When was the dog licence abolished in the UK: 1977, 1985, 1988?

⑬ What is the capital of the Dominican Republic?

⑭ In cricket, what does MCC stand for? 🔅

⑮ Who was the father of the last tsar of Russia?

⑯ In which film does James Mason play Professor Humbert Humbert?

QUIZ 77

① What wakes up the Sleeping Beauty? ☼

② In computer language, what does MODEM stand for?

③ Queen Margrethe II became monarch of which country in 1972?

④ What is the French word for 'town'?

⑤ Eadweard Muybridge was a pioneer in what?

⑥ What was the name of Dick Turpin's horse? ☼

⑦ Which famous palace once had 14,000 fountains?

⑧ What is nine cubed?

⑨ Europe's largest glacier is in which country?

⑩ Which planet is closer to Earth – Mars or Venus? ☼

⑪ Name the English philosopher and economist, John Stuart . . .

⑫ What was Franklin Roosevelt before he became US president?

⑬ Which actor twice played Dr Who in films?

⑭ Which English city has a Hoe and a Sound? ☼

⑮ Chionophobia is a fear of what?

⑯ What is the capital of Papua New Guinea?

QUIZ 78

① Which watery animal can you turn WENT into?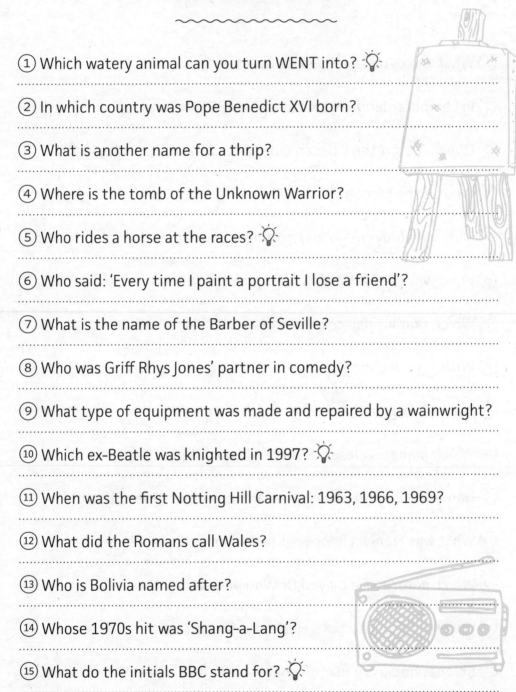

② In which country was Pope Benedict XVI born?

③ What is another name for a thrip?

④ Where is the tomb of the Unknown Warrior?

⑤ Who rides a horse at the races?

⑥ Who said: 'Every time I paint a portrait I lose a friend'?

⑦ What is the name of the Barber of Seville?

⑧ Who was Griff Rhys Jones' partner in comedy?

⑨ What type of equipment was made and repaired by a wainwright?

⑩ Which ex-Beatle was knighted in 1997?

⑪ When was the first Notting Hill Carnival: 1963, 1966, 1969?

⑫ What did the Romans call Wales?

⑬ Who is Bolivia named after?

⑭ Whose 1970s hit was 'Shang-a-Lang'?

⑮ What do the initials BBC stand for?

⑯ What is the lightest weight category in boxing?

QUIZ 79

① Who is the smallest and youngest Teletubby?

② Film star Anthony Quinn was a native of which country?

③ Who was the Greek god of the underworld?

④ What is an analgesic?

⑤ A filly is a young female what?

⑥ Where in the UK were DeLorean cars manufactured?

⑦ What is the main wine-growing region of California?

⑧ 'The Modern Prometheus' is the subtitle of which classic novel?

⑨ What range of hills forms the border between England and Scotland?

⑩ Who is the patron saint of Scotland?

⑪ London Bridge can be seen in which US state?

⑫ How was Vladimir Illyich Ulyanov better known?

⑬ What date is Bastille Day in France?

⑭ A baby whale is called a what?

⑮ What would you buy from a French *boulangerie*?

⑯ In which European city is the Schönbrunn Palace?

QUIZ 80

1. Which Muppett plays the piano? 💡

2. What film was George Clooney's directorial debut?

3. Who does Martin Freeman play in *The Office*?

4. What is floating debris at sea called?

5. Who founded the Christian Science movement?

6. Which English king died at the Battle of Hastings? 💡

7. What is the Italian word for chicken?

8. Which US state is north of Arkansas?

9. In which British city is the Bridgewater Concert Hall?

10. What building is on a bottle of HP Sauce? 💡

11. A salmon that has spawned is called a what?

12. Who competed in the first-ever Twenty20 international?

13. What, in a geographical context, is a maelstrom?

14. Who (in full) was LBJ?

15. Tom Daley is a world champion what? 💡

16. What was the name of Edward Heath's yacht?

QUIZ 81

1. Who visits the land of Lilliput on his travels? 🔆

2. A passepied is a type of what?

3. Does Bryn Terfel sing tenor or bass?

4. What animal is a *Canus lupus*?

5. Which two letters in front of ICE mean you can cut a cake? 🔆

6. When it's noon at GMT, what time is it in Qatar?

7. What do the Americans call jam?

8. London Zoo is located in which park?

9. What is the name of the high school in *Glee*? 🔆

10. Politician Jeremy Thorpe was married to which concert pianist?

11. Who led the mutineers on HMS *Bounty*?

12. In which year did the Queen celebrate her Silver Jubilee?

13. A statue of which footballer was unveiled at Everton in 2001?

14. Amps are a unit for measuring what? 🔆

15. Which comic came first, *The Beano* or *The Dandy*?

16. Who is the wife of King Juan Carlos of Spain?

QUIZ 82

① Who took James walking in the air? ☀

② Express 3/10 as a decimal.

③ What is the third letter of the Greek alphabet?

④ Who created the fictional Larkins family?

⑤ What word goes with meat, dog and roll? ☀

⑥ In which country were the 19th-century Anglo-Ashanti wars fought?

⑦ What does IMF stand for?

⑧ When was Terry Waite kidnapped in Beirut: 1985, 1987 or 1989?

⑨ Who does Keira Knightley play in *The Pirates of the Caribbean*? ☀

⑩ What does the name Zoe mean?

⑪ Who is the author of the *Twilight* books?

⑫ What was the dispersion of Jews beyond Israel called?

⑬ Name the US city largely destroyed by an earthquake in 1906.

⑭ Which English king led a campaign for literacy and learning?

⑮ How many sporting events are there in a decathlon? ☀

⑯ What is the port of Edinburgh?

QUIZ 83

① Who was London Zoo's most famous resident in the 60s and 70s?

② What drink is served on the Polar Express?

③ In which year did Singapore fall to the Japanese?

④ Which royal park is near Hampton Court?

⑤ With which sport was the 18th-century Hambledon Club associated?

⑥ What jingling musical instrument do you bang and shake?

⑦ Which future James Bond posed nude for an art class?

⑧ What are unwanted items thrown overboard at sea called?

⑨ Which former First Lady's memoirs were entitled *My Turn*?

⑩ What wild dog can you make out of DOING?

⑪ When did food rationing finally end in the UK?

⑫ What did Wilhelm Röntgen invent?

⑬ Which poet received a peerage in 1884?

⑭ What is the second largest fishing port in France?

⑮ In the Bible, who are Cain and Abel's parents?

⑯ What relation was Kaiser Wilhelm II to Queen Victoria?

QUIZ 84

① Which poet won the Nobel Prize in Literature in 1995?

② What does a caterpillar turn into? 🔆

③ The Koran is a holy book for which religion?

④ Who was made commander of the New Model Army in 1645?

⑤ Which nuclear scientist was jailed in the UK in 1950 for spying?

⑥ What imaginary line divides the earth into north and south? 🔆

⑦ Does *ante* mean before or after?

⑧ What is the turbulence behind a vessel called?

⑨ Complete the name of this town: Barrow in . . .

⑩ Who are Santa's little helpers? 🔆

⑪ What was John Lennon's 1972 backing group?

⑫ In which country is Puerto Bolivar?

⑬ What is the larger barrel, a butt or a tun?

⑭ Who was Wimbledon's first Ladies Champion?

⑮ Can you spell the full word for a hippo? 🔆

⑯ 'Brumaire' in the French Revolutionary calendar means what?

QUIZ 85

① How many prime numbers are there between 50 and 60?

② What is the name of Homer Simpson's pet lobster? ⋆

③ The Haflinger pony comes from which European country?

④ Pierce Brosnan made his screen debut in which gangster film?

⑤ Which two letters in front of APE make a fruit? ⋆

⑥ By what name is an elk known in North America?

⑦ What phrase means an overthrow of government?

⑧ On which sea is the port of Murmansk?

⑨ What is the first book in the Bible? ⋆

⑩ Who became Children's Laureate in 2011?

⑪ What is the world's largest lizard?

⑫ What is the proper name for 'parrot disease'?

⑬ Who did James VI of Scotland become?

⑭ Where in England was the broadcaster Alistair Cooke born?

⑮ Reykjavik is the capital of which country? ⋆

⑯ Which golfer is nicknamed 'Walrus'?

QUIZ 86

① Who sings 'Bare Necessities' with Mowgli in *The Jungle Book*? 💡

② What are the principal colours on the Peruvian flag?

③ Which great hall at Windsor Castle was gutted by fire in 1992?

④ Who had a 2003 hit with 'Leave Right Now'?

⑤ Where do the Lost Boys live in *Peter Pan*? 💡

⑥ Who was known as 'Stormin' Norman'?

⑦ What is Oberon in *A Midsummer Night's Dream*?

⑧ Which flying insect is sometimes called 'Devil's Arrow'?

⑨ Which flower is sometimes known as 'Traveller's Joy'?

⑩ Which English king lost his head in 1649? 💡

⑪ What is the name of Virginia's vast natural harbour?

⑫ Who did the All Blacks beat 145–17 in the 1995 World Cup?

⑬ What is the surname of Buffy the Vampire Slayer?

⑭ What is the world's fastest land animal? 💡

⑮ Complete the name of this town: Ashby de la . . .

⑯ Which make of bicycle shares the name of an English explorer?

QUIZ 87

(1) Bryn is Welsh for what?

(2) How many monsters are there in *Where the Wild Things Are*?

(3) Who played Vicki Vale in the 1989 film *Batman*?

(4) What is the regulation height of a tennis net at the centre?

(5) Who eats 'snozzcumbers' and drinks 'frobscottle'?

(6) What are racing pigeons kept in?

(7) Where did Robert Louis Stevenson move to in 1890?

(8) Jumbuck is an Australian term for what?

(9) Who wrote a book about himself called *Moonwalk*?

(10) The sloe is the fruit of which bush?

(11) Who was the first UN Secretary General?

(12) And what nationality was he?

(13) What was Scarlett Johansson's first film?

(14) What is the object hit by players of badminton called?

(15) What food item is made from ground almonds, sugar and egg whites?

(16) What is the UK's largest container port?

QUIZ 88

1. Who made a triumphant return to Iran in 1979?

2. What is a sombrero?

3. Which US state is larger in area, Louisiana or Wisconsin?

4. How many stones were used to build the Great Pyramid at Giza?

5. Who led the England cricket tour of Australia in 1982–83?

6. What is bigger, a lion or a tiger?

7. Svetlana Alliluyeva was whose daughter?

8. What does *ipso facto* mean?

9. Michael Fagan achieved fame by entering whose bedroom?

10. Who directed the film *The Pianist*?

11. What does the perfect pet in *Dear Zoo* turn out to be?

12. What was Richard Nixon's middle name?

13. Which tennis player did Chris Evert marry in 1979?

14. Port Chalmers serves which New Zealand city?

15. What is a book written by someone about their own life called?

16. What is the lay term for infectious mononucleosis?

QUIZ 89

① What do grapes grow on?

② What is the German word for 'town'?

③ Who in 1999 became the first Children's Laureate?

④ Which Somerset town stages a major carnival every year?

⑤ Who has friends called Thing One and Thing Two?

⑥ What is an angle of more than 180° called?

⑦ Which Australian prime minister was sacked in 1975?

⑧ Beau Nash was the 'Master of Ceremonies' in which spa town?

⑨ What large animal can you turn THE PANEL into?

⑩ Which 19th-century US poet wrote over a thousand poems?

⑪ Who overthrew Philippine president Ferdinand Marcos in 1986?

⑫ What drug is used to treat malaria?

⑬ How many states are there in the USA: 48, 49 or 50?

⑭ Who was sacked by Yorkshire County Cricket Club in 1986?

⑮ Which son of actor Richard Harris plays a part in TV's *Mad Men*?

⑯ With which band was Dave Gilmour singer and guitarist?

QUIZ 90

① In the Roald Dahl story, what is BFG short for?

② The 1856 Treaty of Paris ended which war?

③ Who wrote the book *Mrs Doubtfire*?

④ In which game do players try to reduce their score to zero?

⑤ What is the capital of Scotland?

⑥ Seretse Khama was the first president of which African country?

⑦ Which 60s pop star did Reg Smith become?

⑧ Who was the first unmarried US president?

⑨ What book lists items of general knowledge in alphabetical order?

⑩ Which famous English philosopher died in 1970?

⑪ Who carried out the first heart transplant in 1967?

⑫ Which football team did Alf Garnett support?

⑬ Complete the title of the Tennyson poem: 'The Lady of . . .'

⑭ Which saint has the same name as a breed of dog?

⑮ Who was known as the 'Iron Chancellor'?

⑯ Which England cricketer lost an eye in a car accident in 1969?

QUIZ 91

① Which famous general was killed at Khartoum in 1885?

② What live in an aviary?

③ Add the surname to the UK fraternal filmmakers: John and Roy . . .

④ Which disease affects the salivary glands?

⑤ Who was Mary Queen of Scots' second husband?

⑥ What do big game hunters go on?

⑦ Which British playwright died in 1950 at the age of 94?

⑧ What colloquial phrase is used to describe a learned woman?

⑨ When did Bobby Charlton first play for England: 1956, 1958, 1960?

⑩ Nelson Muntz is a bully at which school?

⑪ What is the third tennis Grand Slam event of the year?

⑫ Which monarch ruled between Henry I and Henry II?

⑬ Where would you find the 'Marsh of Sleep'?

⑭ Who were John, Paul and George before The Beatles?

⑮ What flag is shown to the winner in a motor-racing Grand Prix?

⑯ Who once said: 'There is much pleasure to be gained from useless knowledge'?

QUIZ 92

① Which is the largest planet in the solar system?

② Which two letters in front of OWL is what an angry dog does?

③ What is Cambridge University's principal cricket ground?

④ Which American poet wrote 'The Village Blacksmith'?

⑤ Whose catchphrase was 'Heavens to Murgatroyd'?

⑥ Which greedy animal came to tea with a small girl named Sophie?

⑦ Which VW car might be said to have eighteen holes?

⑧ What are lines on a map joining places of equal elevation?

⑨ In which year was The Great Train Robbery: 1963, 1965, 1967?

⑩ Blackpool is on the shore of which sea?

⑪ What is a Venice waterbus called?

⑫ What is the principal ingredient of hummus?

⑬ What does SAS stand for?

⑭ Why do some Australians hang corks from their hat?

⑮ 'Matchstalk Men & Matchstalk Cats & Dogs' was a tribute to whom?

⑯ Which Spanish-born philosopher and writer died in 1952?

QUIZ 93

① What three animals does the mouse meet going to the Gruffalo?

② The 2009 film *Dorian Gray* is based on whose story?

③ What was Cliff Richard's first UK No 1 hit?

④ Which world leader survived an assassination attempt in 1981?

⑤ Who are the three Darling children in *Peter Pan*?

⑥ In which sport do the Salchow, Axel and Lutz figure?

⑦ The term 'motte and bailey' relates to which type of building?

⑧ Scurvy is caused by a deficiency of which vitamin?

⑨ In the film *Elf,* who does Buddy say smells of beef and cheese?

⑩ Who was the first president of Tanzania?

⑪ Which country declared war on Britain in June 1940?

⑫ In the legend, who was blinded by Lady Godiva?

⑬ What is the square root of 576?

⑭ Kabul is the capital of which country?

⑮ In which American classic is Simon Legree the villain?

⑯ And who wrote the book?

QUIZ 94

① Who wrote the play *She Stoops to Conquer*?

② Change one letter and turn TALK into a story.

③ What gives plants their green colour?

④ Which breed of cat has no tail?

⑤ Hydrophobia is another name for what?

⑥ In World War II, what was 'Operation Sealion'?

⑦ What is a camel with one hump called?

⑧ At which sport would you use a penholder grip?

⑨ Which gravel-voiced actor had a hit with 'Wanderin' Star'?

⑩ What is Fuller's Earth?

⑪ What straits link the Gulf of Mexico with the Atlantic?

⑫ Who is Kermit the Frog's nephew?

⑬ Which two UK politicians had air-raid shelters named after them?

⑭ What does FM stand for in radio?

⑮ What do you call a winning serve in tennis?

⑯ What number, when squared, is one third of its cube?

QUIZ 95

1. What do the letters OHMS stand for? 💡

2. Who was the first president of an independent Ghana?

3. What is the initial stage in the construction of a ship?

4. Where is the venue for the 2014 Commonwealth Games?

5. What animal is 'King of the Jungle'? 💡

6. Who was nicknamed 'Brenda' by *Private Eye*?

7. What is artist Jackson Pollock's real first name?

8. 'Barwick Green' is the theme tune of which radio programme?

9. What does *à propos* mean?

10. What special day is on February 14th? 💡

11. In *Great Expectations*, what is Joe Gargery's trade?

12. Which jazz singer was 'Empress of the Blues'?

13. A fletcher is a maker of what?

14. Silicon Valley is adjacent to which US city?

15. How many green bottles were hanging on the wall to begin with? 💡

16. What did President Roosevelt call 7th December 1941?

QUIZ 96

1. What is both a member of the cat family and a make of car? 🔅

2. How does a boa constrictor kill its prey?

3. Who is Sherlock Holmes' brother?

4. In which film did Michael Caine first play Harry Palmer?

5. Which Muppet wants to be a comedian? 🔅

6. In the metric system, what prefix stands for one million?

7. What was Buddy Holly's backing group?

8. Which tennis player was nicknamed 'The Las Vegas Kid'?

9. What was 15th August 1945?

10. Who are the Caped Crusader and Boy Wonder? 🔅

11. Which place name goes with Campden, Norton and Sodbury?

12. Thomas Mann's novel *The Magic Mountain* is set in a what?

13. What did Commander Robert E Peary reach in 1909?

14. Who is always getting who into 'another fine mess'? 🔅

15. What happens when you cut the head off a hydra?

16. Who was the last white president of South Africa?

QUIZ 97

1. Complete the saying: 'As hard as . . .'

2. Who composed 'The Young Person's Guide to the Orchestra'?

3. Which English king had at least 20 illegitimate children?

4. Which English classic novel is set in 17th-century Exmoor?

5. Inside a book you find its what?

6. What was the first mass-produced car?

7. In which human organ is the limbic system?

8. Where in New York was the original Cotton Club?

9. Who plays Dr Watson to Basil Rathbone's Sherlock Holmes?

10. Which insect can jump 130 times its own height?

11. Where were the 1988 Olympic Games staged?

12. To which family of animals does the llama belong?

13. What is the RAF officer cadet training college?

14. In which US state was the first nuclear bomb test carried out?

15. What word can come before ache, land or line?

16. Which 15th-century Dominican monk made his name as a painter?

QUIZ 98

① What does 'fax' stand for?

② Which country invented the pizza? ☼

③ On what would you find a Bézier curve?

④ What is inflammation of the lining of the nose called?

⑤ Who was the last leader of East Germany?

⑥ Thorshavn is the capital of which European island group?

⑦ What vegetable was changed into a golden vehicle? ☼

⑧ *Le Onde* was which Italian pianist's successful album?

⑨ Who edited the *Washington Post* during the Watergate years?

⑩ Which Twenty20 cricketing county is the 'Phantoms'?

⑪ What is the name of *The Simpsons* pet dog? ☼

⑫ Who in 1845 wrote *Modern Cookery for Private Families*?

⑬ What are the stories of Creation called in Aboriginal culture?

⑭ Which Norwegian figure skater became a Hollywood star?

⑮ What is the world's smallest continent? ☼

⑯ In Greek mythology, who was Poseidon's wife?

QUIZ 99

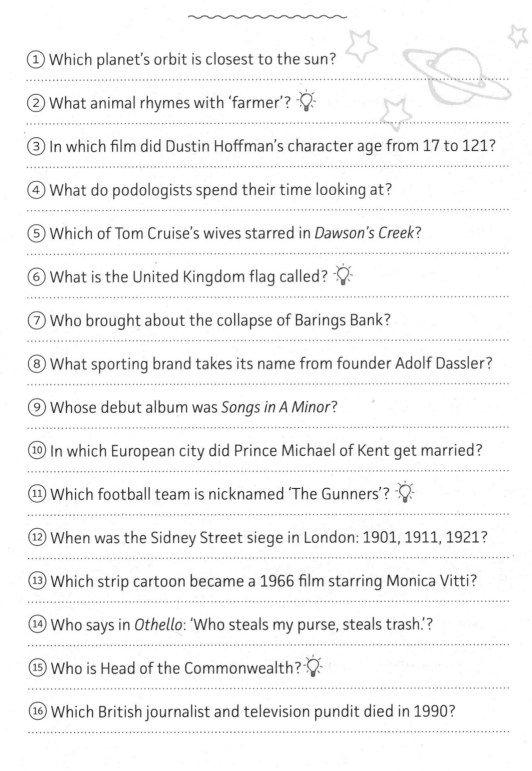

① Which planet's orbit is closest to the sun?

② What animal rhymes with 'farmer'?

③ In which film did Dustin Hoffman's character age from 17 to 121?

④ What do podologists spend their time looking at?

⑤ Which of Tom Cruise's wives starred in *Dawson's Creek*?

⑥ What is the United Kingdom flag called?

⑦ Who brought about the collapse of Barings Bank?

⑧ What sporting brand takes its name from founder Adolf Dassler?

⑨ Whose debut album was *Songs in A Minor*?

⑩ In which European city did Prince Michael of Kent get married?

⑪ Which football team is nicknamed 'The Gunners'?

⑫ When was the Sidney Street siege in London: 1901, 1911, 1921?

⑬ Which strip cartoon became a 1966 film starring Monica Vitti?

⑭ Who says in *Othello*: 'Who steals my purse, steals trash.'?

⑮ Who is Head of the Commonwealth?

⑯ Which British journalist and television pundit died in 1990?

QUIZ 100

① Where does a Mancunian come from?

② Complete the saying: 'As neat as a . . .'

③ Who was the son of the goddess Venus?

④ Sarah Palin was governor of which US state?

⑤ Which is the brightest star in the night sky?

⑥ In which country was the Battle of the Kasserine Pass fought?

⑦ What royal event took place on 2nd June 1953?

⑧ Which top UK fashion designer died in 2010?

⑨ What does CND stand for?

⑩ Who is younger, Paul Simon or Art Garfunkel?

⑪ What kind of insect is a termite?

⑫ In which year was the Festival of Britain?

⑬ What do the initials stand for in W B Yeats?

⑭ Which Yeats poem begins: 'I will arise and go now . . .'?

⑮ Creatures that live both on land and in water are called what?

⑯ Which Twenty20 cricketing county is the 'Dragons'?

QUIZ 101

1. What birds are used for racing and carrying messages? ☀

2. Who was the leader of Nicaragua's Sandinista rebels?

3. Which country did Italy invade in April 1939?

4. Who wrote: 'Rose is a rose is a rose is a rose'?

5. What building does King Kong climb at the end of the film? ☀

6. Which instrument did jazz musician Art Blakey play?

7. Lake Tahoe is in which US state?

8. Which was the fourth *Star Trek* movie?

9. What does the 'e' in email stand for? ☀

10. What are the flowers of the hazel tree?

11. Which group of UK artists was named after a London suburb?

12. What colour was Donovan's mellow song?

13. Who was the first president of Israel?

14. What is another word for fishing? ☀

15. How old was Seve Ballesteros when he won the 1979 British Open?

16. What is a female camel called?

QUIZ 102

① What on an aircraft is known as 'George'?

② Complete the film title: *The Mask of* . . .

③ What is the name of the dog on the HMV label?

④ Which play is superstitiously known as the 'Scottish Play'?

⑤ What do Americans call a wallet?

⑥ How many legs does a tripod have?

⑦ Who was the author of the Brer Rabbit stories?

⑧ Bryan Ferry was lead singer with which 70s band?

⑨ Which cleric won the 1984 Nobel Peace Prize?

⑩ Which of Laurel and Hardy was English-born?

⑪ Which one of these is a herb: Basil, Beryl, Bruno?

⑫ Who played Sharon Watts in *EastEnders*?

⑬ Julian Bream is a renowned performer on which instrument?

⑭ Who in cricket had Test status first, India or West Indies?

⑮ What mechanical animal do greyhounds chase at a racetrack?

⑯ In which ocean is Norfolk Island?

QUIZ 103

① What colours are on a barber's pole?

② How many stomachs has a cow?

③ For which film was Sean Penn first nominated for an Oscar?

④ What is the capital of the Canadian province of British Columbia?

⑤ How was Tracey Emin's *Everyone I Have Ever Slept With* also known?

⑥ A four-leaved clover is supposed to bring you what?

⑦ Footballer Geoff Hurst played one game of county cricket for whom?

⑧ Who is the author of the *Captain Hornblower* books?

⑨ In which country is Lake Garda?

⑩ What type of boat carries cars and people back and forth?

⑪ Who did Princess Anne marry in 1992?

⑫ Which New Labour Cabinet minister died in 2000?

⑬ What was Matt Monro's job before he became a singer?

⑭ Who played the Sorcerer's Apprentice in *Fantasia*?

⑮ What do you do around a maypole?

⑯ In which year did *Hollyoaks* first hit the sceen?

QUIZ 104

1. How many wives did Henry VIII have? 💡

2. What does *sine qua non* mean?

3. Which English king signed the Magna Carta in 1215?

4. Who directed the 2009 film *Sherlock Holmes*?

5. What part of a book faces outwards on the shelf? 💡

6. Which giant bird legend is common to many Native American tribes?

7. What is the world's largest lake?

8. Which insect transmits malaria?

9. What is the favourite food of a panda? 💡

10. Who wrote the book *Get Shorty*?

11. What instrument measures an aircraft's height in flight?

12. Which vintage US singer was known as 'Mr Nice Guy'?

13. What Japanese food item is wasabi?

14. If you have gastric flu, what part of you is upset? 💡

15. From which animal is Moroccan leather obtained?

16. What special day was celebrated for the first time in 1970?

QUIZ 105

① Who tried to make the shoes fit in *Cinderella*? ⚲

② Which kills more people: AIDS, malaria or TB?

③ What lake is the lowest point in Australia?

④ Elinor Dashwood is a character in which Jane Austen novel?

⑤ What code teaches children about road safety? ⚲

⑥ Who was the first female prime minister of New Zealand?

⑦ When an aircraft flies faster than sound what does it create?

⑧ What dance is synonymous with Vienna?

⑨ In *Battlestar Gallactica* whose call sign is 'Apollo'?

⑩ What is a didgeridoo? ⚲

⑪ Which George Bernard Shaw play features the Salvation Army?

⑫ What kind of fruit is a mirabelle?

⑬ On which river is Madrid located?

⑭ What is the duration of a standard game of American football?

⑮ What is the main tower of a castle called? ⚲

⑯ Who is the unseen narrator of the UK *Big Brother*?

QUIZ 106

① Complete the saying: 'As stiff as a . . .' 💡

② What were the first postage stamps called?

③ Hanuman is the Hindu god of which animal?

④ Who designed the Spitfire?

⑤ What is the word for knives, forks and spoons? 💡

⑥ Who was the 19th-century reformist headmaster of Rugby School?

⑦ Where was Martin Luther King's killer apprehended?

⑧ What do Orson Welles, Aly Khan and Dick Haymes have in common?

⑨ Which annual show in the UK is all about dogs?

⑩ Spell the name of Egypt's ancient rulers? 💡

⑪ What do Americans call a full stop?

⑫ Name the Greenpeace ship blown up in Auckland Harbour in 1985.

⑬ Who were the heavy metal-loving teens in MTV's animated series?

⑭ Which England cricketer's nickname was 'Arkle'?

⑮ What is the symbol for the star sign Pisces? 💡

⑯ Who starred opposite Patrick Swayze in *Dirty Dancing*?

QUIZ 107

1 What sends the Sleeping Beauty to sleep? 💡

2 Which Scottish loch has the most water in it?

3 What is Mach 1?

4 When did Florence Nightingale die: 1890, 1900, 1910?

5 What colour are most sapphires? 💡

6 What cord connects a foetus with the placenta?

7 Name Lord Byron's narrative poem, 'Childe Harold's . . .'

8 How old was Michael Jackson when he died?

9 In which kind of book do you look up words? 💡

10 What do the initials stand for in J B Priestley?

11 And which of his novels was about a concert party?

12 What soap did Natalie Imbruglia appear in?

13 Who was sold to Real Madrid in 2009 for £80m?

14 In the song, what was given on the third day of Christmas? 💡

15 Who founded the Salvation Army in 1878?

16 Who was the original choice for the role of Inspector Clouseau?

QUIZ 108

① Who rang the bell on the Runaway Train?

② What is the only egg-laying mammal?

③ In computer speak, what is mb short for?

④ Which car model could mean a 'small barrel-maker'?

⑤ Who is the head of the Roman Catholic Church?

⑥ What does RSPCA stand for?

⑦ Which New Zealand city is known for its geothermal activity?

⑧ How old was Edward VII when he became king?

⑨ How many 'towns' did Arnold Bennett write about?

⑩ What part of a book is also a type of finger?

⑪ In which year was the Boy Scouts movement founded?

⑫ What song from *Kismet* became an international hit?

⑬ Which instrument did Davy Jones play in The Monkees?

⑭ How many sides does a heptagon have?

⑮ In which 2009 film does Eddie Izzard play a media mogul?

⑯ Americans Jack Kilby and Robert Noyce share the credit for inventing what in 1958?

QUIZ 109

① What did 'Tom, Tom the piper's son' steal? 💡

② Was it Gilbert or Sullivan who drowned in his swimming pool?

③ When was the compact disc invented: 1977, 1979, 1981?

④ Who wrote the lyrics of 'Moon River'?

⑤ What was Count Dracula's favourite drink? 💡

⑥ Who did Jerry Springer play in *The Simpsons*?

⑦ What is the second longest river in the world?

⑧ Which city name does Spain and Ohio have in common?

⑨ Who played Professor Henry Higgins in the 1938 film *Pygmalion*?

⑩ And who wrote the play on which the film was based?

⑪ What bird lays the largest egg? 💡

⑫ The *Blue Peter* pet Freda was what kind of animal?

⑬ A fire devastated which US city in 1871?

⑭ Which flower gives rise to a song in *The Sound of Music*?

⑮ Where does the Queen lay a wreath on Remembrance Sunday? 💡

⑯ In football, what did the Inter-Cities Cup become in 1972?

QUIZ 110

① In Greek mythology, how many eyes did Argos have?

② What colours are the cat's hat in *The Cat in a Hat*? 💡

③ Who leapt to fame in the film *Free Willy*?

④ Where did John the Baptist baptize Jesus?

⑤ By what name is the Society of Friends better known?

⑥ In *The Muppets*, who is Dr Bunsen Honeydew's assistant? 💡

⑦ Which James Bond was once a Mr Universe contestant?

⑧ The suspension bridge was invented in which country?

⑨ What injury did Brad Pitt sustain while playing Achilles in *Troy*?

⑩ What is a ship's kitchen called? 💡

⑪ Who was the first duo to sing 'The Phantom of the Opera'?

⑫ What is the capital of Estonia?

⑬ Which English football club is nicknamed 'The Posh'?

⑭ In the night sky what can be half, full or new? 💡

⑮ Which US state's name ends with three vowels?

⑯ What is the largest town on the Isle of Wight?

QUIZ 111

① What is the number 111 sometimes called?

② Which one of Mickey Mouse's friends is silly and clumsy? ☀

③ On which river is the city of Hull?

④ When was the electric razor invented: 1928, 1938, 1948?

⑤ Which legendary blues singer was born McKinley Morganfield?

⑥ What did Noah see in the sky after the Flood? ☀

⑦ How long did the Iran-Iraq War last?

⑧ Who wrote the lyrics for Andrew Lloyd Webber's musical *By Jeeves*?

⑨ What is Japanese soya bean curd?

⑩ In *Home Alone*, Macaulay Culkin watches TV eating a what? ☀

⑪ When is Thanksgiving Day in the USA?

⑫ In which English county is Leeds Castle?

⑬ Which iconic Greek opera singer was born in New York?

⑭ What is the plural of wolf? ☀

⑮ Who plays Nate Fisher in the TV series *Six Feet Under*?

⑯ In which year was the first-ever Sunday football league game: 1971, 1974, 1977?

QUIZ 112

① What did the Owl and the Pussycat eat with? 💡

② Which child actress won an Oscar for *The Piano*?

③ Tightly packed isobars on a weather map indicate what?

④ Which English monarch was called the 'People's King'?

⑤ Which foreign country can you make out of IGLEBUM? 💡

⑥ How are igneous rocks formed?

⑦ What subject does Will Schuester teach in *Glee*?

⑧ Who was winner of Series 3 of *The X Factor*?

⑨ Which is more senior, a captain or a major? 💡

⑩ Who led the Springboks to victory in the 2007 Rugby World Cup?

⑪ Bruce Forsyth married a 'Miss World' from which country?

⑫ Which major river has its source in the Black Forest?

⑬ How is US outlaw Harry Longabaugh better known?

⑭ Who went *Looking for Richard* in 1996?

⑮ What is a moving staircase called? 💡

⑯ Who married Lady Carina Fitzalan-Howard in 1983?

QUIZ 113

① Who is Winnie-the-Pooh's best friend?

② Which is further east, Hamburg or Munich?

③ What is land endowed to a parish church for income called?

④ Which 20th-century Pope was 'Jolly'?

⑤ In the film *Zeus and Roxanne*, what is Roxanne?

⑥ The Four Noble Truths are fundamental to which religion?

⑦ Who is Sharpay Evans' twin brother in *High School Musical*?

⑧ What part of the eye gives it its colour?

⑨ In Roman mythology, who was the goddess of marriage?

⑩ Where are the Spanish Steps?

⑪ Ash, beech and plane are all types of what?

⑫ The Athenian legislator Draco has given us which modern word?

⑬ Which cricket Twenty20 county is called 'The Steelbacks'?

⑭ In which UK city can you walk the Royal Mile?

⑮ What is the capital of Australia?

⑯ What type of dancing is performed wearing a pair of ghillies?

QUIZ 114

① Complete the saying: 'As free as the ...'

② The Celtic bodhrán is what kind of musical instrument?

③ In which room of the White House does the US president work?

④ Which poet wrote: 'They also serve who only stand and wait'?

⑤ Which prickly plant grows in a desert?

⑥ *Polis* is the Greek word for what?

⑦ Which is the first prime number after 100?

⑧ What was Coldplay's first album?

⑨ Who are always playing cat and mouse with each other?

⑩ Which British prime minister was nicknamed 'Grocer'?

⑪ Who led a slave revolt in Virginia in 1831?

⑫ And who wrote a bestselling novel about his 'Confessions'?

⑬ How is Kernow better known?

⑭ Which prickly plant is the national emblem of Scotland?

⑮ Who is Scottish actor Denis Lawson's more famous nephew?

⑯ Who won the 2011 FIFA Women's World Cup?

QUIZ 115

① At what age do you become an octogenarian?

② Who tries to mend his head with vinegar and brown paper?

③ The Dogger Bank is off which coast of England?

④ Who won three Grammy awards for 'Tears in Heaven'?

⑤ Which English king was 'the Confessor'?

⑥ What does SOS mean?

⑦ How many Pussycat Dolls are there?

⑧ Which military force protects the Vatican?

⑨ How many sporting events are there in a pentathlon?

⑩ At which university is Clare College, Oxford or Cambridge?

⑪ What do Americans call a funny bone?

⑫ The word 'tsunami' comes from which language?

⑬ What does FOW stand for in cricket?

⑭ Which 20th-century dictator was called 'Pineapple Face'?

⑮ What does Neptune hold in his hand?

⑯ Who did Orlando Bloom play in *The Lord of the Rings*?

QUIZ 116

1. Whose heart was two sizes too small?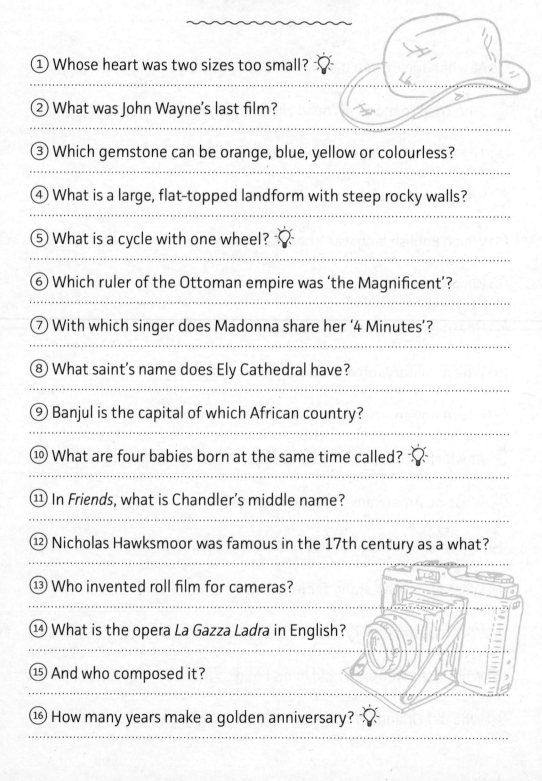

2. What was John Wayne's last film?

3. Which gemstone can be orange, blue, yellow or colourless?

4. What is a large, flat-topped landform with steep rocky walls?

5. What is a cycle with one wheel?

6. Which ruler of the Ottoman empire was 'the Magnificent'?

7. With which singer does Madonna share her '4 Minutes'?

8. What saint's name does Ely Cathedral have?

9. Banjul is the capital of which African country?

10. What are four babies born at the same time called?

11. In *Friends*, what is Chandler's middle name?

12. Nicholas Hawksmoor was famous in the 17th century as a what?

13. Who invented roll film for cameras?

14. What is the opera *La Gazza Ladra* in English?

15. And who composed it?

16. How many years make a golden anniversary?

QUIZ 117

① Who said: 'The play's the thing'?

② Who are Rastamouse, Scratchy and Zoomer? ⭤

③ Meerkats belong to which animal family?

④ What can be Wandering, Snowy or White-winged?

⑤ What is the highest mountain in the world? ⭤

⑥ What is Russian for citadel or fortress?

⑦ How many times did Ian Botham captain England?

⑧ Sheikh Mohammed bin Rashid Al Maktoum rules which country?

⑨ From which animal does venison come? ⭤

⑩ Which is the larger hyena, Brown or Spotted?

⑪ Who had a 2008 hit with 'So What'?

⑫ Which Irish nationalist was the 'Big Fella'?

⑬ Tariffs and quotas are used in which type of war?

⑭ Which cricketer has taken the most wickets ever? ⭤

⑮ Geographically speaking, what is a bill?

⑯ Who directed the 2007 remake of *Sleuth*?

QUIZ 118

① What clothing fabric originated in the French town of Nîmes?

② Who are Mr Bloom's helpers in the nursery? 💡

③ Which city has a football team named Ajax?

④ Which acting duo had a hit with 'I Believe'?

⑤ And which Irish group had a hit with the song before them?

⑥ What is the liquid inside a coconut called? 💡

⑦ Which English king was the 'Merry Monarch'?

⑧ How many counties are there in Northern Ireland?

⑨ Name the only UK woman to be seeded No 1 at Wimbledon postwar.

⑩ What is the world's largest bird of prey? 💡

⑪ When did Patrick Moore first take a look at *The Sky at Night*?

⑫ What was Tommy Steele's job before show business?

⑬ What is the deepest lake in Africa?

⑭ What is the worst thing about a skunk? 💡

⑮ To which floral family does the tulip belong?

⑯ What is a peri: a cocktail, fairy or parakeet?

QUIZ 119

① Complete the saying: 'As sly as a . . .'

② What did RFC stand for in World War I?

③ Eritrea was formerly part of which country?

④ Who almost drowned in a lake near Heathrow in 2009?

⑤ How long did the Wright brothers' first powered flight last?

⑥ Where do Curious George and the Man with the Yellow Hat live?

⑦ Which best-selling British author is a former Dr Barnardo's Boy?

⑧ Who was Britain's only medal winner at the 2006 Winter Olympics?

⑨ Which British wrestler was 'The Man You Love To Hate'?

⑩ Is New York on America's east or west coast?

⑪ Which English monarch was known as 'the Bastard'?

⑫ How is the height of a horse measured?

⑬ What are the Benelux countries?

⑭ What was the cat in *Breakfast at Tiffany's* called?

⑮ Which vegetable has the name of a European capital city?

⑯ Where in the UK was the Atomic Weapons Research Establishment?

QUIZ 120

① Which English city do you come from if you are a 'Brummie'? ☼

② In which month is the Queen's official birthday?

③ *Icky Thump* was whose thumping hit?

④ What is the chemical symbol for sodium?

⑤ Which country is on Egypt's western border?

⑥ Who captained Europe's winning Ryder Cup team in 2002?

⑦ Which Miliband is leader of the Labour Party, David or Ed? ☼

⑧ What tunnel links the Japanese islands of Honshu and Hokkaido?

⑨ Which World War II commander had the nickname 'Bomber'?

⑩ Who were the creators of *Steptoe and Son*?

⑪ What did the sparrow claim to kill Cock Robin with? ☼

⑫ The title of which Billy Wilder film is a type of hat?

⑬ Whose 17th-century *Brief Lives* took 20 years to write?

⑭ 'Jack the Ripper' is cockney rhyming slang for what?

⑮ Which capital city is also the name of a boot? ☼

⑯ Who made an epic journey on his raft Kon-Tiki?

QUIZ 121

① Who was the Roman goddess of corn?

② What colour skirt does Sooty's friend Soo wear? 🔅

③ Blaise Pascal invented the first what in 1642?

④ Which exotic singer's 2011 album was *Born This Way*?

⑤ Into which sea does the River Danube flow?

⑥ Maude Moonshine and Enid Nightshade are whose best friends? 🔅

⑦ Name the two journalists who exposed the Watergate scandal.

⑧ Who wrote the autobiographical novel *Borstal Boy*?

⑨ Which Midlands town is famous for its pork pies?

⑩ What is another name for the Netherlands? 🔅

⑪ In which country was the victorious Duke of Wellington born?

⑫ Who was the drummer in The Monkees?

⑬ What flower is often associated with Buddhism?

⑭ On whose novel is the film *The Damned United* based?

⑮ What does an artist rest his picture on when he's painting? 🔅

⑯ Which UK rugby club's home ground is the Liberty Stadium?

QUIZ 122

1. How many toes has a Pobble? 🔅

2. What is the nickname of the Australian rugby league team?

3. How many chromosomes are there in the human body?

4. Who did Morgan Freeman play in the film *Bruce Almighty*?

5. Who won the first-ever cricket Test match, England or Australia? 🔅

6. Which is the world's lowest major river below sea level?

7. Who wrote the play *The Lady's Not for Burning*?

8. What is the collective name for owls?

9. How many times did Lance Armstrong win the Tour de France?

10. What word can mean a ghost or a spy? 🔅

11. Which airborne service was started in Australia in 1928?

12. The Gaza Strip is bordered in part by which sea?

13. If you're lucky, what might you find at the end of a rainbow? 🔅

14. Which animal is often given the name Brock?

15. Who was defeated at the Battle of Culloden?

16. Merengue is a type of what?

QUIZ 123

① Where is the Grand National run?

② Who live in a monastery?

③ Which is the longest river in Europe?

④ In which sport was the American John Davis a world champion?

⑤ Who in 1961 became the 100th Archbishop of Canterbury?

⑥ What type of fruit are lemons, oranges and grapefruits?

⑦ Who were jointly crowned king and queen of England in 1689?

⑧ What is the fictional Billy Bunter's middle name?

⑨ Which bird is noted for its wisdom?

⑩ What type of musical instrument was a sackbut?

⑪ Who succeeded Alf Ramsey as England football manager?

⑫ What did the record label RCA stand for?

⑬ In which year was the July Plot against Hitler?

⑭ What do otters mainly eat?

⑮ What is the name of Leopold Bloom's wife in the novel *Ulysses*?

⑯ How were many French soldiers transported to the Battle of the Marne in 1914?

QUIZ 124

① Which New York street is associated with advertising?

② How many noughts in a modern trillion?

③ Which country is larger, France or Spain?

④ Who made an airborne escape from London Zoo in 1965?

⑤ In which 1980s film does Julie Andrews take on a male role?

⑥ What used to be home to an Eskimo?

⑦ How was architect Charles-Edouard Jeanneret-Gris better known?

⑧ What is a sinus?

⑨ Barcelona is in which region of Spain?

⑩ Brazil, hazel and monkey are all varieties of what?

⑪ January takes its name from which Roman god?

⑫ Which French king was guillotined in 1793?

⑬ What does GDP stand for?

⑭ Which UK artist turned up as a folk singer in *Frasier*?

⑮ In which Charles Dickens novel will you find Mr Micawber?

⑯ Who was the only Briton to win the Iron Cross in World War II?

QUIZ 125

① Which animal ran up the clock? 💡

② The Sirocco and the Mistral are both what?

③ What colour is a bloodstone?

④ Which royal residence is in Norfolk?

⑤ Which golfer has the nickname 'El Niño'?

⑥ With which art movement is painter René Magritte associated?

⑦ Which English seaport is nearest to France? 💡

⑧ Where in ancient Greece was Theseus king of?

⑨ Which poem begins: 'Should you ask me, whence these stories'?

⑩ Whose name was synonymous with Broadway follies?

⑪ Who travels in a spacecraft? 💡

⑫ Which movie star was the son of a Billingsgate fish porter?

⑬ Who was the first American to orbit the earth?

⑭ Which Beach Boy was acquitted of draft evasion in 1967?

⑮ What connects the centre of a bicycle wheel to its outer edge? 💡

⑯ Who makes the first move in a game of chess?

QUIZ 126

① On which part of an aircraft are the ailerons?

② What do some birds do in winter? ⌁

③ In which UK city is The Crucible theatre?

④ Who did Agnes Gonxha Bojaxhiu maternally become?

⑤ Which Archbishop of Canterbury crowned the Queen in 1953?

⑥ What colour do you add to blue to make it green? ⌁

⑦ Who plays Dawn Tinsley in *The Office*?

⑧ What is the highest judicial body in the USA?

⑨ Gangster star Edward G Robinson was born in which country?

⑩ Which cheese shares its name with an English gorge? ⌁

⑪ What does the S stand for in Winston S Churchill?

⑫ Who was the second wife divorced by Henry VIII?

⑬ In football, who is England's highest-ever goal scorer?

⑭ What is Ermintrude in *The Magic Roundabout*? ⌁

⑮ How many cards are there in a standard tarot pack?

⑯ What was the last album The Beatles recorded?

QUIZ 127

① Where would you wear a *chapeau*?

② What type of food is spaghetti? 🔅

③ Which Italian star made 12 films with Sophia Loren?

④ In which country did the Great Trek take place in 1836?

⑤ What is the smallest British coin? 🔅

⑥ Which Welsh river is longer, the Taff or the Teifi?

⑦ What is gneiss: Iranian cheese, space debris or a type of rock?

⑧ Which ex-England cricket captain co-wrote the thriller *Testkill*?

⑨ What does a carnivore eat? 🔅

⑩ Around what did New York's wits assemble at the Algonquin Hotel?

⑪ What is Homer Simpson's favourite beer?

⑫ Which poem begins: 'Twas the night before Christmas . . .'?

⑬ Knossos was the centre of which ancient civilization?

⑭ What can be an island or something warm to wear? 🔅

⑮ LIONESSES is an anagram of what word?

⑯ How many years were there between Stanley Matthews' first and last England caps?

QUIZ 128

1. What honour was bestowed on Charlie Chaplin in 1975?

2. DIY is short for what?

3. Who wrote 'The Battle Hymn of the Republic'?

4. Which jazz musician was known as 'Bird'?

5. In ballet, what does *sur les pointes* mean?

6. What does a fishermen use worms for?

7. Who is fictional detective Lord Peter Wimsey's manservant?

8. Which legendary All Black was nicknamed 'Pine Tree'?

9. Who plays Inspector Clouseau's servant in the *Pink Panther* films?

10. Which of the Seven Dwarves has the longest name?

11. Where does the River Tagus meet the Atlantic Ocean?

12. Which English city has a church with a crooked spire?

13. What is the USA's biggest selling mail order catalogue?

14. Which Siamese prince was a well-known motor-racing driver?

15. What in Scotland is Hogmanay?

16. Elmer Bernstein composed the music for which famous Western?

QUIZ 129

① What kind of diet was Jack Sprat on? 💡

② Which Tchaikovsky symphony is called the *Pathétique*?

③ Who made the first manned balloon flight in 1783?

④ What was banned from US television in 1971?

⑤ Which saint's day is on the 23rd of April? 💡

⑥ What does a philatelist collect?

⑦ Who wrote a series of novels called *La Comédie Humaine*?

⑧ Which US state came into being first, Alabama or Georgia?

⑨ Who did Reese Witherspoon play in the biopic *Walk the Line*?

⑩ Manhattan is part of which large city? 💡

⑪ What does the word uxorious mean?

⑫ MATRICIDE is an anagram of which word?

⑬ Who wrote a controversial biography of Princess Diana in 1992?

⑭ What do herbivores eat? 💡

⑮ How many times did Geoffrey Boycott captain England?

⑯ What is Japan's native religion?

QUIZ 130

① Who wrote *Tarka the Otter*?

② Which two major French rivers form the Gironde estuary?

③ What word means wise or is a herb?

④ When did the Sydney Opera House open: 1973, 1975, 1977?

⑤ What is Britain's oldest colony?

⑥ Rice grows in a what?

⑦ Which UK coin is not in general circulation?

⑧ What was Noel Coward's middle name?

⑨ 'Cavatina' is the theme music for which 1978 movie?

⑩ What tasty treat is made from the cocoa bean?

⑪ Who did Windsor Davies play in *It Ain't Half Hot Mum*?

⑫ How is 1 Canada Square better known?

⑬ Who composed *Clair de Lune*?

⑭ The emu is a native bird of which country?

⑮ In which English city was Cary Grant born?

⑯ And what was his real name?

QUIZ 131

① Who was England's manager at the 1990 FIFA World Cup?

② Where do Fireman Sam and his firefighters live?

③ Philosophically speaking, epistemology is the theory of what?

④ From which country does Moselle wine come?

⑤ In which year was John F Kennedy assassinated?

⑥ Who composed 'The Minute Waltz'?

⑦ What word can be a flying creature or something you take to the wicket?

⑧ Lady Anne Hyde was the mother of which British monarch?

⑨ What flower is named after the Swedish botanist Anders Dahl?

⑩ Which English cricket county begins with 'M'?

⑪ Where in Washington is the US Congress?

⑫ What was the Pharos of Alexandria?

⑬ What classical instrument did Jascha Heifetz play?

⑭ Who was the 'Fat Owl of the Remove'?

⑮ What is the control centre on a ship?

⑯ On which bank of the Seine is the Sorbonne?

QUIZ 132

① What colour are a Siamese cat's eyes?

② Who wrote the play *Romeo and Juliet*? 🔆

③ What divides Buda from Pest?

④ 'It Won't Be Soon Before Long' was a hit for what colourful band?

⑤ When was the Battle of the Somme?

⑥ How many players are there in a Rounders team? 🔆

⑦ Which cricketing wife wrote *Cricket XXXX Cricket*?

⑧ Switzerland and Austria share which national flower?

⑨ What does BYO stand for?

⑩ 1+2+3+4+5+6 adds up to what? 🔆

⑪ Who directed the film *The Killing Fields*?

⑫ When was the partitioning of India and Pakistan?

⑬ What was the Kennedy White House known as?

⑭ The collective name for witches is what?

⑮ Who are the native people of New Zealand? 🔆

⑯ *A Child of Our Time* is by which modern British composer?

QUIZ 133

① Which American state begins with 'U'?

② What is a wok used for? ☼

③ Who wrote the play *A Taste of Honey*?

④ When was the Great Fire of London?

⑤ Which British 'royal' married in 1986?

⑥ Who is the person in charge of a train? ☼

⑦ In which German city did the post-war Nazi trials take place?

⑧ What is the name for an ecclesiastical council?

⑨ Which UK driver won at Le Mans five times in the 1970s and 80s?

⑩ Which London cathedral has a dome? ☼

⑪ Chinua Achebe is which country's foremost writer?

⑫ What is the state of a feudal lord called?

⑬ Name the prequel to the 1960s film *Zulu*.

⑭ How many seconds are there in an hour? ☼

⑮ What does China's national flower *Prunus mei* mean?

⑯ Which 'White' African river has tributaries that are 'Red' and 'Black'?

QUIZ 134

① In what century is the TV series *Futurama* set?

② Where does a Scotsman wear a Tam o' Shanter? ☀

③ Which military leader's horse was named Marengo?

④ What does *Plaid Cymru* mean?

⑤ Who wrote the novel *Kangaroo*?

⑥ What is the station porter's name in *The Railway Children*? ☀

⑦ 'Stephen' translated into French becomes what?

⑧ What Aztec flower is a great favourite at Christmas?

⑨ Willemstad is the capital of which Caribbean island?

⑩ Which arm did Lord Nelson lose, left or right? ☀

⑪ Which father and daughter acted together in *New Tricks*?

⑫ What is the NUJ?

⑬ Which English mathematician committed suicide in 1954?

⑭ Who has made three *Shock Value* albums?

⑮ What does a milliner make? ☀

⑯ Which two US rivers meet at Harper's Ferry?

QUIZ 135

① What is a baby hare called?

② Where did Thomas the Tank Engine live?

③ Which French city is the setting for *French Connection II*?

④ And who directed the film?

⑤ Which three countries invaded Egypt in 1956?

⑥ MELON spelt differently becomes which other fruit?

⑦ In *The Archers*, who is Joe Grundy's first great-grandson?

⑧ How does a boatswain traditionally issue his commands?

⑨ Where in Paris is Sacre Coeur?

⑩ 2 x 2 x 3 x 4 x 5 adds up to what?

⑪ Who is the lead 'killer' in The Killers?

⑫ Which country is the world's largest producer of natural gas?

⑬ What union was behind the 1981 Gdańsk shipyard strikes?

⑭ Whose catchphrase in *Fireman Sam* is 'Great balls of fire!' ?

⑮ Which other footballer was Dennis Bergkamp named after?

⑯ In *Pride and Prejudice*, which of the Bennet girls does Charles Bingley marry?

QUIZ 136

① What sort of shop was the Little Shop of Horrors?

② 'qv' is an abbreviation for what?

③ Who is Snoopy's best birdy buddy?

④ What is a cooked and pickled flower bud?

⑤ In which film does Matt Damon play a delusional liar?

⑥ What kind of ship was the first nuclear-powered surface vessel?

⑦ Who does a bride marry?

⑧ What word can come before saucer, Scotsman and squad?

⑨ Who was wrongly accused of spying by the French army in 1894?

⑩ On which isle is the seaside town of Margate?

⑪ What does blowing your own trumpet mean?

⑫ The 'New World Symphony' is number what by Dvořák?

⑬ What shape is a Martello tower?

⑭ In *Scrabble*, what is the letter J worth?

⑮ What colour are Superman's shorts?

⑯ Which sportsman was England's last double international at football and cricket?

QUIZ 137

① Who plays Bob Cratchit in *The Muppet Christmas Carol*? 💡

② What is a sitar?

③ In *Futurama* who is Philip J Fry's love interest?

④ Whose name is synonymous with the first waterproof garment?

⑤ What is a mariner? 💡

⑥ Which war prompted the New York Draft Riots?

⑦ What is a wampee: a fruit, tent or tropical wind?

⑧ Which radio show featured Min and Henry Crun?

⑨ How was Indian prime minister Rajiv Gandhi killed?

⑩ What sound makes the time signal on radio – pips or bleeps? 💡

⑪ Who does Richard Harris play in *Unforgiven*?

⑫ What is the 'Old Man of Hoy'?

⑬ 'Naughty but nice' was the advertising slogan for what?

⑭ And which famous novelist wrote the line?

⑮ What river is Liverpool on? 💡

⑯ Who have been Scottish League Champions most, Celtic or Rangers?

QUIZ 138

① Who did Adolf Hitler marry in 1945?

② In *Star Wars*, who is Han Solo's co-pilot? 💡

③ What is Britain's oldest museum?

④ Who replaced Mutya Buena as a Sugarbabe?

⑤ Which US state was purchased from the French in 1803?

⑥ What is a bird of prey beginning with 'B'? 💡

⑦ In the song, what was broken by the man in Monte Carlo?

⑧ The Italian opera *La Cenerentola* is known in English as what?

⑨ Where is La Scala opera house?

⑩ In the world of sport, what was 'Mick the Miller'?

⑪ Which English King Henry founded Eton College?

⑫ What is the capital of Spain? 💡

⑬ Who was Stephen Spielberg's first wife?

⑭ What was the name of George Stephenson's first locomotive?

⑮ The caribou is what type of animal? 💡

⑯ What kind of food was hokey-pokey?

QUIZ 139

1 Which sport has birdies, eagles and albatrosses?

2 Complete the saying: 'As cool as a . . .' 💡

3 Where is the historic city of Syracuse?

4 What is an itinerant mender of pots and pans?

5 In which country was Katie Melua born?

6 Who threatens to gobble up the Three Billy Goats Gruff? 💡

7 Which wife of Ronald Reagan was not his First Lady?

8 What is the highest point on the North American continent?

9 Which cricket county's Twenty20 side is the 'Carnegies'?

10 What did a boy want so much he swapped his dad for them? 💡

11 Who did Theo Walcott score a hat-trick against in 2008?

12 Which film musical was called *Vaselina* in Spanish?

13 Who did Wallis Simpson divorce in 1936?

14 How many colours are there in the rainbow? 💡

15 Who was the fallen angel who became the Devil?

16 What sequel followed *Get Shorty* ten years later?

QUIZ 140

① Nathaniel Winkle is a character in which Charles Dickens novel?

② Tigress, Monkey, Crane, Viper and Mantis are in which gang?

③ On which bank of the Seine is The Louvre?

④ Which port serves Perth, Australia?

⑤ In which year did Henry Ford build his first car?

⑥ What is nautical speed measured in?

⑦ With what sport is Raymond van Barneveld associated?

⑧ What was the name of Winston Churchill's wife?

⑨ The Yvonne Arnaud Theatre is in which UK city?

⑩ What does KFC stand for?

⑪ What word describes a container for holy relics?

⑫ Which Mahler symphony was used for the film *Death in Venice*?

⑬ Who created the fox-hunting character Jorrocks?

⑭ Which of the Seven Dwarves has the shortest name?

⑮ Crystal is for a wedding anniversary of how many years?

⑯ Which is further north, King's Lynn or Norwich?

QUIZ 141

① New York is on which river?

② What did the emperor's new clothes cover? 💡

③ 'Germinal' in the French Revolutionary calendar means what?

④ Who wrote the 19th-century novel *Germinal*?

⑤ In *The Magic Roundabout*, what does Mr Rusty do? 💡

⑥ Which Olympic event does Bill Travers win in the film *Geordie*?

⑦ What are will.i.am, apl.de.ap, Taboo and Fergie?

⑧ William IV had how many children by his mistress Mrs Jordan?

⑨ What is a male bee? 💡

⑩ In Greek mythology, who was the son of Ares and Aphrodite?

⑪ What are the French high-speed trains called?

⑫ Which carbohydrate causes jam to gel?

⑬ What bird is a symbol of fertility?

⑭ Who was the first to put Muhammad Ali on the canvas?

⑮ What comes out of volcanoes red hot and bubbling? 💡

⑯ Canada has a coastline on which three oceans?

QUIZ 142

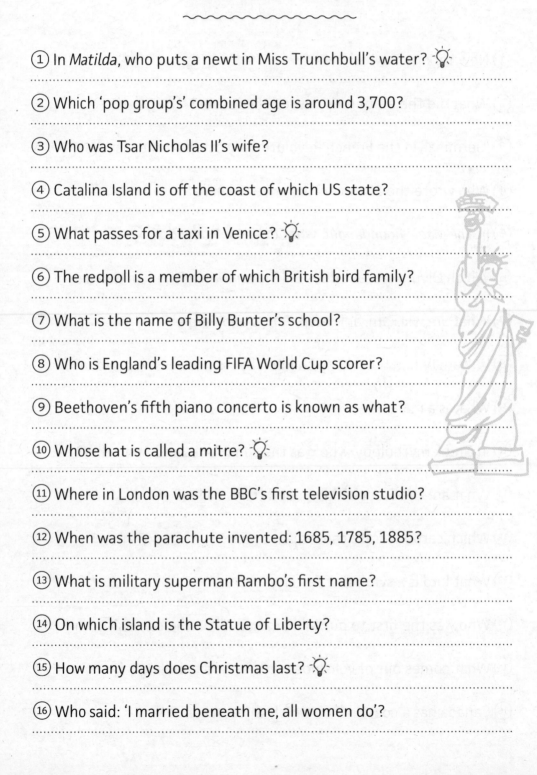

① In *Matilda*, who puts a newt in Miss Trunchbull's water? 💡

② Which 'pop group's' combined age is around 3,700?

③ Who was Tsar Nicholas II's wife?

④ Catalina Island is off the coast of which US state?

⑤ What passes for a taxi in Venice? 💡

⑥ The redpoll is a member of which British bird family?

⑦ What is the name of Billy Bunter's school?

⑧ Who is England's leading FIFA World Cup scorer?

⑨ Beethoven's fifth piano concerto is known as what?

⑩ Whose hat is called a mitre? 💡

⑪ Where in London was the BBC's first television studio?

⑫ When was the parachute invented: 1685, 1785, 1885?

⑬ What is military superman Rambo's first name?

⑭ On which island is the Statue of Liberty?

⑮ How many days does Christmas last? 💡

⑯ Who said: 'I married beneath me, all women do'?

QUIZ 143

1. What are crisps called in the USA?

2. Complete the saying: 'Mad as a . . .' 💡

3. Salop is an abbreviation of which county name?

4. What nationality is film director Wim Wenders?

5. Which cat is particularly well shod? 💡

6. When did the Pilgrim Fathers sail for America?

7. What do queen ants lose after mating?

8. Which father and daughter recorded 'Something Stupid'?

9. Name the first UK football club to have its badge on its shirt.

10. In which county is Land's End? 💡

11. Which pasta is quill-shaped?

12. What nationality was the singer Jacques Brel?

13. What is a judogi?

14. Which London railway station is the name of a famous battle? 💡

15. What is adobe?

16. Who wrote the song 'Me And Julio Down By The Schoolyard'?

QUIZ 144

① Which saint's day is on the 17th of March?

② Can you name the twins in *Rugrats*?

③ What is Latin for 'king'?

④ The Statue of Liberty was a gift from which nation?

⑤ Which major US river flows through Kentucky and Tennessee?

⑥ What does Ace Ventura search for?

⑦ When did the composer Mozart die: 1771, 1781, 1791?

⑧ What was Leslie Nielsen's code name in *Spy Hard*?

⑨ In which Olympic event did Carl Lewis win four gold medals?

⑩ On which vessel would you find a periscope?

⑪ Which is New York's most celebrated theatreland restaurant?

⑫ What is a volcanic vent called?

⑬ Which Hollywood star was known as the 'Sweater Girl'?

⑭ What were soldiers who fought on horseback called?

⑮ In surfing, what are 'Ankle Busters'?

⑯ What is a Mae West?

QUIZ 145

① How many bits in a byte?

② What is Bert's job in *Mary Poppins*?

③ What was Brandon Flowers' first album?

④ Which archbishop became president of Cyprus?

⑤ Who was the last High King of Ireland?

⑥ What colour fur has Top Cat?

⑦ Which is the largest country in Central America?

⑧ What is a connoisseur of good food called?

⑨ What does *tête-à-tête* literally mean?

⑩ What number comes next: 2, 4, 8, 16, 32 . . . ?

⑪ 'The Chorus of the Hebrew Slaves' comes from which opera?

⑫ Whose computer always says no in *Little Britain*?

⑬ What insect is a Garden Tiger?

⑭ In which film is the line: 'We'll always have Paris.'?

⑮ What are the letters in the alphabet that are not vowels called?

⑯ *Only Dad* was whose first novel?

QUIZ 146

1. Detective Superintendent Foyle polices which seaside town?

2. What really fell on Chicken Licken's head? 💡

3. Who wrote *One Flew Over the Cuckoo's Nest*?

4. In which US state is Tulsa?

5. Who sang 'Urban Hymns' in 1997?

6. Who does Norman Osborn turn into in *Spider-Man*? 💡

7. In which year was the Wall Street Crash?

8. *Bach* is a term of affection in which language?

9. Where is Britain's National Space Centre located?

10. What smooth fabric is made with the help of worms? 💡

11. Which Elvis hit came first, 'All Shook Up' or 'Jailhouse Rock'?

12. Who ordered the execution of any Cambodian wearing glasses?

13. In the world of finance, what does ISA stand for?

14. What is often called the 'champagne of tea'?

15. What colour do you add to red to make orange? 💡

16. What tourist attraction was erected in London to celebrate the new millennium?

QUIZ 147

① Mr Spock in *Star Trek* comes from which planet? 🔆

② Who is the creator of Paddington Bear?

③ What does a palaeontologist study?

④ Which Scottish city is on the site of an extinct volcano?

⑤ What is a country's official song called? 🔆

⑥ In which country was the slave Spartacus born?

⑦ What is the German name for Aix-la-Chapelle?

⑧ Where is the Kingsmead Test cricket ground?

⑨ Which poem begins: 'I must go down to the seas again . . .'?

⑩ What did knights in armour do at tournaments? 🔆

⑪ Who, at 29, was the youngest actor to play Hamlet on film?

⑫ In which English county is Hever Castle?

⑬ What instrument did jazz musician Ben Webster play?

⑭ The film *The Servant* was based on whose novel?

⑮ Which team sport is played on horseback? 🔆

⑯ Which 60s group did Otis Williams co-found?

QUIZ 148

① Medically speaking, what is 'Vet' short for?

② Where is the International Court of Justice?

③ What can be a bus or a chocolate bar?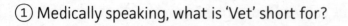

④ The aria 'One Fine Day' comes from which opera?

⑤ Which group's 1973 album was *Band on the Run*?

⑥ What was a cemetery called in the Wild West?

⑦ In which country was the philosopher Jean-Jacques Rousseau born?

⑧ Who wants everyone to 'Keep dancing'?

⑨ How many seconds in an hour and three-quarters?

⑩ Who wrote the 12th-century *History of the Kings of Britain*?

⑪ What does UEFA stand for?

⑫ What is the centre of a target called?

⑬ Which English monarch declared 'I will be good'?

⑭ What is the capital of Fiji?

⑮ How often does a biennial flower?

⑯ How many states are there in Australia: six, eight or ten?

QUIZ 149

1. Who wears a ten gallon hat? 💡

2. Who succeeded Harold Wilson as prime minister?

3. Where is General Santos International airport?

4. Which virtuoso percussionist was born in Scotland in 1965?

5. What is the word for a picnic basket? 💡

6. *Ocean Drive* was which UK duo's debut album?

7. What was the British Home Guard originally called?

8. Where were the 2006 Commonwealth Games held?

9. Who was Robin Hood's clerical companion? 💡

10. What is the monster's name in the epic poem *Beowulf*?

11. In rugby, what is the short side between scrum and touchline?

12. Which film role do Robert Stephens and Robert Downey Jr share?

13. How old was Theo Walcott when he won his first England cap?

14. What can be a type of boat or the introduction of something?

15. What is the capital of New Zealand? 💡

16. Who was the head of German military intelligence executed by Hitler in 1945?

QUIZ 150

1 Alice Nimbletoes is whose best friend?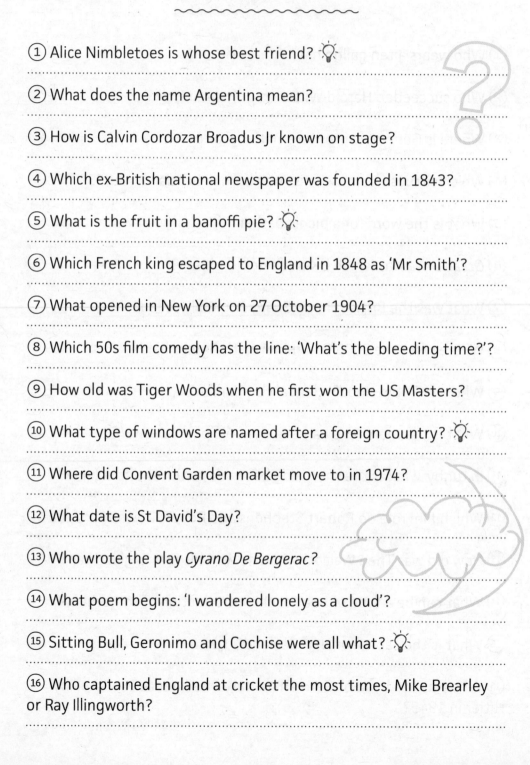

2 What does the name Argentina mean?

3 How is Calvin Cordozar Broadus Jr known on stage?

4 Which ex-British national newspaper was founded in 1843?

5 What is the fruit in a banoffi pie?

6 Which French king escaped to England in 1848 as 'Mr Smith'?

7 What opened in New York on 27 October 1904?

8 Which 50s film comedy has the line: 'What's the bleeding time?'?

9 How old was Tiger Woods when he first won the US Masters?

10 What type of windows are named after a foreign country?

11 Where did Convent Garden market move to in 1974?

12 What date is St David's Day?

13 Who wrote the play *Cyrano De Bergerac*?

14 What poem begins: 'I wandered lonely as a cloud'?

15 Sitting Bull, Geronimo and Cochise were all what?

16 Who captained England at cricket the most times, Mike Brearley or Ray Illingworth?

QUIZ 151

① In motor racing, what does a red and yellow striped flag signal?

② What shape is a rugby ball?

③ Why is Mr Spock in *Star Trek* so called?

④ What is the chemical symbol for strontium?

⑤ Anchorage is on which North American coast?

⑥ Mary Ann Nichols was whose first victim?

⑦ What flower is worn for those who fought and died in war?

⑧ To which bird did John Keats compose an ode?

⑨ What flower is also known as 'Batchelor's Button'?

⑩ Who composed the opera *William Tell*?

⑪ Which American state is the title of a musical?

⑫ What was invented first, the machine gun or revolver?

⑬ Which French word means a middle-class person?

⑭ Who is Coldplay's drummer?

⑮ Who did Anakin Skywalker become?

⑯ In the Bible, who is turned into a pillar of salt?

QUIZ 152

① In which country was Joseph Stalin born?

② Which Mr Man never stops talking?

③ To which island did Napoleon retire in 1814?

④ What is the drink *sake* made from?

⑤ What do hippologists study?

⑥ A *samurai* is a Japanese what?

⑦ Vectis was the Roman name for which part of England?

⑧ Who marched the Israelites around the walls of Jericho?

⑨ In the Bond films, which actor succeeded Bernard Lee as M?

⑩ Which English queen is a London railway station?

⑪ Which part of Cyprus belongs to Turkey, north or south?

⑫ Aung San Suu Kyi is a political activist in which country?

⑬ On which 60s TV show did the Osmond Brothers come to fame?

⑭ In which sport do you hit a ball through a hoop with a mallet?

⑮ Where is the source of the Rhine?

⑯ Kerry Hill is a breed of which animal: cat, dog or sheep?

QUIZ 153

① What is IQ short for?

② Where does a hampster store its food? 🔆

③ What food did a diplodocus eat?

④ Who does Elizabeth Taylor play in *National Velvet*?

⑤ What do fibre optics transmit?

⑥ Who lived in wigwams? 🔆

⑦ The port of Hamburg is on the southern shore of which river?

⑧ What is the world's oldest Sunday newspaper?

⑨ Which ever-expanding 'Library' was first published in 1905?

⑩ Who are Rocco and Brooks? 🔆

⑪ What is a fogou: a Cornish cave or a Celtic foot soldier?

⑫ Where each day does the 'Ceremony of the Keys' take place?

⑬ Who was born and raised at the Daisy Hill Puppy Farm?

⑭ Which Shaffer wrote the play *Equus*, Anthony or Peter?

⑮ What type of animal is a rat? 🔆

⑯ Where is the Sheikh Zayed Cricket Stadium?

QUIZ 154

① Which Little Miss is never on time? 💡

② What country borders Chile to the east?

③ Which urbane film star started life as Reginald Carey?

④ Who was Queen Mary I's mother?

⑤ A woman who is head of a family is called a what?

⑥ Dogs are colour blind – true or false? 💡

⑦ When did Gibraltar become a British colony: 1713, 1723, 1733?

⑧ Which 60s pop group was noted for its humorous parodies?

⑨ Who said: 'The lamps are going out all over Europe . . .' ?

⑩ What feline word describes a quick snooze? 💡

⑪ Who stole fire from Mount Olympus to give to mankind?

⑫ Which English cleric was known as the 'Red Dean'?

⑬ Which TV Rebus came first, John Hannah or Ken Stott?

⑭ Who is the so-called 'Queen of Shops'?

⑮ Which canal was built first, Panama or Suez? 💡

⑯ Who had a 70s album called *The Six Wives of Henry VIII*?

QUIZ 155

① In a 2002 film, Colin Farrell is held hostage in a what?

② Complete the saying: 'As clean as a . . .'

③ What is 'Stinking Bishop'?

④ Johnny Vegas appeared in which Charles Dickens TV drama?

⑤ Which French tennis star was nicknamed the 'Bounding Basque'?

⑥ Which is larger in size, Canada or the USA?

⑦ *A Doll's House* and *Ghosts* are by which playwright?

⑧ In which direction is Hebrew script written?

⑨ Which Scottish football team does Rod Stewart support?

⑩ What can be a salad leaf or a firework?

⑪ If you are nyctophobic what are you afraid of?

⑫ Who had a No 1 in 2000 with 'Life Is A Rollercoaster'?

⑬ In which ocean are the British-administered Chagos Islands?

⑭ Who were known in Scotland as 'gaugers'?

⑮ What is a set of drums called?

⑯ What nationality was the 16th-century theologian John Calvin?

QUIZ 156

1. What is a female horse called? 💡

2. Who is the person responsible for keeping official records?

3. What is Reuters?

4. Which bottle is larger, a Methuselah or Nebuchadnezzar?

5. What change of letter turns PALE into a strong wind? 💡

6. Who was William Wordsworth's diary-keeping sister?

7. What is Hugh Grant's middle name?

8. Which birds are known as 'Mother Carey's chickens'?

9. In which Middle East country are the Elburz Mountains?

10. What is the name of the badly behaved blue bear on TV? 💡

11. Which football club's home ground is The Valley?

12. Osiris is a god in which mythology?

13. Where is the 'Land of the Rising Sun'? 💡

14. Who wrote the novel *Earthly Powers*?

15. What type of food item is a macadamia?

16. In which country did the Romans build the Antonine Wall?

QUIZ 157

① What are you doing if you are 'tickling the ivories'?

② Who took 20 years to return home from the Trojan War?

③ What was the third film in the *Harry Potter* series?

④ 'You're The One That I Want' is a song from which film musical?

⑤ Which Mr Man lives in a teapot-shaped house?

⑥ What in the sea are *Porifera*?

⑦ Which Smith was a show-jumping champion?

⑧ Who succeeded William McKinley as US president in 1901?

⑨ What was Germany's wartime military intelligence agency called?

⑩ Which US state is in the Pacific Ocean?

⑪ Who directed the film *Trainspotting*?

⑫ Which UK rugby team's home ground is Thomond Park?

⑬ In which US state did the Battle of Wounded Knee take place?

⑭ What money changes hands in France, Germany and Spain?

⑮ St Willibrord is the patron saint of which European country?

⑯ Which 60s hit was re-released as a charity single in 1989?

QUIZ 158

1. Who did Billie Piper play in *Dr Who*?

2. From which county did the 19th-century Tolpuddle Martyrs come?

3. What language is spoken by Venetians?

4. How many gallons in a barrel: 12, 24 or 36?

5. With what profession is Harley Street associated?

6. Which of the cats in *Cats* has magical powers?

7. What was Take That's comeback album?

8. Which Cromwell lived longest, Oliver or Thomas?

9. Which member of The Platters died in 1992?

10. How often have France been runners-up in the Rugby World Cup?

11. In which country is a kimono traditionally worn?

12. What is the name of Billy Bunter's sister?

13. TV chat wise, how is Lawrence Harvey Zeiger better known?

14. Which Royal Naval rank is sometimes referred to as a 'snotty'?

15. How many Deadly Sins are there?

16. What colour ribbon is for breast cancer awareness?

QUIZ 159

① Whose face 'launched a thousand ships'?

② How many whiskers should a cat have: 16, 24 or 30?

③ If you are both left- and right-handed, what are you?

④ Who was the founder of the Ballets Russes?

⑤ What are the first three words in the Bible?

⑥ Which Smith wrote *I Capture the Castle*?

⑦ Complete this 1973 film title: *Deaf Smith and Johnny* . . .

⑧ What in the Netherlands are polders?

⑨ Which sport requires bows and arrows?

⑩ Who was the last viceroy of India?

⑪ Where is home to the marine iguana?

⑫ In which century was the English Court of Star Chamber?

⑬ How old was Saddam Hussein when he was executed?

⑭ Who creates chaos in the kitchen in *Gastronuts*?

⑮ When was the Battle of Verdun?

⑯ Who said: 'Nothing happened in the sixties except that we all dressed up.'?

QUIZ 160

① Which novelist won the Nobel Prize in Literature in 2003?

② Chop suey is a dish from which country?

③ What is crime committed via the Internet?

④ 'A wonderful bird is the pelican . . .' Why? 🔅

⑤ What is the state capital of Kansas?

⑥ Which police force claims always to get its man?

⑦ What were the names of the flying Wright Brothers?

⑧ Which Mr Man lives in Coldland? 🔅

⑨ In which UK city is the Radcliffe Camera?

⑩ What keeps a whale warm?

⑪ Who wrote the 16th-century philosophical work, *The Prince*?

⑫ What kind of herring puts you off the scent? 🔅

⑬ In the Old Testament, which book follows Numbers?

⑭ What does quotidian mean?

⑮ Who survived cancer to win the Grand National in 1981?

⑯ Where are there cats' eyes as far as you can see? 🔅

QUIZ 161

① Where would you find a dormer window?

② When do we all go round the mulberry bush?

③ With which Beatles' song did Peter Sellers have a hit?

④ What UK team reached the semi-finals of the 2011 Rugby World Cup?

⑤ Which actor was best known as Hopalong Cassidy?

⑥ What is also known as the anemonefish?

⑦ How many leagues under the sea did Jules Verne write about?

⑧ Which Wiltshire town is famous for manufacturing carpets?

⑨ Who is the Greek goddess of springs and fountains?

⑩ The Brickfielder is a hot, dry northerly wind in which country?

⑪ In what part of your body is the iris: ear, eye or nose?

⑫ Who declared: 'When the President does it, that means that it's not illegal.'?

⑬ In what profession is the prestigious Pritzker Prize awarded?

⑭ What is a male deer called?

⑮ What is the capital of Sardinia?

⑯ How many Scottish kings were called Malcolm?

QUIZ 162

① Which Beatle's song was 'My Sweet Lord'?

② Who is the animal hero in *Tinga Tinga Tales*? 💡

③ In the car world, what does SUV stand for?

④ What was Mika's debut album?

⑤ Change one letter and turn CASE into money? 💡

⑥ What is the square hat worn by academics?

⑦ Which cricket county's home ground is Grace Road?

⑧ What kind of creature is a loggerhead?

⑨ Where do you go for an eye test? 💡

⑩ What does 'Hobson's choice' mean?

⑪ Who played the title role in the 1954 film *Hobson's Choice*?

⑫ What was Jeffrey Archer found guilty of in 2001?

⑬ What sort of stone is Bath stone?

⑭ What is the princess' name in *Sleeping Beauty*? 💡

⑮ Irish Peach and Cornish Aromatic are varieties of what?

⑯ FOAF stands for what in Internet chat?

QUIZ 163

① Who plays Link Larkin in the film *Hairspray*?

② When you have a full set of teeth how many will it be? ☀

③ What common British bird is also known as a 'gowk'?

④ Who sat under the shade of a coolibah tree?

⑤ Add the showbiz surname: David, Patricia and Rosanna . . .

⑥ Which country does the food dish paella come from? ☀

⑦ What was Cilla Black's first No 1 hit?

⑧ What does a lepidopterist collect?

⑨ What is an open-sided barn called?

⑩ How many times was Stanley Baldwin prime minister?

⑪ What is a Mafia boss called? ☀

⑫ What is the pointed end of a blacksmith's anvil?

⑬ Who has to help their alien foster parents get acclimatized?

⑭ Where is the city of Petra?

⑮ What is the capital of Poland? ☀

⑯ Who described whom as a 'prophet for the 21st-century'?

QUIZ 164

① In which country is the royal palace of El Escorial?

② What is known as the 'sport of kings'?

③ In the USA, what is someone who works in the docks called?

④ What do you mix with red to make purple?

⑤ Which rapper joins Rihanna under her 'Umbrella'?

⑥ What is the collective noun for racehorses?

⑦ Which Little Misses do everything in pairs?

⑧ What is the largest Gothic church in northern Europe?

⑨ Who does Gary Burghoff play in the TV series *M*A*S*H*?

⑩ In which year was the Cuban missile crisis?

⑪ What is the monstrous Medusa's hair made of?

⑫ Which Great Train Robber returned from exile in 2001?

⑬ Rossano Brazzi made his Hollywood debut in which 'female' film?

⑭ If you changed a £5 note into 5p coins how many would you get?

⑮ Which disease does the Ambrosia beetle spread?

⑯ What is the only strictly marine herbivorous mammal?

QUIZ 165

① What instrument does Yo-Yo Ma play?

② Who got his feet wet trying to command the waves?

③ Mistress of the Robes makes sure who is dressed properly?

④ Which snooker player was known as the 'Romford Robot'?

⑤ Complete the saying: 'Like a red rag to a . . .'

⑥ Where is the Lincoln Center for the Performing Arts?

⑦ What badge does a newly qualified pilot receive?

⑧ Pram is an abbreviation of which word?

⑨ The bongo is what kind of animal?

⑩ How many teeth does a cat have: 24, 30 or 36?

⑪ Which John was 'Public Enemy No 1'?

⑫ What was the first UK city to be a 'Capital of Culture'?

⑬ Which club did Alex Ferguson manage before Manchester United?

⑭ In which country was Símon Bolívar born?

⑮ Which Test cricket team wears a baggy green cap?

⑯ 'Bloody-nosed' and 'screech' are types of which insect?

QUIZ 166

① Which UK film company was synonymous with horror movies?

② What is longer, a metre or a yard? 🔅

③ The Willis Tower is in which US city?

④ Who composed the original theme music for *Dr Who*?

⑤ In which French city was Joan of Arc burnt at the stake?

⑥ What English rugby club shares the name of an insect?

⑦ Which game is played on a chequerboard but isn't chess? 🔅

⑧ In which country was the far-sighted Nostradamus born?

⑨ Where was the Muhammad Ali-George Foreman rumble in the jungle?

⑩ Which port is on the Atlantic side of the Panama Canal?

⑪ What is a baby rabbit called? 🔅

⑫ What causes a blue moon?

⑬ What spends its life standing on its head?

⑭ Newman Noggs is a character in which Dickens novel?

⑮ What can be something painful on your toe or a field of cereal? 🔅

⑯ ASPIRANT is an anagram of which word?

QUIZ 167

① Which evil person kidnaps dalmation puppies for their fur? 🔅

② What is foot and mouth disease called in the USA?

③ Which Apache hero's name means 'One Who Yawns'?

④ To what bird family do puffins, razorbills and guillemots belong?

⑤ What is a costard: an apple, floppy hat or heraldic device?

⑥ In which city is the magnificent Hagia Sophia?

⑦ What can be darning, knitting or sewing? 🔅

⑧ Which two former US presidents died on the same day in 1826?

⑨ What Notts town shares its name with New Jersey's largest city?

⑩ Bobby 'Boris' Pickett found fame with what song?

⑪ Which singing animals are Alvin, Simon and Theodore? 🔅

⑫ What nationality is movie director James Cameron?

⑬ Which 2008 sporting venue was known as the 'Bird's Nest'?

⑭ Name the reclusive American writer who died in 2010.

⑮ In *Tracy Beaker*, what is Elm Tree House better known as? 🔅

⑯ 'Goodbye, Farewell and Amen' was the last episode of which long-running TV series?

QUIZ 168

① *The Misfits* was which Hollywood legend's last film?

② Which tiny girl is found in a flower?

③ The port of Mocha is in which country?

④ Early houses were constructed using wattle and what?

⑤ What 'johns' are something to wear in winter?

⑥ In which sport is David Bryant a supreme champion?

⑦ According to Shakespeare, life is a tale told by a what?

⑧ Which canal links London and Birmingham?

⑨ In an American car, which side is the steering wheel?

⑩ What colour is a female Chalk-hill Blue butterfly?

⑪ Which World War II heroine did Anna Neagle portray on film?

⑫ What is deeper water, bathypelagic or mesopelagic?

⑬ Who was the first US driver to win the F1 World Championship?

⑭ In which establishment was Abraham Lincoln shot?

⑮ Which city's nickname is 'The Big Apple'?

⑯ Whose own last words were: 'Last words are for fools who haven't said enough.'?

QUIZ 169

① Which Mr Man is round and yellow and very cuddly? 🔆

② Who won an Oscar for her role as Edith Piaf?

③ What is 1666 in Roman numerals?

④ Which sport has a short leg and a long leg? 🔆

⑤ In Nordic mythology, what was Odin's ring called?

⑥ Who composed the opera *Lucia di Lammermoor*?

⑦ Which director of silent films invented false eyelashes?

⑧ What future English monarch played at Wimbledon in 1926?

⑨ What is the ditch around a castle wall called? 🔆

⑩ Who wrote the novel *The Sound and the Fury*?

⑪ Which sea creature has enough power to illuminate a house?

⑫ Name the port at the southern end of the Suez Canal.

⑬ What in the UK was nationalized first, coal or the railways?

⑭ Which country's motto is 'Liberty, Equality, Fraternity'? 🔆

⑮ Who wrote the devotional work, *Imitation of Christ*?

⑯ Which island was awarded the George Cross for heroism?

QUIZ 170

① Which of Coldplay's albums means 'Long live life'?

② If you raise a false alarm what do you cry? 💡

③ Who does Gemma Arterton play in *Quantum of Solace*?

④ Johann Zoffany was best known for painting what?

⑤ Basic slag, a bi-product of steel manufacturing, is used as what?

⑥ What is the toy train in the Night Garden? 💡

⑦ Whose 2006 Christmas No 1 was 'A Moment Like This'?

⑧ Which period came first, palaeolithic or chalcolithic?

⑨ Who was the first sports commentator to be knighted?

⑩ Parmesan cheese comes from which country? 💡

⑪ What is the top prize at the Venice Film Festival?

⑫ Who is the creator of Asterix?

⑬ What lives in the abandoned shells of other creatures?

⑭ Which Bonaparte became king of Spain in 1808?

⑮ What number will the next King Charles be? 💡

⑯ Add the fraternal sporting surname: Kamran and Umar . . .

QUIZ 171

① What did Mortimer Mouse change his name to? 💡

② Where was the singer Paolo Nutini born?

③ What is the main vegetable ingredient in moussaka?

④ In which South African city is the Castle of Good Hope?

⑤ What seaside sweet has its name down the middle? 💡

⑥ Who is the patron saint of civil servants?

⑦ The leotard was named after a famous French what?

⑧ What kind of insect is a Small Postman?

⑨ Which US president received an honorary knighthood in 1989?

⑩ On a ship, is starboard left or right? 💡

⑪ What sport is divided into chukkas?

⑫ Which Californian port is a major US Naval base?

⑬ What was the name of the first US space shuttle?

⑭ Who directed the 2006 film *World Trade Center*?

⑮ Bubbles the chimpanzee was a good friend of which singer? 💡

⑯ In which activity is a dibber or dibble used?

QUIZ 172

① Who resigned as England's rugby manager in 2011?

② What are an elephant's tusks made of?

③ Which ex-Beatle was stabbed by an intruder at his home in 1999?

④ What is the chemical symbol for copper?

⑤ In which year did Cassius Clay become Muhammad Ali?

⑥ Which fruit eaten every day is meant to keep the doctor away?

⑦ What did Dian Fossey study for 18 years in Rwanda?

⑧ Which Russian lake is the deepest in the world?

⑨ In which war did the tank make its first appearance?

⑩ What is larger, a stoat or a weasel?

⑪ Cabrio, Corrado and Jetta are models of which car?

⑫ Who in 1929 won the first Oscar for 'Best Actor'?

⑬ Khaki Campbell and Indian Runner are breeds of what?

⑭ Who vacated No 10 Downing Street on 28 November 1990?

⑮ What is the capital of Iraq?

⑯ Who writes the new 'Dick Francis' thrillers?

QUIZ 173

① What does WYSIWYG stand for in computer speak?

② Who eats all the porridge in baby bears bowl?

③ In cricket, where was the original county ground of Essex?

④ Who wrote *The Mill on the Floss*?

⑤ Which Bernardo Bertolucci film won nine Oscars in 1988?

⑥ Which animal is the symbol of the World Wildlife Organisation?

⑦ What is the Argentinean name for the Falklands?

⑧ Who said: 'I like Mr Gorbachev, we can do business together.'?

⑨ In which US state is Waco, site of the 1993 siege?

⑩ What did Tony Blair convert to in 2007?

⑪ From which direction does the sun rise?

⑫ What kind of implement is an adze?

⑬ For how many years did Queen Victoria reign?

⑭ In popular mythology, a satyr is part man, part what?

⑮ Most wine is made from which fruit?

⑯ In the USA, what commemorative day is on the third Monday in January?

QUIZ 174

① How many cents make a US dollar?

② A lot of bees flying together are called a what?

③ Who won the US Open golf championship in 2011?

④ Rose hips are rich in which vitamin?

⑤ What is Poland's national airline?

⑥ Who traditionally sits on the Woolsack?

⑦ Which sport has a front row, second row and back row?

⑧ What was the name of Lord Nelson's daughter by Lady Hamilton?

⑨ Which former TV presenter created *Ballykissangel*?

⑩ Who was Hollywood's most famous choreographer of the 1930s?

⑪ What can be white, brown or caster?

⑫ What does occidental mean?

⑬ Which bird is the symbol of the RSPB?

⑭ Who was the wife of King Priam of Troy?

⑮ What is the furthest north you can get on Earth?

⑯ Which legendary US bank robber did Lester M Gillis become?

QUIZ 175

① What piece of wood when thrown away always come back?

② How was Prince Harry known at Sandhurst?

③ Mycology is the study of what?

④ Which footballer was PFA Young Player of the Year in 1995/1996?

⑤ How many gold medals did Sir Steve Redgrave win in total?

⑥ When was the Irish Free State established?

⑦ Who played Burt Campbell in the TV soap *Soap*?

⑧ A sea urchin is also known as a what?

⑨ Which classic children's tale did Carlo Collodi write?

⑩ What would you hope to find in an oasis?

⑪ Which artificial international language was devised in 1887?

⑫ What humanitarian organization was founded in 1863?

⑬ Which was the second film in *The Lord of the Rings* trilogy?

⑭ What does the name Austria mean?

⑮ How do cowboys greet each other?

⑯ What is the sign language of bookies?

QUIZ 176

① What colour flowers does a jacaranda tree have?

② Which Arab tribe lives in the desert? 🔅

③ What acid does vinegar contain?

④ Which wife of a president had a musical written about her?

⑤ Who wrote: 'Shall I compare thee to a Summer's day?'?

⑥ 'Up to tricks' is the bingo call for which number?

⑦ If you change a £10 note for 20p coins, how many will you get? 🔅

⑧ Which Roman goddess shares her name with a brand of spread?

⑨ What is the name of Malaysia's Formula One circuit?

⑩ In which country is Mombassa?

⑪ Which queen made some tarts all on a summer's day? 🔅

⑫ In which year was the Tiananmen Square massacre?

⑬ *Rockferry* was whose No 1 album in 2008?

⑭ What is the Spanish equivalent of 'Michael'?

⑮ Who was in charge of law and order in a Wild West town? 🔅

⑯ Which English monarch wrote: 'The Divine Right of Kings'?

QUIZ 177

① With which style of acting was Lee Strasberg identified?

② What number nanny for the Brown children was Nanny McPhee?

③ Which two brothers founded an Anglo-Saxon kingdom in Kent?

④ What does antebellum mean?

⑤ Who did Jacqui Smith succeed as Home Secretary?

⑥ Which great scientist once worked as a clerk in a patent office?

⑦ What is Prince Harry's real first name?

⑧ Who was the 'fastest milkman in the West'?

⑨ 'Laura' was the muse of which 14th-century Italian poet?

⑩ Who won the 2010 Man Booker Prize?

⑪ Which English town was made 'Royal' in 2011?

⑫ Which racing driver was 1992 BBC Sports Personality of the Year?

⑬ What are the rebel fighters in Sri Lanka called?

⑭ Which princess died in a car accident in 1982?

⑮ What is the large iron grating at the entrance to a castle?

⑯ Which actress and singer did Julia Elizabeth Wells become?

QUIZ 178

① 'Single' and 'These Words' were hit songs for whom?

② Complete the saying: 'As dry as a . . . ' ☀

③ What is done to an ice hockey puck to stop it bouncing?

④ Which word can come before killer, like and ship?

⑤ What is the world's most southerly capital?

⑥ *Crêpe* is the French word for which food item? ☀

⑦ What is the artist Cézanne's first name?

⑧ When did Mikhail Gorbachev become leader of the Soviet Union?

⑨ What can be a type of window or a medical instrument?

⑩ Who wrote the poem 'The Owl and the Pussy-Cat'? ☀

⑪ In which TV space series was Capt Del Tarrant a character?

⑫ What is a derrick?

⑬ For what is dB the symbol?

⑭ How many players are there in a rugby league team? ☀

⑮ In Herman Melville's story, who does Billy Budd kill?

⑯ At which ground was the first-ever cricket Test played?

QUIZ 179

① What does the word prolix mean?

② Which Greek island almost gave its name to a lettuce?

③ Who had a coat of many colours?

④ What is the waist-high horizontal bar used by ballet dancers?

⑤ 'Garden gate' is cockney rhyming slang for what?

⑥ What symbols represented the USSR industrial worker and peasant?

⑦ Which town on the River Thames has a Royal Regatta each summer?

⑧ What type of flower is the jonquil?

⑨ What is the German word for the number nine?

⑩ 17 is the square root of what?

⑪ Where did the Chow dog come from originally?

⑫ Dr Crippen was arrested at sea through the first use of what?

⑬ What rank was Hermann Goering?

⑭ Who on TV played the role of Aunt Sally in *Worzel Gummidge*?

⑮ What is the title of Wallace and Gromit's horror film?

⑯ Which French driver had a career total of 51 Grand Prix wins?

QUIZ 180

① Who plays Tracy Turnblad's mother in the film *Hairspray*?

② Whose home is in Gotham City?

③ What is the first day of Lent?

④ Whose stately home is Longleat?

⑤ Which cheese has holes in it not caused by mice?

⑥ What is the second largest planet in the Solar System?

⑦ For which film did Frank Sinatra win an Oscar in 1954?

⑧ What date is Michaelmas Day?

⑨ Claude William Dukenfield was which funny man's real name?

⑩ What do you mix with black to get grey?

⑪ In which country is Mount Kilimanjaro?

⑫ Who headed the Vichy government in wartime France?

⑬ Which US presidential candidate in 2008 was a Vietnam war hero?

⑭ What is the capital of Afghanistan?

⑮ Who won the 2010 British motor-racing Grand Prix?

⑯ What did Ferruccio Lamborghini make before luxury cars?

QUIZ 181

① Which Little Miss has very long legs and is very gymnastic?

② In Internet chat, what is AAMOF short for?

③ Who was the creator of Billy Bunter?

④ Which female animal is a jenny?

⑤ In fishing, what is a fyke?

⑥ What can be a dance or something you get water from?

⑦ Who was King Charles I's wife?

⑧ Nemesis was the Greek goddess of what?

⑨ Where is the football club Juventus based?

⑩ What Sunday is a week before Easter Sunday?

⑪ Where is known as 'La Belle Province'?

⑫ Whose solo debut album was *Diva*?

⑬ What is South Africa's currency?

⑭ Complete the simile: 'As rich as . . .'

⑮ Who is headmaster of Hogwarts School?

⑯ Where in the UK was the first civilian bombing death recorded in World War II?

QUIZ 182

① What does the initial stand for in George W Bush?

② In the film *Ratatouille*, what is the rat's name?

③ When would you wear a hacking jacket?

④ On which island is Pearl Harbor?

⑤ Which king was born at Tintagel?

⑥ Which mythological twins are said to have founded Rome?

⑦ Which composer and classical guitarist share the same name?

⑧ What is 10° Celsius in Fahrenheit?

⑨ Why does Pinocchio's nose keep growing?

⑩ Who composed *Fantasia on a Theme by Thomas Tallis*?

⑪ Which British nurse did the Germans execute in 1915?

⑫ Who was Australia's first rugby World Cup-winning captain?

⑬ What is the currency of Denmark?

⑭ In which country are Audi cars made?

⑮ Who was the first-ever combat soldier to win a double VC?

⑯ Which famous UK comedy was remade in 2004 starring Tom Hanks?

QUIZ 183

① Which children's novel begins: 'How's the bellyache, then?'?

② Which meat-eater switches to sushi in the film *Madagascar*? ·̣̇Ω·

③ What in Australia is the MCG?

④ Oenology is the study of what?

⑤ Henry Temple was the name of which great British statesman?

⑥ After how many years did England win back the Ashes in 2005?

⑦ Whose 'Unchained Melody' made it to No 1 in 1995?

⑧ What colour sashes did Puritans wear in the English Civil War?

⑨ Fandango, Mazurka and Tarantella are all types of what?

⑩ Prince Charles is the Duke of which county? ·̣̇Ω·

⑪ The ohm is a measurement of what?

⑫ What kind of insect is a ladybird? ·̣̇Ω·

⑬ In which park is Rotten Row?

⑭ Who wrote the four gospels in the New Testament? ·̣̇Ω·

⑮ What word can follow fan, green or trouser?

⑯ Who in the commercials went 'Clunk click, every trip'?

QUIZ 184

① Which animal never forgets? 💡

② Who presented *The Antiques Roadshow* for 19 years?

③ Which UK cathedral was destroyed by bombs in November 1940?

④ What is a hotel pageboy called in the USA?

⑤ How many sides has a rectangle? 💡

⑥ In archaeological terms, what is a barrow?

⑦ Who won the 2009 Cricket County Championship?

⑧ What is parthenogenesis?

⑨ Which gate was reopened in Berlin in 1989?

⑩ What is the central region of England known as? 💡

⑪ Which three states border California?

⑫ Is the moon yin or yang?

⑬ From which region of Italy does Chianti wine come?

⑭ Who was son and heir of Haitian dictator 'Papa Doc' Duvalier?

⑮ What is the opposite of 'add'? 💡

⑯ Which song went No 1 for both Harry Nilsson and Mariah Carey?

QUIZ 185

① What is the RSC?

② 'Peter Piper picked a piece of pickled pepper' is a what? ☀

③ In the USA, what date is Groundhog Day?

④ Which product's slogan was 'Full of Eastern promise'?

⑤ Montpelier is the capital of which US state?

⑥ What is a baby horse called? ☀

⑦ Which Polish general had a helicopter named after him?

⑧ What does the word obfuscate mean?

⑨ Who was the first man to fly solo across the Atlantic?

⑩ Which word can come after pencil, money and lunch? ☀

⑪ In which year did Sachin Tendulkar make his Test debut?

⑫ The opera *Die Zauberflöte* is called what in English?

⑬ By what name was Ethiopia formerly known?

⑭ In the natural world, what is a bug?

⑮ In which adventure story is Blind Pew a character? ☀

⑯ Which ex-cavalry officer won two BRITS in 2006?

QUIZ 186

① What is RSVP short for?

② How many holes are there on a Chinese Checkers board?

③ What did Mrs Frederick C Little's second son turn out to be?

④ On whose novel was the film *Death in Venice* based?

⑤ The Conciergerie in Paris served both as a palace and as a what?

⑥ A cricket bat is made from the wood of which tree?

⑦ What word describes a deadlock or impasse?

⑧ Who was the first to swim the English Channel?

⑨ What is an area of high atmospheric pressure called?

⑩ How many musicians play in a septet?

⑪ Which footballer was PFA Young Player of the Year in 2005/2006?

⑫ Who did Coldplay's Chris Martin marry in 2003?

⑬ Through which gate did prisoners in the Tower of London pass?

⑭ What is a USB flash drive?

⑮ Where is the Millennium Stadium?

⑯ Which stage musical won a record number of Tony Awards in 2001?

QUIZ 187

① Where was the birthplace of the prophet Muhammad?

② What Irish fairy is usually a mischievous old man?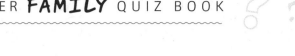

③ How many points for an aircraft carrier in the game Battleships?

④ What is the large East Anglian inlet of the North Sea called?

⑤ Buffetiers, guards of the monarch's food, became known as what?

⑥ Which item of footwear was named after a famous general?

⑦ What is Rigoletto in Verdi's opera of the same name?

⑧ Which country's national emblem is a hexagram?

⑨ What insect's larva is the bloodworm?

⑩ Rumba, salsa and samba are all what?

⑪ What do crutches on a boat support?

⑫ In *The Lone Ranger*, what is the name of Tonto's horse?

⑬ Which Greek sorceress turned Odysseus' crew into swine?

⑭ How many Nobel Prizes are awarded each year?

⑮ What is the opposite of 'to admit'?

⑯ Which oppressed family lived in Wimpole Street?

QUIZ 188

① *We Need to Talk about Kevin* is a prize-winning novel by whom?

② What is the fourth vowel from the end of the alphabet?

③ Who married actor Anthony Booth shortly before her death in 1986?

④ What poems begins: 'When I consider how my light is spent . . .'?

⑤ Who replaced Kerry Katona of Atomic Kitten in 2001?

⑥ What is the part of Earth south of the equator called?

⑦ If you are lachrymose, what are you?

⑧ What is measured on the Richter Scale?

⑨ What is Wales' 'Holy City'?

⑩ Which animal can be red, fallow or roe?

⑪ In which Spanish city do the bulls run through the streets?

⑫ Which word can come before ball, glass and sore?

⑬ Who lent his name to the Lean Mean Grilling Machine?

⑭ In motor racing, what does a white flag indicate?

⑮ Who creates the steps and movements for a dance routine?

⑯ What catastrophe infected England in 1665?

QUIZ 189

① Who was the forerunner of the London policeman?

② Which children's classic animal story first appeared in 1908?

③ What is the capital of Japan?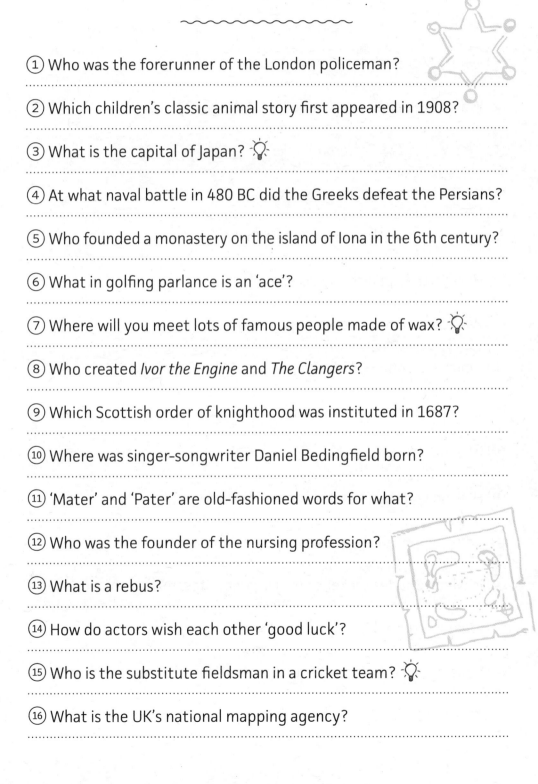

④ At what naval battle in 480 BC did the Greeks defeat the Persians?

⑤ Who founded a monastery on the island of Iona in the 6th century?

⑥ What in golfing parlance is an 'ace'?

⑦ Where will you meet lots of famous people made of wax?

⑧ Who created *Ivor the Engine* and *The Clangers*?

⑨ Which Scottish order of knighthood was instituted in 1687?

⑩ Where was singer-songwriter Daniel Bedingfield born?

⑪ 'Mater' and 'Pater' are old-fashioned words for what?

⑫ Who was the founder of the nursing profession?

⑬ What is a rebus?

⑭ How do actors wish each other 'good luck'?

⑮ Who is the substitute fieldsman in a cricket team?

⑯ What is the UK's national mapping agency?

QUIZ 190

① Who is Mumble's love interest in *Happy Feet*?

② What is the chemical symbol for hydrogen?

③ Who wrote *The Canterbury Tales*?

④ Which Hollywood star was known as the 'It Girl'?

⑤ Can you name the parrot in Enid Blyton's *Adventure* books?

⑥ How do the Spanish say goodbye?

⑦ Who created the choreography for *West Side Story*?

⑧ Which instrument did jazz musician Miles Davis play?

⑨ Who was Australia's prime minister for 18 years?

⑩ What is the world's slowest mammal?

⑪ How do you calculate the area of a rectangle?

⑫ Who composed the music for the ballet *Coppélia*?

⑬ In which Charles Dickens novel is James Steerforth a character?

⑭ What is a runnel?

⑮ Which group of islands are off the southwest coast of England?

⑯ What does the Latin phrase *mea culpa* mean?

QUIZ 191

① Who is the pig in *Charlotte's Web*? 🔦

② Where was the singer Mika born?

③ The island of Nantucket is off the coast of which US state?

④ At which major film festival is the 'Golden Bear' the top prize?

⑤ What can be a Chinese boat or a load of rubbish? 🔦

⑥ In Greek mythology, how many Furies were there?

⑦ What is a social gathering of Scottish music and dance called?

⑧ In the phonetic alphabet which word is used for W?

⑨ Ferns don't have seeds, what do they have?

⑩ What is BT short for? 🔦

⑪ What can be used for storing grain or missiles?

⑫ Add the showbiz surname: Bruce, David, Keith, Robert . . .

⑬ What brings the exhibits to life in *Night at the Museum*?

⑭ In which sea is the Great Barrier Reef?

⑮ Which famous rugby club is nicknamed the 'Ba Ba's'? 🔦

⑯ Who were the rival families in *Romeo and Juliet*?

QUIZ 192

① What is the capital of India?

② Which Mr Man just can't get things right?

③ In which style of wrestling are holds below the waist forbidden?

④ What was the FIFA World Cup trophy originally called?

⑤ How many triangular sides does a tetrahedron have?

⑥ What can be a set of clothes or a set of cards?

⑦ Which UK politician was nicknamed 'Hezza'?

⑧ What kind of aircraft is the Harrier?

⑨ What does the word 'karaoke' mean?

⑩ Which ingredient makes bread rise?

⑪ What was the 2009 Christmas No 1 in the UK?

⑫ Post, smock and tower are types of what working building?

⑬ What was the first colour movie to win an Oscar as 'Best Film'?

⑭ 'Pugilist' is an old-fashioned word for a what?

⑮ The Thomas Cup is a world championship trophy for which sport?

⑯ On which continent are the McMurdo Dry Valleys?

QUIZ 193

① 'The Fat Of The Land' went to No 1 around the world for whom?

② In *Big Baby* who is always saying 'Oh, Bongo!'?

③ Which gate separates consecrated and unconsecrated ground?

④ Which US president advised: 'Speak softly and carry a big stick'?

⑤ What was Gandalf's second ring?

⑥ What is 17 ÷ 100?

⑦ What does the word ubiquitous mean?

⑧ Who does Helen Mirren play in *Prime Suspect*?

⑨ Which popular cricket commentator died in 1994?

⑩ Ciabatta, Naan and Pitta are all types of what?

⑪ How many more wives than Henry VIII has Mickey Rooney had?

⑫ What meat is used in the Italian dish *saltimbocca*?

⑬ Which famous US car was named after a French explorer?

⑭ Which cricketer was knighted in 2007?

⑮ What is the opposite of 'affirmative'?

⑯ Which legendary Scottish hero did Robert MacGregor become?

QUIZ 194

① Who do the Bright Sparks have to beat in *Beat the Boss*?

② For which football club did Robbie Savage play most?

③ What is *mal de mer*?

④ Who wrote *The Constant Gardener*?

⑤ What bird can be golden or bald?

⑥ King George VI was known to his family as who?

⑦ The Welsh motto 'Cymru am byth' means what?

⑧ Which US president was born Leslie Lynch King Jr?

⑨ Which old language is spoken in Scotland – Garlic or Gaelic?

⑩ What happened in the University Boat Race of 1912?

⑪ What do you get when you multiply ½ x ½?

⑫ Who is the patron saint of cooks?

⑬ Dialling from the UK, what is the telephone prefix for Germany?

⑭ In *Madagascar*, Julian XIII is king of which animals?

⑮ Who ordered Sir Walter Raleigh's execution?

⑯ What does *à la mode* mean?

QUIZ 195

1. Is President Obama a Democrat or a Republican?

2. What is super villain Oswald Chesterfield Cobblepot III's alias? 💡

3. Which colourful singer's real name is Alecia Beth Moore?

4. In which year was the Munich Agreement?

5. What is a house that has no upstairs called? 💡

6. Is heat yin or yang?

7. What crime-detection aid is dactyloscopy?

8. Who ordered the dropping of the first atomic bomb?

9. Coppicing trees encourages what?

10. What is a pepo: a fish, a flower or a fruit? 💡

11. Which superstar's children's book was called *The English Roses*?

12. What is the name of the toreador in the opera *Carmen*?

13. A Welsh poppy is what colour?

14. Springfield is whose home town? 💡

15. What is the theme tune of *Desert Island Discs*?

16. What is the meaning of the name Texas?

QUIZ 196

① Who wrote the TV series *Dinnerladies*?

② What is the New Zealand women's rugby team called?

③ Which edible gentleman's last words were 'I'm all gone.' ? 💡

④ Cortina, Consul and Zephyr were models of which car?

⑤ Mast is the fruit of which tree?

⑥ Which country first had parking meters: Japan, UK or USA? 💡

⑦ Who plays Colonel Pickering in the film *My Fair Lady*?

⑧ Which revolutionary did Lev Davidovitch Bronstein become?

⑨ What was Dan Brown's first novel, published in 1998?

⑩ What is a metropolis? 💡

⑪ Which Smith unilaterally declared Rhodesia's independence?

⑫ What is the square root of 144?

⑬ Which senior judge presides over the Court of Appeal?

⑭ What do the initials stand for in W G Grace?

⑮ What number will Britain's next King William be? 💡

⑯ Which English monarch was called 'Gloriana'?

QUIZ 197

① Whose ring did the Jackdaw of Rheims steal?

② What does the word purloin mean?

③ Who sculpted the statue of 'The Three Graces'?

④ Which word can follow leg, tea and wind?

⑤ Who has won the football World Cup more often, Brazil or Italy?

⑥ When was the Act of Union between England and Scotland?

⑦ Which German composer married the daughter of Franz Liszt?

⑧ What is the lower house of the US Congress?

⑨ Who was the first black athlete to win gold at a Winter Olympics?

⑩ What phrase means 'the latest possible moment'?

⑪ Who was the wife of Zeus?

⑫ What is the smallest breed of dog?

⑬ When was Mafeking relieved: 1900, 1901, 1902?

⑭ From which country does the word chintz originate?

⑮ What motorway links London and Wales?

⑯ Who was the English Monkee?

QUIZ 198

① In Greek mythology, who built the labyrinth on Crete?

② In the nursery rhyme, where did Doctor Foster go to? 🔆

③ What arch frames the front of a stage in a theatre?

④ Which US president won the Nobel Peace Prize in 1919?

⑤ How many items are there in four and a half gross?

⑥ When was the first motor-racing grand prix: 1906, 1912, 1920?

⑦ What 'pm' is 21.00 hours? 🔆

⑧ Who played Philip Marlowe in the 1978 remake of *The Big Sleep*?

⑨ Which Jacobean dramatist co-wrote plays with Francis Beaumont?

⑩ Whose soul goes marching on?

⑪ In *Nina and the Neurons*, who is the baby of the group? 🔆

⑫ What, according to the Bible, 'goeth before destruction'?

⑬ Who wrote about his years in Paris in *A Moveable Feast*?

⑭ Which country hosts the Sun City Open golf tournament?

⑮ What is a mushroom? 🔆

⑯ What is a ha-ha when it isn't a laugh?

QUIZ 199

① What is the last book in Louisa M Alcott's famous trilogy?

② In *Bear Behaving Badly* what is Crazy Keith? ☼

③ Which Roald Dahl story became a musical in 2011?

④ Where on the human body are the plantars?

⑤ Name the space station launched by the Soviet Union in 1986.

⑥ What is England's northernmost county? ☼

⑦ Who did Elizabeth Fry replace on the reverse of a £5 note?

⑧ Which railway line was the LMS?

⑨ Who wrote the novel *Frankenstein*?

⑩ What is tossed at Scottish highland games? ☼

⑪ In *Little Britain* who insists 'I'm a laydee'?

⑫ Which is the world's oldest parliament?

⑬ The wapiti is what kind of animal?

⑭ Pebbles stuck naturally together are called what?

⑮ What is the opposite of 'accidental'? ☼

⑯ Which England bowler took a hat-trick against New Zealand at Hamilton in 2008?

QUIZ 200

① What does curiosity kill? ☼

② Who wrote the poem 'The Lady of the Lake'?

③ What is the proper name for quicksilver?

④ Who was 'Il Duce'?

⑤ In what special oven is pottery baked? ☼

⑥ What was Lonnie Donegan's 'old man' by profession?

⑦ Which team included Mr T?

⑧ What is the capital of Croatia?

⑨ Alfred the Great was king of where?

⑩ The Albert Hall is named after the husband of which queen? ☼

⑪ What is a pawnbroker's sign?

⑫ Who played the title role in the 1964 film *The Pawnbroker*?

⑬ What is the GMC?

⑭ In *Midsomer Murders*, where is the police station?

⑮ What large, angry dog did Sherlock Holmes come across? ☼

⑯ What do Americans call a nappy?

QUIZ 201

① About whose arrival did Handel compose a piece of music?

② Whose catchphrase is 'Booyakasha!'?

③ Who plans to capture the world in *Cats and Dogs*?

④ According to the proverb, what is the soul of wit?

⑤ Who is known as 'The Father of Medicine'?

⑥ What is a long sand hill called?

⑦ 'Monticello' was the home of which US president?

⑧ Which pop star became a UNICEF Ambassador in 2001?

⑨ In *Gossip Girl*, who is Serena's ex-best friend?

⑩ Can you make a jockey out of RIVER by changing one letter?

⑪ Who wrote the novel *For Whom the Bell Tolls*?

⑫ And which poet was the source of the title?

⑬ Which athlete became MP for Falmouth and Cambourne in 1992?

⑭ What can't 'Muggles' perform?

⑮ In which country was Chris de Burgh born?

⑯ What is a clove hitch?

QUIZ 202

① Multiply 0.07 x 1000 and what do you get?

② Who played the title role in the film *Desperately Seeking Susan*?

③ Valentine's Day falls under which Sign of the Zodiac?

④ The Darling is a major river in which country?

⑤ Whose debut album was *PCD*?

⑥ Where in the human body do you find platelets?

⑦ Which TV presenter spends his time with Animals at Work?

⑧ The musical *Les Miserables* is based on whose 19th-century novel?

⑨ Blazon is the formal language of what?

⑩ Who was Elizabeth I's mother?

⑪ What sport did Dr James Naismith found in 1891?

⑫ Name the father and son explorers, John and Sebastian . . .

⑬ Where in Russia is Yalta?

⑭ What is the opposite of emigration?

⑮ Who does Tim McInnerny play in *Blackadder Goes Forth*?

⑯ What is a Jewish minister or teacher called?

QUIZ 203

① Academically speaking, what does LSE stand for?

② How many decades in 200 years?

③ Which novel begins: 'Robert Langdon awoke slowly.'?

④ Which artist founded the Royal Academy in 1768?

⑤ What is an abacus used for?

⑥ Which one tennis Grand Slam title eluded Ivan Lendl?

⑦ What is the longest snake in the world?

⑧ Add the food item: 'I Gave My Love A . . .'

⑨ What is a state of lawlessness and disorder?

⑩ In which sport does a night watchman play a part?

⑪ What territory did Jacques Piccard explore?

⑫ Whose catchphrase was: 'You can't see the join'?

⑬ Where in the human body is the occipital bone?

⑭ How many languages can you speak if you are bilingual?

⑮ The Siege of Ladysmith was in which war?

⑯ What was a flintlock?

QUIZ 204

① In *Wallace and Gromit*, what is Wallace's favourite cheese?

② What is 32° Fahrenheit in Celsius?

③ Tyrol is a province of which country?

④ Who is the author of the *Alex Rider* children's books?

⑤ Which driver was the 1997 Formula One world champion?

⑥ How many holes are there in a standard golf course?

⑦ What for the British was the first major battle of World War I?

⑧ What is the US equivalent of the Foreign Office?

⑨ Where in the UK is Parkhurst Prison?

⑩ Which Australian state is an island?

⑪ Who composed the opera *Norma*?

⑫ What was Sri Lanka previously called?

⑬ The adjective asinine relates to which animal?

⑭ Who had a mega hit with *100 Songs From A Life In Music*?

⑮ What is a large American cattle farm called?

⑯ What do Phil Tufnell, Kerry Katona and Joe Swash have in common?

QUIZ 205

① Which of Henry VIII's wives was called 'The Mare of Flanders'?

② Who is the farmer's dog in *Shaun the Sheep*? ☀

③ In measuring a horse, how big is a hand?

④ How did Gestapo chief Heinrich Himmler die?

⑤ Which character sings 'Bali Ha'i' in the musical *South Pacific*?

⑥ Which word rhymes with cow and is used on a farm? ☀

⑦ The Sutherland Trophy is a major prize at which film festival?

⑧ What is the New Zealand rugby league team called?

⑨ Which UK prime minister was nicknamed the 'Welsh Wizard'?

⑩ Who wrote *The Story of Tracy Beaker*? ☀

⑪ What, geographically speaking, is chorology?

⑫ How was the yeti otherwise known?

⑬ What is actor David Jason's real name?

⑭ In which country is the city of Tampico?

⑮ Name the other half: French and . . . ☀

⑯ Who was the first pop star to be made a Fellow of the Roya College of Music?

QUIZ 206

① Which Little Miss would be the perfect partner for Mr Clever?

② How many micrometres in a millimetre?

③ In which film did Ingrid Bergman play missionary Gladys Aylward?

④ What are Kirsty and Phil's surnames?

⑤ Who foiled the 40 thieves?

⑥ What is the opposite of alkaline?

⑦ Which wartime broadcaster from Germany was called 'Lord Haw Haw'?

⑧ When were the first BRIT awards: 1973, 1975 or 1977?

⑨ Which UK bird is extinct: Great Auk, Great Hawk or Great Lark?

⑩ What in the sporting arena is a discobolus?

⑪ Whose dictionary was first published in 1755?

⑫ The robin belongs to which family of birds?

⑬ Which Elizabethan dramatist wrote *The Duchess of Malfi*?

⑭ What does *ex gratia* mean?

⑮ What is the opposite of 'major'?

⑯ In the TV ads for which car were Nicole and Papa a double act?

QUIZ 207

① Who stole Christmas in the Dr Seuss book? ☀

② In which German city was Beethoven born?

③ The film *Cold Mountain* was based on whose novel?

④ *Life Thru A Lens* was whose first solo album?

⑤ What do the initials stand for in T E Lawrence?

⑥ Which breakfast cereal goes 'Snap, Crackle and Pop'? ☀

⑦ What is a dry gulch that is occasionally filled with water?

⑧ Which Greek god was noted for his pipes?

⑨ Where is the TV comedy series *The League of Gentlemen* set?

⑩ What word rhymes with prawn and is something you blow? ☀

⑪ Which famous book begins: 'Stately plump Buck Mulligan . . .'?

⑫ The hoppus cubic foot was used to measure the volume of what?

⑬ Pumpernickel is a type of what?

⑭ What can be a flowering shrub or an implement for sweeping?

⑮ Which ocean has the deepest point? ☀

⑯ In which Shakespeare play is Friar Laurence a character?

QUIZ 208

① What kind of trees does a genealogist study?

② Yogi Bear hangs out in which park?

③ In which city is the European Parliament?

④ 1 gigabyte equals how many megabytes?

⑤ In political and military terms what is the opposite of a hawk?

⑥ How long is a football match?

⑦ In which book of the Bible is the story of Noah's Ark told?

⑧ Martina Navratilova defected to the USA from which country?

⑨ Where in England is the summer solstice festival held?

⑩ What is the capital of Holland?

⑪ Who was the unfortunate captain of HMS *Bounty*?

⑫ What relation is Nicolas Cage to Francis Ford Coppola?

⑬ Who was the first batsman to score 11,000 runs in Tests?

⑭ What does BP stand for at some service stations?

⑮ What degree of burns is life threatening?

⑯ In which English town was The Verve rock band formed in 1989?

QUIZ 209

① What are trees that seasonally shed their leaves called?

② What is the name of the speakeasy in *Bugsy Malone*?

③ Which singer stood guard over the Queen Mother's coffin in 2002?

④ When was the metric system adopted in France: 1699, 1799, 1899?

⑤ What is a loom used for?

⑥ In *The Three Musketeers* which one was played by Oliver Reed?

⑦ Where in London is the Strangers' Gallery?

⑧ Who led the miners' strikes of the 1980s?

⑨ What is the outermost colour of a rainbow?

⑩ On which Hebridean island is Fingal's Cave?

⑪ What does the O stand for in David O Selznick?

⑫ When did Queen Victoria celebrate her Diamond Jubilee?

⑬ On which Caribbean island was the singer Rihanna born?

⑭ How does a thrush break snail shells to get to the inside?

⑮ Where in the USA would you go for a quick divorce?

⑯ What do time and tide wait for?

QUIZ 210

① Which leaves can soothe a nettle's sting?

② What breed of dog is Gromit supposed to be? 💡

③ A nautical mile is how many metres?

④ Amiens is in which region of France?

⑤ What is a Portuguese man-of-war? 💡

⑥ 'Suicide is Painless' is the theme tune of which TV sitcom?

⑦ Who directed the film *Easy Rider*?

⑧ Which poet wrote the stories *Adventures in the Skin Trade*?

⑨ What animal is the video game character *Sonic*? 💡

⑩ A thick-knee is what type of bird?

⑪ What number president is Barack Obama?

⑫ Which US chess grand master died in 2008?

⑬ Who played the put-upon Mr Barraclough in *Porridge*?

⑭ How long is a rugby match? 💡

⑮ What is New Zealand's longest navigable river?

⑯ The French word *goût* means what?

QUIZ 211

① Who is in charge of the Pontypandy fire station? 💡

② Which Scottish hero was known as Braveheart?

③ What are olfactory organs?

④ Shiraz is a city in which country?

⑤ Where in London does the Trooping of the Colour take place? 💡

⑥ In which year did Captain Scott die: 1908, 1910, 1912?

⑦ Which biblical character was noted for his wisdom?

⑧ How old was Lester Piggott when he rode his first winner?

⑨ Who was JD in *Lock, Stock and Two Smoking Barrels*?

⑩ Was Pablo Picasso a footballer, painter or chef? 💡

⑪ What is the most northerly point of mainland Britain?

⑫ Holly the computer featured in which TV comedy series?

⑬ What is Birmingham's principal railway station?

⑭ Which Strauss composed the opera *Der Rosenkavalier*?

⑮ What is the opposite of servant? 💡

⑯ Elizabeth St Michel was married to which famous diarist?

QUIZ 212

① Which *X Factor* contestant has her own fashion line called Dee V?

② Spitfires and Hurricanes helped to win which battle in 1940?

③ Which 2009 film cost an eye-watering $300m dollars to make?

④ In *Treasure Island* what is the name of Long John Silver's parrot?

⑤ What is a series of dots between words called?

⑥ Does a prologue come at the beginning or the end of something?

⑦ Which English queen spent her childhood at Hatfield House?

⑧ Alan Parker made a film of which Roddy Doyle book?

⑨ What is another word for gristle?

⑩ Who helps the hens escape in *Chicken Run*?

⑪ Which country has a parliament building called the 'Beehive'?

⑫ What word can be a small bird or a unit of speed?

⑬ Which instrument did jazz musician Woody Herman play?

⑭ Tennis at Wimbledon is played on what surface?

⑮ Which general was known as the 'Desert Fox'?

⑯ Who was the first non-human to win an honorary Oscar?

QUIZ 213

① Who was the glamorous puss in *Cats*? 💡

② Which German city is associated with a type of sausage?

③ Who was the first rap artist to win an Oscar for Best Song?

④ Adelaide is the capital city of which Australian state?

⑤ How many wings does a flea have? 💡

⑥ Which British comedian shared the name of a seaside resort?

⑦ What does *savoir faire* mean?

⑧ Dens Park is which Scottish football club's home ground?

⑨ Who was the first woman in space?

⑩ What decoration is the GCVO?

⑪ Yann Martel won the Booker Prize in 2002 for which novel?

⑫ Which English king was known as 'Rufus'?

⑬ In which US city are Brooklyn and the Bronx? 💡

⑭ Whose first film together was *Woman of the Year*?

⑮ Leukophobia is a fear of what colour?

⑯ Who has a wooden eye in *Pirates of the Caribbean*? 💡

QUIZ 214

① What does the word tardy mean?

② Who is Yogi Bear's constant companion?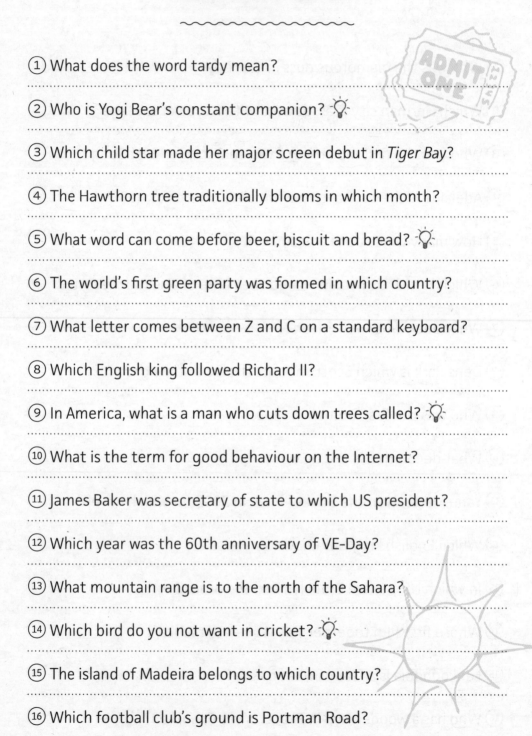

③ Which child star made her major screen debut in *Tiger Bay*?

④ The Hawthorn tree traditionally blooms in which month?

⑤ What word can come before beer, biscuit and bread?

⑥ The world's first green party was formed in which country?

⑦ What letter comes between Z and C on a standard keyboard?

⑧ Which English king followed Richard II?

⑨ In America, what is a man who cuts down trees called?

⑩ What is the term for good behaviour on the Internet?

⑪ James Baker was secretary of state to which US president?

⑫ Which year was the 60th anniversary of VE-Day?

⑬ What mountain range is to the north of the Sahara?

⑭ Which bird do you not want in cricket?

⑮ The island of Madeira belongs to which country?

⑯ Which football club's ground is Portman Road?

QUIZ 215

① Which Elizabeth was younger when she came to the throne, I or II?

② Complete the saying: 'A rolling stone gathers no . . .'

③ Who wrote the award-winning children's book *The New Policeman*?

④ In what US state is the Colorado Desert?

⑤ Who directed himself in *Mary Shelley's Frankenstein*?

⑥ In which Italian city is a boat handier than a car?

⑦ Who was referred to as the 'Teflon President'?

⑧ Add the missing food item in this song title: 'Big . . .'

⑨ What city name can be a type of shoe, shirt or trousers?

⑩ Where is the 'International Rescue' base in *Thunderbirds*?

⑪ In the phonetic alphabet, P is for what?

⑫ Which British prime minister was 'The Grand Old Man'?

⑬ When it's not a riddle what is a monkey-puzzle?

⑭ Baruch Spinoza was a 17th-century what?

⑮ Plants crossed from different species are called what?

⑯ Who on stage is Stefani Joanne Angelina Germanotta?

QUIZ 216

1. Who is the central character in *Breakfast at Tiffany's*?

2. What is the 'toad' in toad in the hole? 🔆

3. How many dozens are there in a gross?

4. Which flamboyant British film director died in 2011?

5. Who was known as 'The Sun King'?

6. What rhymes with tickle and is used to cut long grass? 🔆

7. Bratislava is the capital of which European country?

8. What is the peregrine falcon's main source of food?

9. In the *Katy* series of children's books what is Katy's surname?

10. The islands of the West Indies are in which sea? 🔆

11. For whom did Bob Dylan write 'Lay Lady Lay'?

12. How many *Harry Potter* books are there?

13. What fruit is used to make a traditional Christingle?

14. Which former stand-up wrote the novel *Gridlock*?

15. How many lanes has an Olympic-size swimming pool: 8, 10 or 12? 🔆

16. What does hyperbole mean?

QUIZ 217

1. Who is Robinson Crusoe's island companion?

2. Who was the first European to win the US Masters?

3. From which country does Ludo come?

4. Which Nazi flew to Scotland on a secret mission in 1941?

5. Is 'flamenco' a bird, a dance or a flower?

6. Which London street became a sign of the 'Swinging Sixties'?

7. 'Lara's Theme' came from which film?

8. And who composed the music?

9. Eros, Nysa and Hektor are all astronomically what?

10. What numerical confectionery is sprinkled on cakes?

11. Which three 'Dames' were in *Tea with Mussolini*?

12. From what part of France does a Breton come?

13. The Goodwin Sands are at the entrance to which straits?

14. Which instrument did jazz musician Charles Mingus play?

15. Which Humberside chemical plant exploded in 1974?

16. In *Gavin & Stacey*, where in Essex is Gavin from?

QUIZ 218

① Who plays Sam Witwicky in the *Transformers* films?

② What breed of dog is Scooby-Doo? 🔦

③ Who was the first footballer to score 100 premiership goals?

④ What instrument did comedian George Formby play?

⑤ How many bottles in a Salamanazar?

⑥ What is a network of secret agents? 💡

⑦ In which country are the holy cities of Mecca and Medina?

⑧ Which 1970s fitness pioneer wrote *The Complete Book of Jogging*?

⑨ Where in London is the Hayward Gallery?

⑩ What are Japanese pocket monsters called? 💡

⑪ In which year was the Battle of El Alamein?

⑫ Which Jones was a Renaissance architect?

⑬ Who did the Prince Regent become in 1820?

⑭ Which fruitcake is named after a Scottish city?

⑮ What is the opposite of a valley? 🔦

⑯ 40° Celsius is what in Fahrenheit?

QUIZ 219

① Which country is called the Emerald Isle? 💡

② What do you get if you cross a Labrador with a poodle?

③ Which league football team is nicknamed 'The Pirates'?

④ Who is Elton John's long-time partner?

⑤ What is the name of Phileas Fogg's manservant? 💡

⑥ 'Old Glory' is a popular name for which national flag?

⑦ What sort of criminal is a 'dip'?

⑧ Who wrote *The Pathfinder* and *The Deerslayer*?

⑨ What element is found in bones and shells?

⑩ Postman Pat delivers letters in which village? 💡

⑪ The kelvin is a unit of what?

⑫ What nationality was the painter Joan Miró?

⑬ On which river is Washington DC?

⑭ What do Americans call a sofa?

⑮ What is an online journal or column called? 💡

⑯ Who played the title role in Oliver Stone's film *Alexander*?

QUIZ 220

① What is the moveable indicator on a computer screen?

② What are Hacker T Dog and Dodge hoping to achieve? 💡

③ Who was Amy Pond's husband in *Doctor Who*?

④ What are gnocchi?

⑤ Tic-tac-toe is another name for which popular game?

⑥ What instrument does a flautist play? 💡

⑦ In which film did Tommy Lee Jones make his screen debut?

⑧ What is the largest primeval forest left in Europe?

⑨ *The Lord of the Rings* is set in which magical world? 💡

⑩ In the proverb, whose work is never done?

⑪ Which city staged the word premiere of *Les Misérables*?

⑫ What comes with a thirteenth wedding anniversary?

⑬ Ten dekalitres are equal to how many hectolitres?

⑭ What is another word for a bumper car? 💡

⑮ Who won the women's tennis US Open in 2000 and 2001?

⑯ What is a VJ?

QUIZ 221

① What does Wallace (in *Wallace and Gromit*) spend most of his time doing? ⚲

② In bingo, what number is 'Heinz'?

③ Which is the one golf major Lee Trevino didn't win?

④ What is the first name of the French writer Colette?

⑤ What creepy crawly can you make out of PARCEL TRAIL? ⚲

⑥ When is Harry Potter's birthday?

⑦ Which Bush was governor of Florida?

⑧ In World War II what was the WLA?

⑨ What is the capital of Paraguay?

⑩ Who is the wise master of the Jade Palace in *Kung Fu Panda*? ⚲

⑪ Which John Wayne film won him his only Oscar?

⑫ What is the cakewalk?

⑬ Which tree can be Goat, Bay or Creeping?

⑭ What did Dionicio Cerón win in London three times in the 1990s?

⑮ How many 'arms' do most starfish have? ⚲

⑯ Which poem begins: 'If you can keep your head . . .'?

QUIZ 222

① Who looks after the post office in *Postman Pat*?

② If you are myopic, what are you?

③ The *Cutty Sark* was what type of ship?

④ Who said: 'You are old, Father William'?

⑤ What aircraft might be mistaken for an elephant?

⑥ Which Dutch explorer is Tasmania named after?

⑦ What date was D-Day?

⑧ Which British prime minister was a Huddersfield Town supporter?

⑨ What is the opposite of 'supporter'?

⑩ *For Want of a Nail* was which broadcaster's first novel?

⑪ What is the study of plants called?

⑫ On which Formula One circuit is the 'Coca-Cola Curve'?

⑬ Whose debut album was *The Piper At The Gates Of Dawn*?

⑭ Where in Sussex did William the Conqueror land in 1066?

⑮ To quadruple something what do you multiply it by?

⑯ Which five Arab countries largely make up the Maghreb?

QUIZ 223

1. Which mother has her own pantomime?

2. The film *The Iron Giant* is based on which children's story?

3. Which chess piece can only move diagonally?

4. Which superhero is James Howlett?

5. Change DANCE into a type of spear by changing one letter.

6. Which artist painted several pictures of sunflowers?

7. Who sang the theme song in *Avatar*?

8. Which apostle was the brother of Peter?

9. What does a lack of rain cause?

10. Who is the author of the Inspector Wexford books?

11. What do climbers put on their boots for a firmer footing?

12. Which animal is also called a 'desert rat'?

13. What is the lead in pencils made from?

14. Which US president was a student at Oxford University?

15. How many musicians play in an octet?

16. Which US time zone is AKST?

QUIZ 224

① Who was the winner of *Strictly Come Dancing* 2010?

② Which singing trio's follow-up film was 'The Squeakquel'?

③ On which type of surface is the French tennis Open played?

④ Who wrote and directed the film *Bugsy Malone*?

⑤ ESP is an abbreviation of what?

⑥ Which pirate had a dark, hairy chin?

⑦ What is the capital of Lebanon?

⑧ In which year was *Punch* magazine founded: 1841, 1851, 1861?

⑨ Which golfer won the 2005 US Open?

⑩ Who wrote *Alice in Wonderland*?

⑪ Which nobleman did ex-model Victoria Lockwood marry?

⑫ Who invented the Dambusters' bomb?

⑬ By what name was Harare previously known?

⑭ Brogues, clogs and moccasins are all types of what?

⑮ Who wrote the play *A Day in the Life of Joe Egg*?

⑯ In *The Godfather II* who plays Fredo Corleone?

QUIZ 225

① Which Little Miss is even smaller than Mr Small?

② What does PTO stand for?

③ How many degrees are there in a turn and a half?

④ In *Harry Potter* what is the Snape family home?

⑤ What part of your body does a chiropodist look after?

⑥ Which cricket county's Twenty20 side is called 'The Royals'?

⑦ Who was the leader of the PLO who died in 2004?

⑧ *The Rachel Papers* was whose first novel?

⑨ Which sport has a 'chinaman' and a 'googly'?

⑩ Which car is famous for looking like an insect?

⑪ Who is younger, Jenson Button or Fernando Alonso?

⑫ Which Australian media tycoon changed the face of cricket?

⑬ What was September 1939 to April 1940 called?

⑭ Which UK city has more people living in it – Glasgow or Leeds?

⑮ Where in England is the Roodee Racecourse?

⑯ Which fictional sleuth, other than Sherlock Holmes, resided in Baker Street?

QUIZ 226

① What strikes back in *Star Wars*?

② Is a blue chip investment good or bad?

③ How many lines in a sonnet?

④ *Back to Bedlam* was whose bestselling album of the 2000s?

⑤ In which Roald Dahl book is 'wormy' spaghetti served up?

⑥ Which is the larger partridge, Grey or Red-legged?

⑦ What does a numismatist collect?

⑧ Bizzie Lizzies are a type of what: fly, flower or lizard?

⑨ How many carats is pure gold?

⑩ What is your proboscis?

⑪ Duck, fustian and hessian are all what?

⑫ Who would use a jacquard for work?

⑬ Who was Russia's first leader after the tsar's abdication?

⑭ If you bumped your funny bone what part of you would hurt?

⑮ What is 'Adam's Ale'?

⑯ Who starred in the 1963 version of *The Nutty Professor*?

QUIZ 227

① Who changes a frog's life by giving it a kiss?

② Michael Jackson's hit song 'Ben' was originally written for whom?

③ Members of what profession are called to the Bar?

④ What is a puffball?

⑤ Which of these is a herb: Ambrose, Primrose or Rosemary?

⑥ What is the experimental Dr Jekyll's first name?

⑦ Which Swedish actress was married to Peter Sellers?

⑧ What part of a plant catches pollen?

⑨ Which member of 'Take That' has a colourful name?

⑩ Who climbed Mt Everest with Edmund Hillary?

⑪ Which Michael went around the world in 80 days?

⑫ What are the vast grasslands of Russia called?

⑬ How many lines in a quatrain?

⑭ What deadly creature is a Black Mamba?

⑮ Johannesburg is the capital of which South African province?

⑯ Which country was renamed the Khmer Republic in 1970?

QUIZ 228

① What do Americans call a pushchair?

② Ziggy the genie pops out of what in *Trust Me, I'm A Genie*?

③ Who invented the first official postage stamp?

④ What legendary creature was the Kraken?

⑤ Who circumnavigated the globe non-stop in his boat *Suhaili*?

⑥ If you cross a puppet with a marionette what do you get?

⑦ Which sign of the Zodiac spans July and August?

⑧ Hazel is whose brother in *Watership Down*?

⑨ What meadow flower's botanical name is *Ranunculus acris*?

⑩ Who wrote *Winnie-the-Pooh*?

⑪ Andorra lies between which two countries?

⑫ Who is Hercule Poirot's secretary?

⑬ In *ER* it's a gurney, what is it in a British hospital?

⑭ What type of artist makes statues out of marble?

⑮ Which country ended its civil war in 1994?

⑯ What bag lady launched 'I'm not a plastic bag' for Sainsbury's?

QUIZ 229

① Where in England is the Isle of Dogs?

② Which pet dog's birthday is the 12th of February?

③ How is the 17th-century Rebecca Rolfe better known?

④ Which French actor-director made *Mr Hulot's Holiday*?

⑤ How many days are there in an advent calendar?

⑥ Which Australian fast bowler retired from Test cricket in 2010?

⑦ In which country is the region of Cappadocia?

⑧ Which product claimed it helped you work, rest and play?

⑨ What is a female pig called?

⑩ Which member of The Bachelors was not a 'Cluskey'?

⑪ What is the capital of Ethiopia?

⑫ Which King George married Caroline of Brunswick?

⑬ What is Hungary's currency?

⑭ Which Irish author wrote the *Barrytown* trilogy?

⑮ What carry electricity cables overland?

⑯ Which 60s pop group's name was a tribute to Buddy Holly?

QUIZ 230

1. According to the saying, what may a cat look at? 💡

2. What word can be newborn kittens or something to put in the bin?

3. In which Henrik Ibsen play is the Troll King a character?

4. Who was the 1782 naval Battle of Trincomalee between?

5. What is mincemeat made from? 💡

6. Who wrote the World War II novel *King Rat*?

7. Karlheinz Stockhausen is a modern what?

8. St Petersburg is at the head of which gulf?

9. What is Europe's largest native swan?

10. In which sea is the island of Malta? 💡

11. What is the highest number on the Richter Scale?

12. Birmingham is the largest city in which US state?

13. A zebu is what type of animal?

14. What is mainland Britain's most easterly port?

15. Which game involves knights, bishops and castles? 💡

16. Who played the estranged couple in the film *Kramer vs Kramer*?

QUIZ 231

① What is the last day of Christmas called?

② Who composed the 'Oxford Symphony'?

③ Is an elver a female elf, a baby eel or an elephant's ear?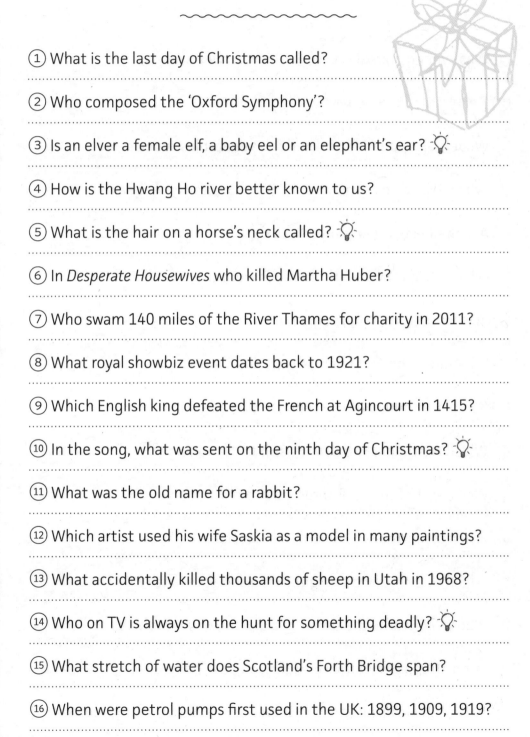

④ How is the Hwang Ho river better known to us?

⑤ What is the hair on a horse's neck called?

⑥ In *Desperate Housewives* who killed Martha Huber?

⑦ Who swam 140 miles of the River Thames for charity in 2011?

⑧ What royal showbiz event dates back to 1921?

⑨ Which English king defeated the French at Agincourt in 1415?

⑩ In the song, what was sent on the ninth day of Christmas?

⑪ What was the old name for a rabbit?

⑫ Which artist used his wife Saskia as a model in many paintings?

⑬ What accidentally killed thousands of sheep in Utah in 1968?

⑭ Who on TV is always on the hunt for something deadly?

⑮ What stretch of water does Scotland's Forth Bridge span?

⑯ When were petrol pumps first used in the UK: 1899, 1909, 1919?

QUIZ 232

① What young animal is the mischievous Olivia?

② 'Cello' is short for what?

③ What is an appetizer of sliced raw vegetables called?

④ Which inland sea connects the Black Sea to the Aegean?

⑤ A man's best friend is his what?

⑥ Which child movie star's memoirs were titled *Little Girl Lost*?

⑦ In which US city is Carnegie Hall?

⑧ What does the Latin phrase *bona fide* mean?

⑨ Complete the proverb: 'What can't be cured must be ...'

⑩ Which Australian bird sounds as if it is laughing?

⑪ Which star of musicals directed the film *Hello Dolly*?

⑫ When did President Richard Nixon resign?

⑬ Which of Zimbabwe's neighbours also begins with Z?

⑭ Whose 'Epistle' is the penultimate book of the New Testament?

⑮ In which sporting activity might you do a 'bellyflop'?

⑯ What Ben Elton/Andrew Lloyd Webber musical is about football?

QUIZ 233

① Which English king was called 'The Conqueror'? ☼

② What was the route of Britain's first public steam railway?

③ Who first played the title role in the musical *Evita* on stage?

④ In which sport can you 'catch a crab'?

⑤ On what kind of green do you play a short form of golf? ☼

⑥ In what event did Daley Thompson win two Olympic gold medals?

⑦ Who played Hamlet in a 1990 film version of the play?

⑧ What is the traditional dessert on Thanksgiving Day in the USA?

⑨ George Balanchine was famous in which field of the arts?

⑩ What four-letter word can follow brief, nut or pillow? ☼

⑪ The gas firedamp is found where?

⑫ What does the German word *reich* mean?

⑬ Who wrote *The Return of the Native*?

⑭ Dakar is the capital of which country?

⑮ Where did Prince William and Kate Middleton get married? ☼

⑯ What was the *Guardian* newspaper previously called?

QUIZ 234

① CIA is short for what?

② What did Little Jack Horner put his thumb into? 💡

③ Which Oxford college has no undergraduates?

④ What is a tall four-sided pillar with a pyramidal top?

⑤ Which children's author was knighted in 2009?

⑥ What can be blue, brown, black or crossed? 💡

⑦ Who is the spiritual leader of Tibet?

⑧ Which British playwright started life as Tom Straussler?

⑨ What is Del Boy's company called in *Only Fools and Horses*?

⑩ In what glass tank do you keep fish and other sea creatures? 💡

⑪ Which Welsh singer made her screen debut in *Patagonia* in 2010?

⑫ On water taps in France what replaces the letters H and C?

⑬ Who was the female co-star in the Crosby/Hope 'Road' movies?

⑭ In which studio would you use a clapper board? 💡

⑮ Which Gerald was a zoologist, writer and broadcaster?

⑯ Who wrote *The Alexandria Quartet*?

QUIZ 235

① 'Yours Truly, Angry Mob' was a No 1 for whom?

② Who more than anything wanted to be a sheep-pig?

③ What nationality is the writer Milan Kundera?

④ Which snooker champion is nicknamed 'The Whirlwind'?

⑤ What is a taipan: a boat, a saucepan or a snake?

⑥ Whose radio slogan is 'I'm listening'?

⑦ What is pyorrhoea?

⑧ Name the silent star of *The Sheikh* and *Blood and Sand*.

⑨ What is a Morning Glory?

⑩ What do you look at in a planetarium?

⑪ Paul Tortelier was a virtuoso performer on which instrument?

⑫ What is a baby pigeon?

⑬ Newscasters read from a what?

⑭ Which county plays cricket at the Rosebowl?

⑮ What were French medieval singer-songwriters called?

⑯ Which US president said: 'If you want a friend in Washington, get a dog.'?

QUIZ 236

① Which African horse looks like a pedestrian crossing

② When did the League of Nations come into being?

③ What is the opening of San Francisco Bay to the Pacific?

④ Who invented the most commonly used system of shorthand?

⑤ Which teeth leave you none the wiser?

⑥ What does the word verisimilitude mean?

⑦ Who did Harold Macmillan follow as prime minister?

⑧ Where was the reception centre for immigrants entering New York?

⑨ Which former England Test cricket captain is a psychoanalyst?

⑩ What is a female sheep?

⑪ Which Irish playwright won the 1969 Nobel Prize in Literature?

⑫ What is the state capital of Oregon?

⑬ In *Harry Potter*, who is 'The Keeper of the Keys'?

⑭ Which sailor had water everywhere . . . yet not a drop to drink?

⑮ Which ocean is to the west of Ireland?

⑯ What is the 'Red Rose' county, Lancashire or Yorkshire?

QUIZ 237

① Who is the creator of Wallace and Gromit?

② Which of the seven dwarves wears glasses?

③ Who took the Russian throne from her husband Tsar Peter III?

④ What was the title of the first Discworld novel?

⑤ How is 30 St Mary Axe, London, better known?

⑥ Who played the title role in Ken Russell's film *Tommy*?

⑦ How many funnels did the *Titanic* have?

⑧ Which familiar TV weather forecaster retired in 2000?

⑨ In *EastEnders* what was Kathy Mitchell's maiden name?

⑩ How many were there in The Osmonds?

⑪ What is like a housing estate for rabbits?

⑫ In which century was Leonardo da Vinci born?

⑬ Annapurna is in which mountain range?

⑭ Which controversial US comedian died of an overdose in 1966?

⑮ Who has the job of looking after the country's Budget?

⑯ Who in 2000 won the first rugby Six Nations Championship?

QUIZ 238

① Which Mr Man is long, yellow and as thin as a rake? ☀

② Where is the Isle of Sheppey?

③ What country borders Syria to the north?

④ Which popular British cheese ceased production in 1992?

⑤ What building has lots of different shops in it? ☀

⑥ Which three heads of state met at Yalta in 1945?

⑦ The writer Samuel Johnson was a doctor of what?

⑧ Whose last words were: 'I shall hear in heaven.'?

⑨ What flowery word can come after apple, cherry and May? ☀

⑩ Cool, Nice and Oz are all what?

⑪ What term is an unnaturally high singing voice for a man?

⑫ Who directed *Billy Elliot* on stage and on film?

⑬ What is a large sea-going fishing boat called? ☀

⑭ According to the proverb, what is required to make bricks?

⑮ Name the family in John Steinbeck's novel *The Grapes of Wrath*.

⑯ The 2011 Wimbledon singles champions each earned how much in prize money?

QUIZ 239

① To where in Scotland did people elope?

② Who is Shaun the Sheep's enemy?

③ Which John was a celebrated British economist?

④ What does porcine mean?

⑤ Tasmin Little plays what musical instrument?

⑥ A stitch in time saves . . . how many?

⑦ Who was murdered on the Ides of March?

⑧ And what date is the Ides of March?

⑨ What is unglazed brownish-red earthenware called?

⑩ Where will you find a Canterbury Bell: church, ship or garden?

⑪ Nnamdi Azikiwe became which country's first president in 1963?

⑫ What synthetic substitute is 200 times sweeter than sugar?

⑬ Who was born in 1959, was never a baby and never grows old?

⑭ What are black and white and play a tune?

⑮ Which English city centre is called 'The Bull Ring'?

⑯ What does 'Cosa Nostra' mean?

QUIZ 240

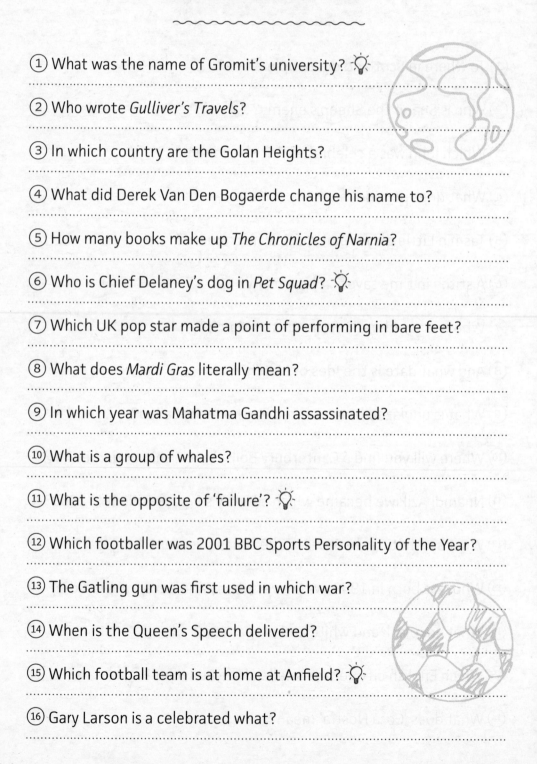

① What was the name of Gromit's university?

② Who wrote *Gulliver's Travels*?

③ In which country are the Golan Heights?

④ What did Derek Van Den Bogaerde change his name to?

⑤ How many books make up *The Chronicles of Narnia*?

⑥ Who is Chief Delaney's dog in *Pet Squad*?

⑦ Which UK pop star made a point of performing in bare feet?

⑧ What does *Mardi Gras* literally mean?

⑨ In which year was Mahatma Gandhi assassinated?

⑩ What is a group of whales?

⑪ What is the opposite of 'failure'?

⑫ Which footballer was 2001 BBC Sports Personality of the Year?

⑬ The Gatling gun was first used in which war?

⑭ When is the Queen's Speech delivered?

⑮ Which football team is at home at Anfield?

⑯ Gary Larson is a celebrated what?

QUIZ 241

1. Who described England as 'a nation of shopkeepers'?

2. Where was champion cyclist Mark Cavendish born?

3. Which queen wanted Alice's head? 💡

4. How many horses pull a Russian troika?

5. The film *Funny Girl* was about which US actress and comedienne?

6. Which Smith was an 18th-century clergyman, journalist and wit?

7. What are peas naturally packed in? 💡

8. Which poet lived at Dove Cottage in Grasmere?

9. What is the last letter of the Greek alphabet?

10. In which country were the first-ever Olympic Games held? 💡

11. Which Roman emperor appointed his horse a consul?

12. Whose 'Merry Christmas Everybody' was a mega hit in 1973?

13. Who lent his name to London's most prestigious theatre awards?

14. What is the name EMI short for?

15. Who climbs tall buildings to carry out repairs? 💡

16. What is the outside of a circle called?

QUIZ 242

① What is the UK equivalent of the Oscars?

② What does a caterpillar become?

③ Which 'James Bond' is the son of a policeman?

④ What was the notorious herbicide used by the US in Vietnam?

⑤ Which was the first three-time winner of the Grand National?

⑥ Whose catchphrase was 'Now *that's* magic.'?

⑦ What ice cream, fruit and jelly dessert comes in a tall glass?

⑧ Who was the bespectacled comedy star of the silent screen?

⑨ Which Roman general wrote a history of the Gallic Wars?

⑩ Who lives in The Palace of the Vatican?

⑪ Who wrote the novel *The Age of Innocence*?

⑫ What were usually inserted through the holes of a pillory?

⑬ How many 'Pomp and Circumstance' marches did Elgar compose?

⑭ What was raised from the sea in 1982 after 437 years?

⑮ Which stretch of water can you cross by plane, train or boat?

⑯ What does probity mean?

QUIZ 243

1 What did evil pirates make their prisoners walk? 💡

2 Which Michael was the principal dancer in *Riverdance*?

3 What became the Democratic Republic of the Congo?

4 Who founded the Persian Empire?

5 What is an Indian clay oven called?

6 If it is 11am now, what time will it be in four hours? 💡

7 Who wrote the poem 'Stop All the Clocks'?

8 What fruit normally goes into a strudel?

9 Which is colder, Mars at night or an iceberg? 💡

10 What landmark New York building was bombed in 1993?

11 Who went around the world in 108 minutes in 1961?

12 What birds were used in coal mines to warn of gas?

13 In which country was the composer Percy Grainger born?

14 Actions speak louder than . . . what? 💡

15 What can you drive with an HGV licence?

16 What aid to broadcasting did Aleksandr Popov invent in 1895?

QUIZ 244

① Who is the voice of Wallace in *Wallace and Gromit*?

② What rhymes with trolley and rounds up sheep? 💡

③ Who didn't see a hurricane coming?

④ What was the 17th-century poet Robert Herrick's day job?

⑤ Who was the creator of Tarzan?

⑥ Which country's flag has a red dragon on it? 💡

⑦ In which city was the painter Canaletto born?

⑧ The opera *Carmen* is based on whose story of the same name?

⑨ What word means gaudy and in bad taste?

⑩ Who became James Bond in 2005? 💡

⑪ What was writer Boris Pasternak forced to decline in 1958?

⑫ Who was the Battle of Marathon in 490 BC between?

⑬ In which US state is Princeton University?

⑭ What part of a horse does a farrier take care of? 💡

⑮ How and when did John F Kennedy Jr die?

⑯ Which skyscraper dominates Taiwan's skyline?

QUIZ 245

① Which ancient city did Pericles rule?

② What is known as the 'Silver Screen'? 💡

③ Who is queen of the fairies in *A Midsummer Night's Dream*?

④ In which year was Michael Jackson's *Thriller* released?

⑤ Which famous battle took place in 1066? 💡

⑥ Who addressed poems to a mouse, a louse and a haggis?

⑦ Tom Pinch is a character in which Charles Dickens novel?

⑧ Which batsman scored a record 197 first-class 100s in his career?

⑨ Do you smell, touch or hear an aroma? 💡

⑩ What is a fop?

⑪ A cat is often a witch's what?

⑫ What were LPs made of?

⑬ Who played Maid Marion to Errol Flynn's Robin Hood?

⑭ Which ape has the longer arms, a gibbon or an orang-utan? 💡

⑮ 'Chicane' is the alias of which UK songwriter/producer?

⑯ Which Michael was head of an acting dynasty?

QUIZ 246

① Who was the Roman god of fire?

② Who is the Princess Royal? ☀

③ In which country did the Women's Institute movement begin?

④ Where did Monet paint his famous water lily pictures?

⑤ What can be a bloomer, a cob or a cottage? ☀

⑥ What 70s film was about an accident in a US nuclear power station?

⑦ In computer speak, what is a TIFF?

⑧ What is the process of adding a soundtrack to a piece of film?

⑨ Which is the second book of the *Narnia Chronicles*?

⑩ What wood was Robin Hood's bow made from? ☀

⑪ Which piece of music celebrates Napoleon's retreat from Moscow?

⑫ What is the crack in a glacier called?

⑬ How many people have escaped from Alcatraz prison?

⑭ What lizard-like creature can change its colour? ☀

⑮ What is further east, Montreal or Ottawa?

⑯ For which film did Ron Howard win 'Best Director' Oscar in 2002?

QUIZ 247

① What do the initials stand for in MI6?

② Complete the title: *Phantom of the* . . .

③ How old was Benedict XVI when he became Pope?

④ Which Yorkshire cricketer played for England at the age of 18?

⑤ If you suffer from ochlophobia what are you afraid of?

⑥ In which board game is there a Grand Master?

⑦ How was the emperor Lucius Domitius Ahenobarbus better known?

⑧ Who composed the *Symphonie fantastique*?

⑨ Are voles herbivores or carnivores?

⑩ What county cream teas are famous?

⑪ On which island was the ancient city of Knossos?

⑫ Who invented the miner's safety lamp in 1816?

⑬ Which diminutive US singer won his first BRIT in 1985?

⑭ What do two people sing?

⑮ Who in the Bible sold his birthright for a mess of potage?

⑯ What do Americans call a pimple?

QUIZ 248

① When, according to the song, do we go gathering nuts?

② How is the eye disorder strabismus more commonly known?

③ What is partially cooking a pastry base before adding the filling?

④ Where can you see the Rosetta Stone?

⑤ In the film, which three animals made 'The Incredible Journey'?

⑥ Which children's book begins: 'Where's Papa going with that axe'?

⑦ How did suffragette martyr Emily Davison die in 1913?

⑧ In which TV sitcom was Sharon Theodopolopoudos a character?

⑨ Bysshe was the middle name of which English poet?

⑩ Double Gloucester, Stilton and Brie are all types of what?

⑪ Who had a hit album called *1999* in 1982?

⑫ What is Canada's national animal?

⑬ What was the UK's first nuclear submarine?

⑭ Which beetle is particularly bad news for the potato?

⑮ Which movie hero's nickname is an American state?

⑯ What is the currency of Brazil?

QUIZ 249

① Which Terry Pratchett book is about an island boy called Mau?

② What game combines pictures and a dictionary? 💡

③ What is a citizen of Moscow called?

④ What does the word ingenuous mean?

⑤ Oscar Wilde and Bernard Shaw were born in which country?

⑥ In which TV series do you enter the Time Sewers? 💡

⑦ What can be a cafeteria or a flask for carrying water?

⑧ Which ex-Genesis artist won two BRITS in 1987?

⑨ Who replaced Winston Churchill at the Potsdam Conference in 1945?

⑩ Which football team is at home at White Hart Lane? 💡

⑪ Which Chinese dynasty came first, Ming or Qing?

⑫ Which was the first US city lit by electricity?

⑬ Which postwar England captain suffered from epilepsy?

⑭ What shape is a swallow's tale? 💡

⑮ Which Russian playwright is also famous for his short stories?

⑯ What does a lexicographer compile?

QUIZ 250

1. What is between red and green on a traffic light? 💡

2. Whose novel *Small Island* was published in 2004?

3. What is the diameter of a golf hole?

4. Which Mendelssohn composition was first called *The Lonely Island*?

5. What 'feathery' word can follow blue, black and song? 💡

6. Michael Barrett is which vibrating pop singer's real name?

7. Which monarch said: 'I will make you shorter by a head.'?

8. What did US anti-war demonstrators burn in the 1960s?

9. Name the major British artist who died in 2011.

10. What do they make at the Royal Mint? 💡

11. Which mint is supposed to be too good to hurry?

12. What is a cribo: a fish, a snake or a monkey?

13. Who returned to No 10 Downing Street in October 1951?

14. In which country is Bondi Beach? 💡

15. 'I'll Stand By You' was a No 1 for which group in 2004?

16. What does a sphygmometer measure?

QUIZ 251

① Who composed the music for *Once Upon a Time in America*?

② What is pink, fluffy and sugary and comes on a stick? 💡

③ Which gymnast twice achieved a perfect score at the 1976 Olympics?

④ Graham Greene's novel *A Burnt Out Case* is set in which country?

⑤ What is usually the smallest room in the house? 💡

⑥ Which London embassy was seized by terrorists in 1980?

⑦ What Latin term describes the cast of characters in a play?

⑧ Who played Detective Andy Sipowicz in *NYPD Blue*?

⑨ In what units do you measure X-rays?

⑩ Which English seaside resort has a Golden Mile? 💡

⑪ What in 40s and 50s America did HUAC stand for?

⑫ In which country was Alexander the Great born?

⑬ What type of aircraft was a Sunderland?

⑭ Iran was previously known as what?

⑮ What name is an African lake, a queen and a railway station? 💡

⑯ Complete the title of this Charles Dickens story: 'The Cricket on the . . .'

QUIZ 252

1. What are made of snips and snails and puppy-dog tails?

2. Where can you see Michelangelo's painting *The Creation of Adam*?

3. Who played Charles Ryder in the original *Brideshead Revisited*?

4. To which region of Oceania do Fiji and Vanuatu belong?

5. What is .621371 of a mile?

6. Who founded the Turkish Republic?

7. The name of which fish also means 'to struggle'?

8. Snub, aquiline and retroussé are all shapes of what?

9. In *Around the World in 80 Days* what is Phileas Fogg's club?

10. In which country did the Battle of Waterloo take place?

11. Who on the tennis court was 'Little Mo'?

12. Which musical instruction means 'becoming quieter'?

13. In which century did the 'Black Death' decimate Europe?

14. Name the famous violinist who died in 1999: Yehudi . . .

15. What does a Member of Parliament represent?

16. Which US city is known as 'The Big Easy'?

QUIZ 253

① What does the word nefarious mean?

② Which of Horrid Henry's friends is always hungry? 💡

③ Is a houndstooth pattern spots, checks or stripes?

④ How many lines has a clerihew?

⑤ Which French artist died in Polynesia in 1903?

⑥ What is the opposite of 'advance'? 💡

⑦ John Buchan wrote about how many steps?

⑧ A 'Nutmegger' is an inhabitant of which US state?

⑨ Which wedding anniversary does coral represent?

⑩ Who is the singer in the band Radiohead?

⑪ If you have a 'heart of gold', what are you? 💡

⑫ Banquo is a character in which Shakespeare play?

⑬ Where in the USA was trad jazz born?

⑭ Club, hero and torpedo are all types of what?

⑮ The Irrawaddy is the principal river of which country?

⑯ What is in the middle of a Baked Alaska? 💡

QUIZ 254

① In which Sheridan play is Mrs Malaprop a character?

② What is Israel's parliament?

③ Egg yolks and olive oil mixed together make what?

④ Who is Little Grey Rabbit's hedgehog friend?

⑤ What is a small floral bouquet worn by women?

⑥ Why is golfer Fred Couples nicknamed 'Boom Boom'?

⑦ On which river is the Somerset town of Frome?

⑧ What do you do at the start of a hockey match?

⑨ Who was the third spirit to visit Scrooge in *A Christmas Carol*?

⑩ Which king allegedly had the princes in the Tower killed?

⑪ Who was Tom Sawyer's best friend?

⑫ Which H G Wells novel became *Half a Sixpence*?

⑬ AFD stands for which food process?

⑭ What flower is meant to bring you good luck?

⑮ Otitis-media is an infection of what?

⑯ Which island is between England and Ireland?

QUIZ 255

① Who wrote the *Master and Commander* books?

② Mungojerrie and Rumpleteazer are thieving . . . ?

③ A priest who is removed from sacred orders is what?

④ What political party was formed in China in 1921?

⑤ Which Christian feast day is on Whit Sunday?

⑥ What does Venice's Rialto Bridge span?

⑦ How do you feel if you are on 'Cloud Nine'?

⑧ In what group of islands is Guadalcanal?

⑨ What was the last western nation to abolish slavery?

⑩ Which children's book is about all sorts of knickers?

⑪ Which conductor founded the 'Proms'?

⑫ What military weapon is an AAM?

⑬ Dotterels, dowitches and drongos are all what?

⑭ In which sport does the loser throw in the towel?

⑮ Name the character played by Queen Latifah in *Chicago*.

⑯ Whose parties changed the face of kitchenware?

QUIZ 256

① Who are the ghost-like creatures in the *Moomin* books? 💡

② What is the symbol on the front of a Lamborghini?

③ Who composed *The Water Music*?

④ Who wrote *The Water Babies*?

⑤ In which city is there a statue of C S Lewis with a wardrobe?

⑥ What breed of dog is *Spot*? 💡

⑦ Whose album was *Confessions On A Dance Floor*?

⑧ Who was excommunicated at the Diet of Worms?

⑨ What is a warm wind, a Native American tribe or a helicopter?

⑩ Someone who always has his nose in a book is called a what? 💡

⑪ What is a flight of geese called?

⑫ In World War II, how was the Fieseler Fi 103 better known?

⑬ Who was the winner of *Any Dream Will Do*?

⑭ What mail service was used during the 1870 siege of Paris?

⑮ What is the capital of Denmark? 💡

⑯ Which growing fish is called a fry, smelt and parr?

QUIZ 257

① What super-spy dog's seven languages includes Dolphin? ☼

② Who was the 19th-century author of *Dracula*?

③ What breed of monkey inhabits Gibraltar?

④ Where in London was the 1851 Great Exhibition held?

⑤ What device records a vehicle's speed and travel time?

⑥ Who is the restaurant critic in the film *Ratatouille*? ☼

⑦ Which artistic movement did Dante Gabriel Rossetti help found?

⑧ In which sport would you see a Fosbury Flop?

⑨ Which country had a revolution in 1789?

⑩ What type of thief takes after an animal? ☼

⑪ Which long-time conductor of the Hallé Orchestra died in 1970?

⑫ Whose advertising slogan was 'Say it with Flowers'?

⑬ Cork is in which province of Ireland?

⑭ What is the capital of Norway? ☼

⑮ Which river flows through Ohio, Indiana and Illinois?

⑯ What is shale?

QUIZ 258

① Who composed *The Planets Suite*?

② ESSO stands for what?

③ What is Everton famous for apart from football?

④ Which Egyptian god took the form of a solar disc?

⑤ What is a Scandinavian buffet called?

⑥ Who is Lorna Doone's romantic interest?

⑦ The first Oxford v Cambridge Boat Race was 1819, 1829 or 1839?

⑧ Where is a 62-gun salute fired on the Queen's birthday?

⑨ Which Native American tribe gave its name to a haircut?

⑩ What was Portugal's currency before the euro?

⑪ In which city is Germany's stock exchange?

⑫ And what is it called?

⑬ What is the pirate flag called?

⑭ What militant Chinese secret society was founded in 1896?

⑮ Are the strings on a harpsichord plucked or struck?

⑯ Alan Coren was editor of which magazine?

QUIZ 259

① Who is the teenage detective of River Heights?

② Where was the Hallé Orchestra founded?

③ What colour were Elvis Presley's suede shoes? 💡

④ Angora wool comes from which animal?

⑤ Whose 'Millennium Prayer' made it to No 1 in 1999?

⑥ Smith and Susie are whose brother and sister? 💡

⑦ What is calico made from?

⑧ Which country invaded France in 1870?

⑨ Where did the carioca dance originate?

⑩ Which 1959 film won the same number of Oscars as *Titanic*?

⑪ Which TV show banned pets after more than 50 years? 💡

⑫ At which racecourse is the *Prix de l'Arc de Triomphe* run?

⑬ What organization is AOL?

⑭ What keeps a duffle coat together?

⑮ In *Star Wars* what is Qui-Gon Jinn? 💡

⑯ Who was G K Chesterton's priestly detective?

QUIZ 260

① What is Bombay Duck?

② What are built on beaches to prevent erosion?

③ What breed of dog is Lassie?

④ In the Mark Twain story, how much is the bank note worth?

⑤ What is a mnemonic designed to aid?

⑥ Which US seaside resort is famous for its boardwalk?

⑦ What is a vein of metal ore called?

⑧ Which European city has a famous boys' choir?

⑨ What do the Walrus and the Carpenter eat in *Alice in Wonderland*?

⑩ A principal female singer in opera is called a what?

⑪ In *Dad's Army*, what is Captain Mainwaring's first name?

⑫ Who wrote *20,000 Leagues Under the Sea*?

⑬ What was the first widely used radio receiver?

⑭ Who was the first-ever castaway on *Desert Island Discs*?

⑮ In which country is the Dunc Gray Velodrome?

⑯ Who makes a habit of saying 'Lovely jubbly'?

QUIZ 261

① What dog is of no particular breed?

② How many trombones led the big parade?

③ Who was Britain's first prime minister?

④ Complete the film title: *Five Graves to . . .*

⑤ What is a whip with nine knotted strands of rope called?

⑥ Which is the larger paper size, A4 or A3?

⑦ What is Miss Marple's first name?

⑧ What is the moment of high drama at the end of an episode called?

⑨ Who sang 'Endless Love' with Diana Ross?

⑩ What road runs from Admiralty Arch to Buckingham Palace?

⑪ Which Shakespeare play begins: 'Tush! Never tell me!'?

⑫ What letter in Morse code is 'dash dash dash'?

⑬ On the Isle of Man who has the title 'Lord of Mann'?

⑭ When did tea first arrive in England: 1615, 1651 or 1705?

⑮ Which country was ceded to Russia in 1809?

⑯ Who is the only tennis player to have achieved two calendar Grand Slams?

QUIZ 262

① *Fidelio* is whose only opera?

② What small flower has white petals and a girl's name? 💡

③ Which ideal embraced knightly virtues, honour and courtly love?

④ What is the smallest state in the USA?

⑤ Add the fraternal sporting surname: Rory and Tony . . .

⑥ Which bird has the same name as a famous wizard? 💡

⑦ What is another name for a dirge?

⑧ Which city is Detective Inspector Rebus' patch?

⑨ What are the Grimm Brothers first names?

⑩ Where will you find your tibia bone – in the arm or leg? 💡

⑪ What word can mean naked or to be an authority on something?

⑫ Which country split into two in 1993?

⑬ What is the BFI?

⑭ Which Yorkshire town is famous for its sticky toffee? 💡

⑮ What BBC TV channel began in 2003?

⑯ Who played Mr Bridger in the original film *The Italian Job*?

QUIZ 263

① Name the policeman in Noddy's Toyland?

② Which ship did Shirley Temple sing about?

③ *X&Y* was whose hit album?

④ A cow that hasn't calved is called a what?

⑤ Which Chinese philosopher had a lot to say?

⑥ What train does a boy have to ride on to believe in Christmas?

⑦ In American football, who are known as 'zebras'?

⑧ What is an open-sided gallery or arcade called?

⑨ Which cast of characters lived at 165 Eaton Place?

⑩ What type of animal are Chip 'n' Dale?

⑪ What is the final resolution of a book, film or play called?

⑫ A white woman in colonial India was addressed as what?

⑬ Where is the Doges Palace?

⑭ What do you call a late summer?

⑮ Which Verdi opera was first performed in Cairo in 1871?

⑯ What type of ship is a VLCC?

QUIZ 264

1. What fantastically nasty beast is a lycanthrope?

2. Which Mr Man wears his hat upside down? 💡

3. What is the name of Tony Soprano's mother?

4. The singer Basshunter is what nationality?

5. What is the French stock exchange called?

6. Which animal is South Africa's national emblem? 💡

7. How many pilgrims sailed on the *Mayflower* in 1620?

8. Which country joined the European Community in 1981?

9. Where did the Beer-Hall Putsch take place in 1923?

10. How many runs are scored off the bat in a maiden over? 💡

11. Who wrote *The Wonderful Wizard of Oz*?

12. In the Bible, which priest anoints Solomon?

13. What is an American vagrant called?

14. Which prehistoric creature's name means 'terrible lizard'? 💡

15. To what activity does the word terpsichorean relate?

16. What is the name of Chief Inspector Tom Barnaby's wife?

QUIZ 265

① Which country was home to Count Dracula? 💡

② In *A Midsummer Night's Dream*, what is Bottom?

③ Who were the first presenters of BBC's *Crimewatch*?

④ Which car's name could be described as an 'earth nomad'?

⑤ What is a treecreeper: a bird, a plant or a snake? 💡

⑥ Which Robert Harris thriller revolves around Bletchley Park?

⑦ Who hit a Test double century in just 153 balls in 2002?

⑧ When did Texas achieve statehood: 1825, 1835, 1845?

⑨ What is a male witch called? 💡

⑩ Who had a 2008 Christmas hit with a 1984 Leonard Cohen song?

⑪ In the financial world what does AIM stand for?

⑫ Which Hollywood star's real name was Issur Danielovich?

⑬ Who is the hero of Evelyn Waugh's *Sword of Honour* trilogy?

⑭ Getting into the Lotus position is part of what activity?

⑮ From which city did the dance *habanera* come?

⑯ Which bear was given super powers by a yellow man covered in green spots? 💡

QUIZ 266

① Who only wants to eat pink yummy treats?

② Which US rock star changed his name but not his sex in 1975?

③ Who played Mrs Bennet in the 1995 version of *Pride and Prejudice*?

④ What were white French settlers in North Africa called?

⑤ In which direction does the sun set?

⑥ Which chemical plant in Bhopal leaked toxic gas in 1984?

⑦ What was Dr McCoy's nickname in *Star Trek*?

⑧ Golf links are always alongside what?

⑨ How do you say 'cheers' in German?

⑩ How many noughts in a million?

⑪ Which nursery rhyme relates to The Black Death?

⑫ Press tycoon Robert Maxwell was born in which country?

⑬ Where was the 1994 FIFA World Cup staged?

⑭ How many Test wickets did Shane Warne end up with?

⑮ What word is opposite to 'professional'?

⑯ What is a tam-tam?

QUIZ 267

① Christine Daaé is the heroine in which musical?

② Who is the kindly sheep dog who looks after Babe?

③ Cayenne and Cayman are models of what car?

④ Which American Civil War general wrote *Ben-Hur*?

⑤ Which famous trio is Athos, Aramis and Porthos?

⑥ What is the French parliament called?

⑦ Who composed the operetta *The Merry Widow*?

⑧ Which former England footballer was known as 'Psycho'?

⑨ What is the soft part at the bottom of your ear called?

⑩ Who finds lots of things 'Cheap as chips'?

⑪ Which UK bestselling author's real name is David Cornwell?

⑫ Name the final film in the 'Magnificent Seven' series.

⑬ Which city has more people living in it – London or Moscow?

⑭ What was the name of Captain Cook's last ship?

⑮ Who wrote the play *The Marriage of Figaro*?

⑯ What shape means to go horribly wrong or awry?

QUIZ 268

1. Who painted *The Monarch of the Glen*?

2. Does the light from a glow-worm comes from its head or its tail? 💡

3. What is army slang for a military prison?

4. Who is Joan Collins' novelist sister?

5. 'Let slip the dogs of war' is a line from which Shakespeare play?

6. According to the song, what is all you need? 💡

7. How many Northern Ireland caps did George Best win: 27, 37, 47?

8. Which detective does Nathaniel Parker portray on TV?

9. What in medieval times was a *jongleur*?

10. Which family lives at 742 Evergreen Terrace? 💡

11. How is Hardaknut Knutsson better known?

12. In a knitting pattern 'psso' means what?

13. Which Brown was a British foreign secretary?

14. What is hot and crossed and eaten at Easter? 💡

15. Which Hollywood superstar once had a job cleaning lion cages?

16. What does the Latin *agnus dei* mean?

QUIZ 269

1. What does a cartographer produce?

2. What is a baby elephant called: a calf, a cub or a jumbo?

3. How is an Arabian hound more commonly known?

4. Which English sausage comes in a coil?

5. The song 'The House Of The Rising Sun' is set in which US city?

6. And for which group was it a hit in the 1960s?

7. What babies are tasty to eat?

8. What is the Salvation Army's newspaper?

9. Who does Ardal O'Hanlon play in *Father Ted*?

10. What animal helps you find your way around a computer screen?

11. What is an animal slaughterhouse called?

12. Who won an Oscar for her role in *Cold Mountain*?

13. Which city in southern France is a major naval base?

14. Brussels is the capital of which country?

15. Who banned eating mince pies on Christmas Day?

16. With what sport is Bisley associated?

QUIZ 270

① What item of furniture is a 'tallboy'?

② Whose portrait of Henry VIII defined the king's image?

③ How long did Rip Van Winkle fall asleep for?

④ What annual event takes place at Badminton?

⑤ In which Bond film does Louis Jourdan play the arch villain?

⑥ What was Richard Neville, 16th Earl of Warwick, known as?

⑦ People who don't eat meat are called what?

⑧ Who is the Greek goddess of the rainbow?

⑨ How old was Beatrix Potter when she died in 1943: 67, 77 or 87?

⑩ What tinkling bells are one of the sounds of Christmas?

⑪ The major split in Islam is between which two groups?

⑫ What is a burletta?

⑬ What nationality is motor-racing driver Keke Rosberg?

⑭ In which county is Berwick-on-Tweed?

⑮ Which country can you make out of TILAY?

⑯ Who was the first British monarch to broadcast on Christmas Day?

QUIZ 271

① Who wrote *The War of the Worlds*?

② Which cool couple are famous for their ice cream?

③ Comic verse of poor quality is called what?

④ In which US city is the Battle of Bunker Hill monument?

⑤ Who played the title role in the 2009 film *The Young Victoria*?

⑥ What is a baby goat called?

⑦ Where was Adolf Hitler's mountain stronghold?

⑧ In film classification what does PG stand for?

⑨ Whose poem begins: 'Tiger, tiger, burning bright . . .'?

⑩ What fuels the burner on a modern hot-air balloon?

⑪ Which football team is at home at the Emirates Stadium?

⑫ How was the disfigured Joseph Merrick better known?

⑬ Which country is known to its inhabitants as the Fatherland?

⑭ For which football club did Chris Hollins' father John play?

⑮ What important document do you need to travel overseas?

⑯ What was the name of the imperial bodyguard in ancient Rome?

QUIZ 272

① What 'flower' might you eat for Sunday lunch?

② Which artistic movement began in Paris in 1907?

③ How is London's principal river paternally known?

④ Who is the voice of *The Fantastic Mr Fox*?

⑤ What relation to you would your grandfather's grandmother be?

⑥ Where in Scotland is the village of Dollar?

⑦ Little Nell is a character in which Charles Dickens novel?

⑧ How many players in a hurling team?

⑨ Which fatherly insect looks as if it's on stilts?

⑩ How many cents is a dime?

⑪ Who invented pneumatic car tyres?

⑫ What is the native language of the Boers?

⑬ When was Andrew Flintoff BBC Sports Personality of the Year?

⑭ What word can come after bull, gas and wedding?

⑮ A Taser is what type of gun?

⑯ What begins on the 'Glorious 12th' of August?

QUIZ 273

① Which Shakespearean character offers his kingdom for a horse?

② Where are the NATO headquarters?

③ What is the smaller relation of the kangaroo?

④ Which famous motorcycling circuit is located in Cheshire?

⑤ What is the full name of Lady Penelope's chauffeur?

⑥ In which sport might you try a *riposte*?

⑦ Who used a bow and arrow to make people fall in love?

⑧ What is the common name for calcium carbonate?

⑨ In *Cheers*, what is Norm's profession?

⑩ Who built the first working monoplane?

⑪ In which country is the Grand Canyon?

⑫ Which epic Hollywood star began life as John Charles Carter?

⑬ A female cat is called a what?

⑭ What is Washington's five-sided symbol of military might?

⑮ What is the political wing of the IRA?

⑯ Who was the first Wallabies winger to win 100 Test caps?

QUIZ 274

1. 'Twelve little girls all in line, and the littlest one is . . .'? 💡

2. C*anard* is French for what?

3. Walt Kowalski in *Gran Torino* is a veteran of which war?

4. In which capital city is the Abbey Theatre?

5. What is a baby seal called? 💡

6. Which major US volcano erupted in 1980?

7. What is the international dialling code for Italy?

8. Who painted *The Potato Eaters*?

9. Which country's head of state is based in the Blue House?

10. What does TMS stand for in radio sports coverage? 💡

11. Who went from *The Sopranos* to *Nurse Jackie*?

12. What two sea coasts does Morocco have?

13. Most of the regional departments of France are named after what?

14. Whose words are used in the hymn 'Jerusalem'?

15. What term means to shift responsibility to another?

16. In *The Great Ghost Rescue*, what is Humphrey the Horrible's brother George? 💡

QUIZ 275

① What time was it when the mouse ran up the clock?

② Dr William Penney developed the UK's first what?

③ Who became Poet Laureate in 2009?

④ What is the number of the *M*A*S*H* unit?

⑤ Which sport is known as 'The Summer Game'?

⑥ Who sang the title song in the film *Die Another Day*?

⑦ The Great Hall of the People is in which city?

⑧ Who heads the Cold Case Unit in *Waking the Dead*?

⑨ Who perform dangerous acts on behalf of movie stars?

⑩ Which amphibian can you sometimes find lodged in your throat?

⑪ What lacy Spanish shawl is worn over the head and shoulders?

⑫ With which sport are the Queensbury Rules associated?

⑬ What is the name of Prospero's daughter in *The Tempest*?

⑭ What does to throw down the gauntlet mean?

⑮ Which US state is called the 'Aloha State'?

⑯ *Parsifal* is an opera by which German composer?

QUIZ 276

① Birds of a feather . . . do what?

② Which muscle separates the chest from the abdomen?

③ Who founded the Methodist Church?

④ What was lost and regained in the poems of John Milton?

⑤ A carousel at a fairground is another name for what?

⑥ What is 100° Fahrenheit in Celsius?

⑦ In Dave Dee, Dozy, Beaky, Mick and Tich, what did Mick play?

⑧ Vexillology is the study of what?

⑨ What do baseball players call a 'dinger'?

⑩ Where is 'The Windy City': Chicago, New York or Las Vegas?

⑪ Which US writer's real name was Nathan Wallenstein Weinstein?

⑫ On what would you expect to see a mural?

⑬ In which city did Tony Bennett leave his heart?

⑭ What is held out as a gesture of peace?

⑮ In boxing, what is a TKO?

⑯ Who played Guinan in *Star Trek: The Next Generation*?

QUIZ 277

① Where were the famous Hanging Gardens?

② Complete the saying: 'It never rains but it . . . '

③ What is the Greek equivalent of the letter B?

④ Which 1971 novel by William Peter Blatty became a hit movie?

⑤ What breed of dog was Rin Tin Tin?

⑥ Who is Homer Simpson married to?

⑦ How many annual solstices are there?

⑧ What do lugworms live in?

⑨ Dylan is the Celtic god of what?

⑩ What is a large group of seagulls called?

⑪ The adjective ovine relates to which animal?

⑫ What is the name of Superintendent Foyle's wartime driver?

⑬ Who scored the most Test hundreds, Graham Gooch or David Gower?

⑭ What is the cube root of 216?

⑮ What is the part of a nut that you eat called?

⑯ Joseph Goebbels was born with which physical disability?

QUIZ 278

① Rudolph the reindeer has a very shiny what? 💡

② When did council tax replace the poll tax: 1991, 1993, 1995?

③ In which classic tale will you find yourself in Brobdingnag?

④ Which of cricket's Waugh twins was nicknamed 'Afghanistan'?

⑤ What is your belly button really called? 💡

⑥ What historic relic sits in the lobby of Lloyds of London?

⑦ Who plays Roxie Hart's husband in the film *Chicago*?

⑧ Which is nearer the sun, Neptune or Uranus?

⑨ Who wrote the 2002 award-winning biography of Samuel Pepys?

⑩ What does an invertebrate creature not have? 💡

⑪ In which ballroom dance would you execute a fishtail?

⑫ Which insect is the UK's largest?

⑬ What Hollywood dog was the 'biggest in the world'?

⑭ Does an apiarist look after bees, birds or monkeys? 💡

⑮ Name the father and son novelists, Kingsley and Martin . . .

⑯ What was the name of the world's first nuclear submarine?

QUIZ 279

1. Who took over from Gordon Ramsay in *Hell's Kitchen*?
2. What word rhymes with handles and are worn on your feet?
3. Name the author of *Billy Liar* who died in 2009.
4. Which league football team is known as the 'Hatters'?
5. The kauri is a tree native to which country?
6. What are Starsky and Hutch's first names?
7. Forwards in a rugby game go head-to-head in the what?
8. Which queen married kings of both England and France?
9. An enthusiast of the ballet is called a what?
10. Which order of monks had a 1994 hit with their album *Chant*?
11. What is a baby goose called?
12. In a car, what is the end of the rod attached to the crankshaft?
13. If you are raniform what shape are you?
14. Which sporting father and son are: Peter and Shaun . . . ?
15. What pastry-made dish can be found in the heavens?
16. Mathematically speaking, what is a googol?

QUIZ 280

1. Where do Rupert Bear and his chums live?

2. Which writer of nautical novels was born Richard Patrick Russ?

3. Name the charismatic Pakistan politician assassinated in 2007.

4. In which country is Noh a traditional form of drama?

5. Who disobeys Strega Nona and touches her magic pasta pot?

6. Which two football teams make up the 'Old Firm'?

7. What is American Smooth?

8. What is the geologist's principal tool?

9. Who won a 'Best Director' Oscar for *Silence of the Lambs*?

10. Can you spell the word for mixing dough?

11. What P is a range of colours for designers and printers?

12. A bear market indicates falling or rising share values?

13. On what day of the week did Solomon Grundy die?

14. Which English monarch was the 'wisest fool in Christendom'?

15. What does a SIM card go into?

16. Which 20th-century artist said: 'I paint what I know, not what I see'?

QUIZ 281

① Which national cricket team is called the 'Proteas'?

② What was the winged horse in Greek mythology?

③ In *Winnie-the-Pooh*, who jumps into Kanga's pouch?

④ Which British queen defeated the Romans?

⑤ In the Queen's Birthday Honours what is a CH?

⑥ If you are the *paterfamilias* what are you?

⑦ Who was the first woman speaker of the House of Commons?

⑧ Pet Squad try to keep the world safe from whom?

⑨ In which athletic event might you see a 'Brill Bend'?

⑩ What do you commit if you wilfully lie under oath?

⑪ Which large African animal's name means 'river horse'?

⑫ Which poet wrote: 'Gather ye rosebuds while ye may'?

⑬ Who played Miss Jones in the TV sitcom *Rising Damp*?

⑭ Which queen supposedly said, 'Let them eat cake'?

⑮ Who was the Austrian chancellor killed by Nazis in 1934?

⑯ Which European country can you make out of MYNGREA?

QUIZ 282

1. If you ask a silly question what will you get? 💡
2. How is iron pyrite better known?
3. In which Thomas Hardy novel is Gabriel Oak a character?
4. Who designed Queen Elizabeth II's coronation gown?
5. What word rhymes with panel and is kept in the bathroom? 💡
6. Which is the longer Grand Prix circuit, Monaco or Monza?
7. What relation was the 1975 killer of Saudi Arabia's King Faisal?
8. Which football club has to play ball with Delia Smith?
9. What is a shaman?
10. How many people sit on a jury in a court of law? 💡
11. Who was Louis-Napoleon's empress wife?
12. Which UK songstress was awarded the *Légion d'honneur* in 1999?
13. Who plays Prince Philip in the film *The Queen*?
14. How do kings move in chess?
15. Kingston is the capital of which Caribbean island? 💡
16. Who married producer David Gest in 2002?

QUIZ 283

① What is a baby mole called: a cub, a pup or a molar?

② In the film *Mean Girls*, what is the girls' clique called?

③ Willow bark is an ingredient in which common painkiller?

④ Cremello, Pinto and Roan are all types of what?

⑤ What is 'rotator' spelt backwards?

⑥ Freetown is the capital of which country?

⑦ What does a costermonger sell in a market?

⑧ Which flu virus is H1N1?

⑨ In the police force, what is CID short for?

⑩ Who plays Tim Nice-But-Dim?

⑪ Which alpine call fluctuates between normal and falsetto?

⑫ In which era did the cloche hat first become fashionable?

⑬ What is a bittersweet longing for things past?

⑭ What is the boundary between two countries called?

⑮ What is a remote control for a Wii games console?

⑯ Who is television's choirmaster?

QUIZ 284

① On what day did the big ship sail on the ally-ally-oh?

② What type of rock is limestone?

③ Who was the presenter of *Loose Ends* who died in 2007?

④ What is the name of Don Quixote's squire?

⑤ In the nursery rhyme, who went to bed with his trousers on? 💡

⑥ To which US novelist was actress Claire Bloom married?

⑦ Golfer Michael Campbell is from which country?

⑧ Who led the UK Referendum Party in the 1997 election?

⑨ In which world is Ankh-Morpork a city state?

⑩ What is France's equivalent of the Oscars?

⑪ How does TV chef Ina Garten choose to be known?

⑫ Who wrote *How the Leopard Got His Spots*? 💡

⑬ Whose revolutionary wife was Jiang Qing?

⑭ Which English poet was knighted in 1969?

⑮ Which sporting father and son are: Brian and Nigel . . . ?

⑯ 'Beefy' is the nickname of which famous ex-cricketer? 💡

QUIZ 285

① If you're a dirty rascal, what am I? 🔆

② What are stalactites and stalagmites made of?

③ In which country was J R R Tolkien born?

④ What title did Margaret Thatcher take as a member of the peerage?

⑤ Who does Charlotte save in *Charlotte's Web*? 🔆

⑥ Which football team's anthem is 'I'm Forever Blowing Bubbles'?

⑦ In *'Allo 'Allo* which German officer has a crush on René?

⑧ Name the legendary lovers of the Middle Ages, Abelard and . . .

⑨ Who wrote the play *Entertaining Mr Sloane*?

⑩ How many quadrants in a circle? 🔆

⑪ Pixie-bob and York Chocolate are breeds of what animal?

⑫ Which peer on the run was nicknamed 'Lucky'?

⑬ Who was Gloucestershire cricket captain for 28 years?

⑭ The 2009 film *An Education* is based on whose memoirs?

⑮ Which Dutch painter cut off his ear? 🔆

⑯ Who overtook Bill Gates in 2008 as the world's richest man?

QUIZ 286

1. In which fair city did Molly Malone live?

2. Which Scotsman captained England at cricket?

3. How many English monarchs have been named Mary: 1, 2 or 3? 💡

4. What shape is a rhombus?

5. Who painted *The Blue Boy*?

6. Which little people is the Shire home to? 💡

7. *Going Straight* was the sequel to which long-running UK sitcom?

8. What was the name of Mussolini's residence in Rome?

9. Which French playwright's real name was Jean-Baptiste Poquelin?

10. How old is someone who has reached four score years? 💡

11. Who did Allison Janney play in *The West Wing*?

12. Which Smith won the 1972 Men's Singles title at Wimbledon?

13. Does a *flat* sign in music mean raising or lowering the pitch?

14. Which comedy singing duo are *The Flight of the Conchords*?

15. What is used to mend a broken limb? 💡

16. Which football club's home ground is Camp Nou?

QUIZ 287

① Who is the musical cat in Roobarb's garden? 💡

② What spacecraft flew past Neptune in 1989?

③ Which Pre-Raphaelite artist painted *Ophelia*?

④ How is Simon Templar otherwise known?

⑤ What animal's name starts off with two LL's? 💡

⑥ How many finger holes are there in a tenpin bowling ball?

⑦ What is arteriosclerosis?

⑧ Which vociferous group follows the England cricket team overseas?

⑨ Add the showbiz surname: Ben and Casey . . .

⑩ If that mocking bird don't sing, what will mama buy? 💡

⑪ What was Ernest M Hemingway's middle name?

⑫ Where was Archduke Franz Ferdinand assassinated in 1914?

⑬ Which 1980s film title was an epistle to a Soviet leader?

⑭ Tirana is the capital of which European country?

⑮ Can you turn SKATE into red meat? 💡

⑯ Who wrote *The Railway Children*?

QUIZ 288

① Which foxy TV character goes 'Boom! Boom!'?

② Who swims in a pool of her own tears? 💡

③ What does a phonologist study?

④ Which royal couple started the fashion for Christmas trees?

⑤ Which cricket commentator's nickname is 'Bumble'?

⑥ What word can be a criminal or something a shepherd carries? 💡

⑦ The use of words that repeat a meaning already conveyed is what?

⑧ Which island on the signpost in *M*A*S*H* is 7033 miles away?

⑨ In *Harry Potter* what model is the Weasley's flying car?

⑩ What is a female opossum called – a jill or a puss? 💡

⑪ In physics, Q is the symbol for what?

⑫ What is Shakespeare's longest play?

⑬ Which city is home to *The Royle Family*?

⑭ What is the true shape of the earth?

⑮ What is the name of Dr Dolittle's parrot? 💡

⑯ What was English artist George Stubbs' favourite model?

QUIZ 289

① Whose apple do you have in your throat? 🔆

② Who was the first English artist to be made a Dame?

③ What is two dozen x two score?

④ Add the father and son sporting surname: Graham and Damon . . .

⑤ Which animal does a groom look after? 🔆

⑥ What does subcutaneous mean?

⑦ Which Michael made it big in *Beetlejuice*?

⑧ What is the third book in the *Narnia Chronicles*?

⑨ Where was French revolutionary Jean-Paul Marat when murdered?

⑩ What is a sou'wester when it isn't a wind? 🔆

⑪ Which team did Terry Venables manage from 1984 to 1987?

⑫ Who is the disembodied hand in *The Addams Family*?

⑬ What is the US indicator of stock market prices?

⑭ What nationality is Aida in the opera of the same name?

⑮ Who sings 'Hakuna Matata' to Simba in *The Lion King*? 🔆

⑯ What was Tarzan's real name?

QUIZ 290

① What word does an ampersand denote?

② In what ballet is there a wicked Mouse King?

③ *Julie and Julia* is about which American TV chef?

④ In which century was Michelangelo born?

⑤ Which fictional character lived at Green Gables?

⑥ Which scary animal do you have to ask for the time?

⑦ In which sport was Doug Mountjoy a champion?

⑧ Whose debut operatic album was called *One Chance*?

⑨ When was the first flight over the South Pole: 1919, 1923, 1927?

⑩ What comes after a big freeze?

⑪ Who in 2006 solved the 'Maria problem'?

⑫ Which long-standing Test umpire retired in 2009?

⑬ Mabel Lucie Attwell was known for cute illustrations of what?

⑭ Where would seaweed be on the menu?

⑮ Whose catchphrase is 'Yabba dabba do.'?

⑯ Which king founded the Royal Greenwich Observatory?

QUIZ 291

1. What replaced Roman numerals in Europe?

2. In the films, what sort of a car is Herbie? ϙ

3. Which US state suffered a major quake in 1964?

4. What is a political PR spokesperson called?

5. Which poor orphan asked for more? ϙ

6. Which little girl was the creation of Joyce Lancaster Brisley?

7. What kind of cat does Blofeld in the Bond movies have?

8. When was the Bank of England founded: 1694, 1794, 1894?

9. In *Discworld* what is Great A'Tuin?

10. What sport is played at Edgbaston? ϙ

11. When did Prohibition end in the USA?

12. Nicolae Ceauçescu was the dictator of which country?

13. What is Little Dorrit's first name?

14. Which capital city had an RAF bomber named after it?

15. For what film did Colin Firth win a BAFTA award in 2010?

16. Who is always inviting people to eat his shorts?

QUIZ 292

① Boggis, Bunce and Bean try to stop who from stealing their hens? ☀

② In which year was the first *Harry Potter* book published?

③ Bronchitis is an inflammation of the what?

④ Which Thomas Hardy hero was obscure?

⑤ How many spots has Pongo in *101 Dalmations*? ☀

⑥ Add the father and son sporting surname: Micky and Alec . . .

⑦ Which former child star married John McEnroe in 1986?

⑧ In which Indian city were 300,000 killed in a 1737 earthquake?

⑨ How many James Bond novels did Ian Fleming write?

⑩ Who is Puff the Magic Dragon's little friend? ☀

⑪ In which country was the Battle of the Boyne fought?

⑫ Which detective owned a bloodhound called Pedro?

⑬ *Banjaxed* is the title of which popular celebrity's autobiography?

⑭ What sharp teeth do wolves have? ☀

⑮ Who is the creator of Inspector Maigret?

⑯ In horse racing, what is a female horse under the age of four?

QUIZ 293

① What word can come after fishing, rowing and sailing?

② Thomas Cook's first overseas tour in 1855 was to which city?

③ Which scientist wrote *A Brief History of Time*?

④ What is the common name for sodium chloride?

⑤ Which country gives London a Christmas tree each year?

⑥ Who first illustrated *Alice's Adventures in Wonderland*?

⑦ How many times did Fred Perry win the Men's Singles at Wimbledon?

⑧ Who did Jon Pertwee succeed as Dr Who?

⑨ Ellis Bell was the pen name of which 19th-century English writer?

⑩ What is the first light of day called?

⑪ Which postwar British film star died in 2009 aged 90?

⑫ What is AWOL short for?

⑬ Who is actress Carrie Fisher's mother?

⑭ Which county is larger – Norfolk or Suffolk?

⑮ What is the first prime number?

⑯ Which military leader was called 'the Little Corporal'?

QUIZ 294

① Inspector Harry Callaghan is with which city's police department?

② What prehistoric creature can you make out of SDUNORAI?

③ How many individual towers are there at the Tower of London?

④ What did astronomer Christiaan Huygens invent in 1656?

⑤ Which Sioux chief was killed by police while being arrested?

⑥ In New Zealand, what animal outnumbers the people?

⑦ Who is Jane Eyre's employer?

⑧ Which writer of adventure novels was governor general of Canada?

⑨ Who wrote *The Female Eunuch*?

⑩ Is vindaloo a curry, a river or an outside toilet?

⑪ Who was the last of the Mohicans?

⑫ Which former England footballer was knighted in 2004?

⑬ What colour robes do Benedictine monks wear?

⑭ Who was Samuel Johnson's friend and biographer?

⑮ What do French children leap over instead of a frog?

⑯ Which TV personality became an MP for Chester?

QUIZ 295

① Which poet is the subject of the film *Bright Star*?

② Whose album beat Lady Gaga to No 1 in 2009?

③ Which planet was discovered by William Herschel in 1781?

④ What word means to steal or is a way of cooking something? 🔦

⑤ Who is the Reverend Collins' patron in *Pride and Prejudice*?

⑥ Who says: 'I love you right up to the Moon and Back'? 🔦

⑦ In which sport is Nancy Lopez a champion?

⑧ Which movie star became California's governor in 1967?

⑨ How many eggs are there in three dozen? 🔦

⑩ Which river flows through the Grand Canyon?

⑪ Who plays the title role in the 1976 film *Carrie*?

⑫ Which Dickens novel is about a father and his male offspring?

⑬ Who succeeded Charles De Gaulle as French president?

⑭ What is a sea urchin covered in? 🔦

⑮ In the sporting world, what is the ICC?

⑯ What were the organized killings of Jews in Russia called?

QUIZ 296

① What do the Chinese use instead of knives and forks?

② What was the poet Lord Byron's first name?

③ Who plays the title role in the film *Jeremiah Johnson*?

④ Which country is the world's largest source of opal?

⑤ Name the author of *The Autograph Man* and *On Beauty*.

⑥ What large insect can you make out of GOPHER SPARS?

⑦ Which two actors in *Gavin & Stacey* write the show?

⑧ Which Soviet leader was in office only a year?

⑨ How many times did rugby guru Stuart Barnes play for England?

⑩ Which planet is larger – Mars or Venus?

⑪ For which league football club did Angus Deayton have a trial?

⑫ Which boxer was nicknamed 'Gentleman Jim'?

⑬ The opera *Nabucco* is what name in English?

⑭ Which Arthur Miller play has witchcraft as its theme?

⑮ What is the name of Bill Nighy's character in *Love Actually*?

⑯ Who, in the children's book, 'roared their terrible roars and gnashed their terrible teeth'?

QUIZ 297

① Whose name is missing: '... *and the Great Glass Elevator*'?

② What did Marie and Pierre Curie discover in 1898?

③ How many feet in a fathom?

④ Which ancient Greek dramatist wrote *The Frogs* and *The Birds*?

⑤ Whose art features animals preserved in formaldehyde?

⑥ When was golf last played at the Olympics: 1904, 1908 or 1912?

⑦ Which Smith was *The Fresh Prince of Bel-Air*?

⑧ Who was the last white leader of Rhodesia?

⑨ What animal was the *Blue Peter* pet 'George'?

⑩ Which country beheaded its monarch in 1649?

⑪ What did French Sudan become?

⑫ Where are the CIA headquarters?

⑬ Who were the first FIFA World Cup-winners of the 21st-century?

⑭ What New York borough did the Indians call 'Keskeskeck'?

⑮ Who used to wear bell-bottomed trousers?

⑯ Rod Steiger's Napoleon met whose Wellington in *Waterloo*?

QUIZ 298

① What beetle was sacred to the ancient Egyptians?

② One tonne equals how many kilograms?

③ Which metal is the best conductor of electricity?

④ What garment is worn by women on the Indian subcontinent?

⑤ Whose graffiti was exhibited at Bristol in 2009?

⑥ When connected what do all the bones in the body form?

⑦ What is a glass for sherry and a two-masted yacht?

⑧ *Whaam!* is a work by which American Pop Artist?

⑨ The wheel on India's national flag has how many spokes?

⑩ Add the vowels to make a famous book title: GRN GGS ND HM?

⑪ Who wrote *Watership Down*?

⑫ On what sea is the port of Rotterdam?

⑬ Who led New Zealand to victory in the 2011 Rugby World Cup?

⑭ What is the full name of Gus the theatrical cat?

⑮ How many Oscars did *The King's Speech* win?

⑯ It takes how many people to play a game of backgammon?

QUIZ 299

① What on the bus goes *swish, swish, swish*?

② Dromophobia is a fear of what?

③ Which Russian leader moved into the Kremlin in 1918?

④ Whose 'Video Killed The Radio Star'?

⑤ Which ocean covers more than a third of the earth's surface?

⑥ What controversial novel about teenage violence appeared in 1962?

⑦ Who is Edina's PA in *Absolutely Fabulous*?

⑧ The explosive trinitrotoluene is better known as what?

⑨ What farm vehicle can you make out of RATROCT?

⑩ How many times was driver Jackie Stewart F1 World Champion?

⑪ Which chemical element has the shortest name?

⑫ What sport is played at Valderrama?

⑬ Which English writer is in the title of an Edward Albee play?

⑭ In which city is Wenceslas Square?

⑮ What 'animal' duplicates other people's behaviour?

⑯ In which soap did Patrick Stewart make his debut TV appearance?

QUIZ 300

① Which absent-minded cat lives with the Thomas family?

② What number is 144 the square root of?

③ Which London football club was formerly Dial Square FC?

④ What did the ancient mariner kill in Coleridge's poem?

⑤ Which 60s band started out as The Paramounts?

⑥ Where in Europe is known as the Eternal City?

⑦ In which part of the human body is the cortex?

⑧ What is the capital of Bulgaria?

⑨ In which city was gay activist Harvey Milk murdered?

⑩ Who on TV is never short of a cunning plan?

⑪ In *The Water Babies*, what is Tom's job?

⑫ What is the name of the Steptoes' horse?

⑬ Which Roald Dahl character was named after a foot complaint?

⑭ What is the US version of *Strictly Come Dancing*?

⑮ What joins your upper and lower leg?

⑯ Who composed the opera *Porgy and Bess*?

QUIZ 301

① Who was Black Beauty's first owner?

② Plop the owl is afraid of what?

③ The Giant's Causeway is formed from which volcanic rock?

④ What did mathematician John Napier invent in 1614?

⑤ Who bunked off school for a day off in Chicago?

⑥ What tool is used to gather leaves?

⑦ Which country became independent from China in 939?

⑧ What is Inspector Rebus' first name?

⑨ Who is the older of the tennis Williams sisters, Venus or Serena?

⑩ What medal do you win if you come third?

⑪ Which English city was once known as Deva?

⑫ What did Shylock do for a living?

⑬ Former chancellor Nigel Lawson was editor of which magazine?

⑭ Which TV soap is set in Letherbridge?

⑮ How many days does February have in a Leap Year?

⑯ In which town is playwright Alan Ayckbourn theatrically based?

QUIZ 302

① What word rhymes with bird and is produced from milk?

② Who is the nicest of King Lear's three daughters?

③ What is the common name for ethylene glycol?

④ Which 17th-century Italian artist was wanted for murder?

⑤ Who was the first tennis player to serve 1000 aces in a season?

⑥ Which European country can you make out of TALOSNCD?

⑦ What bird sang in Berkeley Square?

⑧ Which TV comic's props were a stool, a cigarette and a drink?

⑨ What is the word for a female aviator?

⑩ Which long robe was worn in ancient Rome?

⑪ What is the first book in the Stieg Larsson trilogy?

⑫ In which country was the sculptor Eduardo Paolozzi born?

⑬ Which magician shares the name of a Dickens' character?

⑭ What is the chemical symbol for iron?

⑮ Which cricket county plays its home games at the Riverside?

⑯ Which country elected its first black leader in 1994?

QUIZ 303

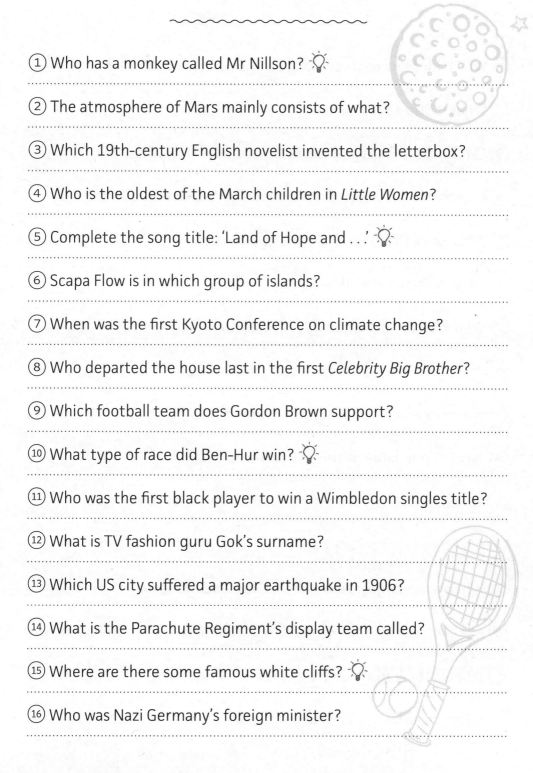

① Who has a monkey called Mr Nillson?

② The atmosphere of Mars mainly consists of what?

③ Which 19th-century English novelist invented the letterbox?

④ Who is the oldest of the March children in *Little Women*?

⑤ Complete the song title: 'Land of Hope and . . .'

⑥ Scapa Flow is in which group of islands?

⑦ When was the first Kyoto Conference on climate change?

⑧ Who departed the house last in the first *Celebrity Big Brother*?

⑨ Which football team does Gordon Brown support?

⑩ What type of race did Ben-Hur win?

⑪ Who was the first black player to win a Wimbledon singles title?

⑫ What is TV fashion guru Gok's surname?

⑬ Which US city suffered a major earthquake in 1906?

⑭ What is the Parachute Regiment's display team called?

⑮ Where are there some famous white cliffs?

⑯ Who was Nazi Germany's foreign minister?

QUIZ 304

① Which Mr Man with very long arms was the first Mr Man of all?

② What is Sting's real name?

③ *Put Out More Flags* and *Vile Bodies* are novels by whom?

④ How are artists Gilbert Proesch and George Passmore better known?

⑤ What does the Cornish word 'oggy' mean?

⑥ What is the capital of Greece?

⑦ Who in *Discworld* is the god of wine and things on sticks?

⑧ What was Russ Abbot's 60s pop group?

⑨ Which video games company's name means 'Leave luck to heaven'?

⑩ What is the name of the RAF aerobatic team?

⑪ Which film was about the mathematician John Forbes Nash?

⑫ A rabbit's tail is called a what?

⑬ What is the largest town on the Shetland Islands?

⑭ MJK Smith played for England at cricket and which other sport?

⑮ What is the largest US state: Alaska, California or Texas?

⑯ American artist Georgia O'Keeffe painted what subject?

QUIZ 305

① Who is missing from the title: '... *and the Bad Hat*'? ⚡

② Which petite US singer was nicknamed 'Little Miss Dynamite'?

③ Henry Moore and David Hockney are both natives of which county?

④ In which play is Blanche DuBois the central character?

⑤ Which two countries are separated by the Kattegat?

⑥ Who is Horrid Henry's loyal vicious hamster? ⚡

⑦ Which type of hat does Captain Mainwaring wear in civvy street?

⑧ Name the Nazi mass murderer assassinated in 1942.

⑨ 'Cowabunga!' is the catchphrase of which quartet?

⑩ What type of pig lives in a forest? ⚡

⑪ Add the footballing fraternal surname: Michael and Brian ...

⑫ Who was the Israeli prime minister assassinated in 1995?

⑬ What kind of hat is associated with Sherlock Holmes?

⑭ The French cheese *brebis* is made from which animal's milk?

⑮ Who removes the wool from a sheep? ⚡

⑯ What can be a sporting total or a musical text?

QUIZ 306

① Which playwright was stabbed to death in Deptford in 1593?

② Cleopatra was queen of which country? ☀

③ Who wrote the *Oedipus* trilogy?

④ Which Indian Test batsman is known as 'The Wall'?

⑤ What can be a pig's home or something painful in your eye? ☀

⑥ Who took over from Humphrey Lyttelton in *I'm Sorry I Haven't A Clue*?

⑦ What do Americans call a baby's dummy?

⑧ Which UK actor died while filming *The Return of the Musketeers*?

⑨ What is fifty more than fifty? ☀

⑩ What is the capital of Ecuador?

⑪ When did the Spanish Civil War begin?

⑫ Where in Italy is Mt Etna?

⑬ Which British knight co-stars in *Shutter Island*?

⑭ Who composed *Carnival of the Animals*?

⑮ What are people forced to leave their homes in wartime called? ☀

⑯ Which US chat-show host collects vintage cars and motorcycles?

QUIZ 307

1. Complete the song title 'When you wish upon a . . .'

2. Who in *The Vicar of Dibley* says: 'No, no, no, no, no, no, yes'?

3. The Exocet missile was developed in which country?

4. Who composed a sonnet 'Upon Westminster Bridge'?

5. In which century was Marco Polo born?

6. Whose best friend is Robby the seal?

7. Which Australian novelist won his second Booker Prize in 2001?

8. What is the company name ICI short for?

9. How many Chemical Brothers are there?

10. What are the bony things either side of your body?

11. What snake delivered a fatal bite to Cleopatra?

12. Which Cornish seaside village is associated with modern art?

13. In which city is Greenwich Village?

14. Who put real sponges in a sponge cake?

15. What religion did Joseph Smith found?

16. Who were this century's first Cricket County Champions?

QUIZ 308

① What can be red or grey and is always cracking nuts?

② Which Australian artist painted a portrait of the Queen in 2005?

③ What US magazine shares the title of a UK 19th-century novel?

④ Who played poet Geoffrey Chaucer in the film *A Knight's Tale*?

⑤ What animal is called the 'Ship of the Desert'?

⑥ At which position did Clive Woodward play rugby for England?

⑦ What is Egypt's currency?

⑧ What was Tokyo previously called?

⑨ Which TV series is reduced to SATC?

⑩ In what sporting activity do you go off *piste*?

⑪ The 1977 film *Slap Shot* features which sport?

⑫ Which ex-ad man is a leading patron of contemporary art?

⑬ In E M Forster's novel of the same name, what is Howard's End?

⑭ Where does Pope John Paul II have an airport named after him?

⑮ What might you wear on your feet when swimming?

⑯ In what sport are Wigan Warriors a leading side?

QUIZ 309

① Charlie Bone is descended from which regal person? ☀

② Which British cartoonist created the image of St Trinian's?

③ Whose memoirs are entitled *Moab is My Washpot*?

④ Enver Hoxha was the communist dictator of which country?

⑤ In which country was the Battle of Blenheim fought?

⑥ What was invented first, the light bulb or the telephone? ☀

⑦ Which is mainland Britain's most northern town?

⑧ The film *A Night to Remember* is about which disaster?

⑨ What was the US infantryman nicknamed in World War I?

⑩ What is a window built into a roof? ☀

⑪ Who was rugby league's 2010 'Man of Steel'?

⑫ In which jail was Oscar Wilde imprisoned?

⑬ What is the name of *The Addams Family* butler?

⑭ *Que será sera* means what?

⑮ What is an aircraft's landing gear called? ☀

⑯ Which poem begins: 'The Curfew tolls the knell of parting day'?

QUIZ 310

1. Whose chair did Goldilocks break? 🔅

2. In which film did Peter Sellers posthumously appear?

3. Who painted *At the Moulin Rouge*?

4. How old was Queen Victoria when she came to the throne?

5. Which US writer's real name was William Sydney Porter?

6. What number comes next: 4, 8, 16, 32 . . .? 🔅

7. What do Larry, Curly and Mo add up to?

8. Who played the title role in the film *Hud*?

9. What is the resident singer in a synagogue called?

10. How many times did Ryan Sidebottom's father play for England?

11. What sweet is an edible fastener? 🔅

12. What does the Maori name for New Zealand, *Aotearoa*, mean?

13. The arm of a mechanical crane is called a what?

14. What is the Latin name for the Northern Lights?

15. True cockneys must be born within the sound of which bells?

16. Which is further north, Edinburgh or Glasgow? 🔅

QUIZ 311

① Who does Bill Sikes murder in *Oliver Twist*?

② How many full bags of wool does 'baa baa black sheep' have?

③ What was the name of the first cloned sheep?

④ Whose husband leaves her in *dinnerladies*?

⑤ Which of these has a tail: baboon, chimpanzee, gorilla?

⑥ A crimper is slang for what?

⑦ Who painted *Children's Games*?

⑧ In which Australian state is the Derwent river?

⑨ Milton Obote was leader of which African country?

⑩ What part of the body is also a place or worship?

⑪ In which country was the 1572 St Bartholomew's Day massacre?

⑫ Ben Ainslie has won three Olympic golds in which sport?

⑬ Who was the woman inside Mrs Merton?

⑭ Which English poet committed suicide at the age of 17?

⑮ What colour blood are kings and queens said to have?

⑯ Which Hollywood superstar was crowned 'King of Cool'?

QUIZ 312

① Turn CHEATER into someone at school?

② Who was Poet Laureate from 1930 to 1967?

③ What is the hardest material in the human body?

④ Who was the second bowler to take 10 wickets in a Test innings?

⑤ What is one-sixtieth of an hour?

⑥ Which Alan wrote the play *The History Boys*?

⑦ Tinnitus affects which of the senses?

⑧ What is the nickname of Egypt's national football team?

⑨ Who plays Rizzo in the film *Grease*?

⑩ What are hanging spikes of frozen water called?

⑪ The Battle of Plassey was fought in which country?

⑫ Who created the 'Angel of the North'?

⑬ In New Zealand, what are 'Pakehas'?

⑭ Which London football club has had the most home grounds?

⑮ What colour do you get if you mix orange with green?

⑯ Mother Ann Lee founded which 18th-century religious movement?

QUIZ 313

① What begins: 'Last night I dreamt I went to Manderley again'?

② Which fish has a rainbow in its name? ☀

③ Which organ in the body also means 'bad temper'?

④ Ngo Dinh Diem was leader of which Asian country?

⑤ What kind of a noise can you make out of RINSE? ☀

⑥ Which actress ended up gold in *Goldfinger*?

⑦ At which sport was Fred Perry a world champion before tennis?

⑧ Which sensational German 'diaries' proved to be a major scam?

⑨ Which pair advised the nation *What Not to Wear*?

⑩ What is snake poison called? ☀

⑪ Which US state is known as the 'Prairie State'?

⑫ What was the name of the computer that cracked the Enigma codes?

⑬ Who is the teenage killer in Graham Greene's *Brighton Rock*?

⑭ 'Bosie' is an Australian cricketing term for what?

⑮ Whose oral histories of the American people were bestsellers?

⑯ What did the old woman who lived in a shoe give all her children to eat? ☀

QUIZ 314

① Which animal howls when the moon is full?

② *The Tin Drum* is a novel by which German author?

③ What is an impish, ugly, mischievous sprite?

④ Who sang 'That's What Friends Are For' with Dionne Warwick?

⑤ What G is a horse-riding competition?

⑥ Which TV chef's parents were both professional actors?

⑦ What was the original name of Boston, Massachusetts?

⑧ Who was the 18th-century author of *The Social Contract*?

⑨ In which year did the All Blacks first tour the UK?

⑩ Which horoscope sign is twins?

⑪ What are the soft spots called on a newborn baby's skull?

⑫ Napoleon and Snowball are characters in which political fable?

⑬ Which English film director was knighted in 2002?

⑭ What is the money put up for contesting boxers called?

⑮ What word can be a student or part of an eye?

⑯ *La fin* is French for what?

ANSWERS

QUIZ 1

1. Bank of England; 2. Crimean War; 3. *A Christmas Carol*; 4. 73; 5. Agatha Christie; 6. Lake District; 7. Two; 8. Red; 9. Stalagmites; 10. Ozone; 11. Six; 12. Spanish Riding School; 13. France; 14. Tanzania; 15. Tigger; 16. 27

QUIZ 2

1. Their letters are in alphabetical order; 2. Gibbs SR toothpaste; 3. Mediterranean Sea; 4. Knot; 5. Infallible; 6. Smell; 7. Alice; 8. North Atlantic; 9. Gallipoli; 10. Captain Ahab; 11. Four; 12. Sheffield Wednesday's; 13. Boat; 14. Charlotte; 15. Wild dog; 16. Three

QUIZ 3

1. Dead Sea; 2. Basil D'Oliveira; 3. Buddha; 4. Prince Edward; 5. Flatiron Building in New York; 6. Statue of Zeus; 7. Karl Marx and Friedrich Engels; 8. Butterfly; 9. Ron Greenwood; 10. El Greco; 11. Anaheim; 12. Horse Chestnut; 13. Toad; 14. Edward VII; 15. Aardvark; 16. Babe

QUIZ 4

1. Replicants; 2. Hive; 3. Winston Churchill; 4. Grasshopper; 5. Matt Cardle; 6. Stonehenge 7. German Nazi Party; 8. Scilly Isles; 9. John Galsworthy; 10. Motor racing; 11. Donald Sutherland; 12. Fifth; 13. Petrograd and Leningrad; 14. St David; 15. Two hours; 16. 'Thou Shalt Not Kill'

QUIZ 5

1. St Clement's; 2. Carbon; 3. Bayonne; 4. Fractions; 5. Cygnet; 6. Rupert Brooke's; 7. Frodo Baggins; 8. Chesapeake Bay; 9. Case; 10. Stuarts; 11. Orange; 12. *Anno Domini*; 13. Arthur Ransome; 14. Knot; 15. Brown; 16. *Midnight's Children*

QUIZ 6

1. Fox; 2. Ear; 3. The Taoiseach; 4. Nimbus; 5. Workhouse; 6. Warren Beatty; 7. United Nations Educational Scientific and Cultural Organisation; 8. BBC's; 9. Old Trafford; 10. T S Eliot; 11. Ainsley Harriott's; 12. New Zealand; 13. Four and twenty; 14. 1917; 15. Lentils; 16. Eminem

QUIZ 7

1. 'Exterminate!'; 2. *The White Tiger*; 3. Shell; 4. Mt Kilimanjaro; 5. 29; 6. 1415; 7. Surfing; 8. The Brontës; 9. Wood; 10. Hanoi; 11. Walmington-on-Sea; 12. Sir Alec Douglas-Home; 13. Snowy Owl; 14. In a church; 15. Skin; 16. 1990

QUIZ 8

1. Pudsey; 2. Herbert George; 3. Clint Eastwood; 4. Top hat; 5. Aslan; 6. Italy; 7. Duke of York; 8. Summer; 9. The Three Musketeers; 10. Domovoi Butler; 11. Alan Partridge (Steve Coogan); 12. Westminster Abbey; 13. Chantilly; 14. Violin; 15. James; 16. The Blue Peter

QUIZ 9

1. Danny Kaye; 2. Nucleus; 3. Fiona; 4. St Mark; 5. Scampi; 6. *Room 101*; 7. Joey; 8. Stanley Baldwin; 9. Kidneys; 10. The Three Graces; 11. Lord's; 12. Three; 13. Darwin; 14. Dan Quayle; 15. Spaniel; 16. *The Return of the King*

QUIZ 10

1. Terry Pratchett; 2. Kanga; 3. Right; 4. Hawser; 5. Radar; 6. Edinburgh; 7. Michelangelo; 8. Catamaran; 9. Ra; 10. Archaeology; 11. Turkey;

12. Lord Palmerston; 13. *Bleak House*; 14. 64; 15. Yellow; 16. Butt

QUIZ 11

1. Raven; 2. Sloane Ranger; 3. Beijing; 4. William Walton; 5. Neck;
6. Belize; 7. Deuce; 8. The Red Baron; 9. Cubism; 10. 1981; 11. St Martin's;
12. Blue; 13. 7/10th; 14. Boston; 15. Pisa; 16. Bill Clinton's

QUIZ 12

1. Las Vegas; 2. Extraterrestrial; 3. Franz Schubert; 4. The atomic bomb
on Hiroshima; 5. Bolivia (Condor); 6. 70%; 7. First floodlit football
international in England; 8. Alexander Pope; 9. *The Big Country*;
10. Camelot; 11. The 13 original colonies; 12. Palm Springs; 13. The
Browns; 14. Pandemic; 15. Photography; 16. Rudyard Kipling

QUIZ 13

1. Cooper; 2. South Africa; 3. Battle of the Little Bighorn; 4. Seine;
5. Red; 6. Blackpool; 7. Doctor; 8. Beans; 9. Brandon Lee; 10. Department
for Environment, Food and Rural Affairs; 11. Det Supt Sandra Pullman;
12. Bank; 13. Russian tea urn; 14. Somalia's; 15. Len Hutton; 16. Neil
Armstrong

QUIZ 14

1. Mice and men; 2. Doe; 3. 30; 4. Marshy swamp; 5. France; 6. Knot;
7. Finch; 8. Charles I; 9. Jersey's Bureau des Etrangers; 10. Po; 11. Haiti
and the Dominican Republic; 12. 1836; 13. Butterflies; 14. Dalmation;
15. Telephone; 16. Sub-atomic particles

QUIZ 15

1. Accra; 2. Rio de Janeiro; 3. Mars; 4. Stormont; 5. Arthur Miller; 6. El
Niño; 7. Andy (in the *Toy Story* films); 8. Reykjavik; 9. Triassic; 10. George
Eliot; 11. Earth; 12. Ayr United; 13. Melanie Griffith; 14. 1973; 15. North
Sea; 16. The Jesuit Order

QUIZ 16

1. Loincloth; 2. James; 3. Blue; 4. Soho; 5. Unit of atmospheric pressure; 6. Los Angeles; 7. Big Brother; 8. Zambezi; 9. Captain (or Colonel) Thomas Blood; 10. Golf clubs; 11. Moses; 12. French Revolution; 13. Sir Frank Worrell; 14. Yorkshire; 15. Harvard; 16. Greece

QUIZ 17

1. Hydrogen; 2. Venus; 3. London Bridge; 4. Dragon; 5. John Paul II; 6. Michigan, New York, Ohio, Pennsylvania; 7. Time; 8. St Vitus; 9. 1986; 10. Two; 11. 20%; 12. Bamber Gascoigne; 13. Nelson; 14. Christchurch; 15. Its breadth at the widest point; 16. Alan Ayckbourn

QUIZ 18

1. Plymouth Argyle; 2. Pilchard; 3. His shadow; 4. Judo (belt); 5. Ivy League; 6. Tower Bridge; 7. Chemical elements; 8. Prague; 9. Archipelago; 10. Seven; 11. Tides; 12. Mike Read; 13. Allen Ginsberg; 14. Michelle; 15. Tony and Hilary Benn; 16. Ali G

QUIZ 19

1. Power; 2. Melbourne; 3. Jeremy Fisher; 4. Charlemagne; 5. *Harry Potter and the Goblet of Fire*; 6. Twice; 7. St George; 8. Bank clerk; 9. COBRA; 10. Algorithmic Language; 11. Sett; 12. Sweden; 13. Acute; 14. Johann Strauss; 15. Eight; 16. Manchester City

QUIZ 20

1. She's a shopkeeper; 2. Great White Way; 3. Turkish; 4. *Alice in Wonderland*; 5. Coco; 6. Nine; 7. Berlin Wall; 8. Troy; 9. Firewall; 10. Meat Loaf's; 11. Type of men's overcoat; 12. Humphry Davy; 13. Tony Blair; 14. Odin; 15. C B Fry; 16. Buffalo

QUIZ 21

1. Duma; 2. Front; 3. Valéry Giscard d'Estaing; 4. Sand; 5. Tina Turner;

6. Canada; 7. An orange ball; 8. Canada (Bay of Fundy); 9. Michael Foale;
10. Prime Minister's; 11. 1900; 12. France; 13. Four; 14. Kermit the Frog;
15. Malcolm X; 16. France

QUIZ 22

1. Table tennis; 2. Mr Blobby; 3. T; 4. Greg Norman; 5. Sir Francis Drake;
6. Violin; 7. 1847; 8. Dead Sea; 9. Bucket; 10. Felt-tip pen; 11. Pudding
Lane; 12. Tiberius; 13. Goliath; 14. Antelope; 15. Mediterranean; 16. Two

QUIZ 23

1. Dipper; 2. Ben Nevis; 3. House of York; 4. Adam's apple; 5. Five;
6. WALL-E; 7. Joyful; 8. Dog; 9. Arctic; 10. Six geese a-laying; 11. Algeria;
12. Australian and New Zealand Army Corps; 13. Jack Black; 14. Mayfair;
15. Washington; 16. Hair stylist

QUIZ 24

1. 'In a beautiful pea-green boat'; 2. Northampton; 3. Hector Berlioz;
4. South China Sea; 5. Jess; 6. Queen Salote; 7. Thorax; 8. Rudolf Nureyev;
9. 13; 10. At the point of death; 11. Richard Nixon; 12. French;
13. Amethyst; 14. Mongooses; 15. Larry Grayson's; 16. 147

QUIZ 25

1. His crown; 2. Blue Moon; 3. Brazil; 4. Wigan; 5. Cook Strait; 6. Houses
of Parliament; 7. Spiro Agnew; 8. Alfred, Lord Tennyson; 9. Battle of
Balaclava; 10. Date; 11. Royal Marines; 12. Protea; 13. Gauchos;
14. A basket called a cesta; 15. Evergreen; 16. Memphis

QUIZ 26

1. Jockey Tony McCoy; 2. Vowel; 3. Otter's; 4. Aberystwyth; 5. Gateshead;
6. Husky; 7. Ulysses Simpson Grant; 8. Botswana and Namibia; 9. The
Great Artesian Basin; 10. Saladin; 11. Eucalyptus; 12. The Priests; 13. The
pocket calculator; 14. Zubin Mehta; 15. Gondoliers; 16. 200 million

QUIZ 27

1. CDLXXXIX; 2. *Titanic*; 3. Atom; 4. Ennio Morricone; 5. Stuart Broad;
6. Seven; 7. 1979; 8. Washington DC; 9. George Gilbert Scott; 10. Charles
II; 11. Cat; 12. Pyrenees; 13. Lord Wilson of Rievaulx; 14. Le Mans;
15. Chess; 16. 17

QUIZ 28

1. Six; 2. Green; 3. Sarah Palin; 4. Bullfighting; 5. Orkneys; 6. Pharoahs;
7. Table Mountain; 8. The Balfour Declaration; 9. Attila; 10. Neptune;
11. Letchworth (Hertfordshire); 12. Mead; 13. 1953; 14. Sea monster;
15. Bag; 16. Plane crash

QUIZ 29

1. 'When I grow rich'; 2. An abacus; 3. Jamie; 4. Harold Wilson; 5. 31;
6. Australia; 7. Deborah; 8. Rome; 9. Doughnuts; 10. Samuel Beckett;
11. Kensington Gardens; 12. France; 13. Paris; 14. China (First Opium
War); 15. Four; 16. Asgard

QUIZ 30

1. Aorta; 2. Wormwood; 3. A map; 4. Johnny Dankworth; 5. *Porgy and Bess*;
6. Compact disc; 7. On its front legs; 8. Huge creature; 9. 'The Soldier' by
Rupert Brooke; 10. Hamelin; 11. Golda Meir; 12. Pangram; 13. Cards;
14. One thousand; 15. Blue star sapphire; 16. Bertrand Russell (1950)

QUIZ 31

1. Hilda; 2. Mausolus'; 3. Sullivan; 4. *Persuasion*; 5. Stanley Falls; 6. Walter
Winterbottom; 7. Alesha Dixon; 8. TASS; 9. John XXIII; 10. Large Hadron
Collider; 11. Peter Piper; 12. Zoophyte; 13. Cleopatra; 14. Emma Watson;
15. Rugby; 16. A baronetcy is hereditary

QUIZ 32

1. The meadows; 2. Worker bees; 3. Everton; 4. Suffolk; 5. Benjamin

Britten; 6. Peter Rabbit's; 7. Gibraltar; 8. Eldred; 9. Divine; 10. Colorado; 11. Berry; 12. *2001: A Space Odyssey*; 13. Errors and Omissions Excepted; 14. Laura Robson; 15. One; 16. Siam

QUIZ 33

1. *Cinderella*; 2. Semicolon; 3. Franklin Roosevelt; 4. Metric system; 5. Excalibur; 6. Delaware; 7. *The Times*; 8. Japan's; 9. 1492; 10. Buddha; 11. Supernumerary; 12. *Lycée*; 13. Kevin Pietersen; 14. Richard Condon; 15. Order of the Garter; 16. Kathmandu

QUIZ 34

1. O J Simpson's; 2. Daisy; 3. Plantagenet; 4. Edinburgh; 5. Dodecanese; 6. Pup; 7. La Pasionaria; 8. Eel; 9. Alfred Nobel; 10. M1; 11. Ten; 12. Boo Boo; 13. Some; 14. St Patrick; 15. British Home Stores; 16. Connecticut

QUIZ 35

1. Halloween; 2. Admiral Lord Nelson; 3. Drum; 4. Capricorn; 5. Jack Sparrow; 6. Sonny and Cher; 7. 1960; 8. Ivan IV (the Terrible); 9. Water vole; 10. *The Tracey Ullman Show*; 11. French; 12. Rajiv Gandhi; 13. *In the Heat of the Night*; 14. Nonet; 15. France; 16. Adams

QUIZ 36

1. Huey, Dewey and Louie; 2. Dr Martin Luther King; 3. Guernsey; 4. Nitrogen; 5. Ewe; 6. Lyndon Johnson; 7. Mirage; 8. Edith Piaf's; 9. Sails; 10. 1776; 11. Hull City's; 12. Juneau; 13. Runner Chris Chataway; 14. Infrasonic; 15. Wishy Washy; 16. John Philip Sousa

QUIZ 37

1. Tinky Winky; 2. Stephen; 3. Intercostal; 4. *Man of La Mancha*; 5. Chromium; 6. Tintin's; 7. Breeches; 8. 'The Clock'; 9. Isle of Man's; 10. Houses of Parliament; 11. Lady Jane Grey; 12. Mt Fujiyama; 13. St Lucia; 14. *Bonjour*; 15. Graham Gooch; 16. Cary Grant and Marlon Brando

QUIZ 38

1. The Queen; 2. Nana; 3. None; 4. Pyrrhic victory; 5. Walter Mondale;
6. Rabbits; 7. Alexander II; 8. Lizard Point; 9. *On the Waterfront*; 10. Four;
11. In its head; 12. Books; 13. Via an ad in *Stage* magazine; 14. Roy
Jenkins, David Owen, William Rodgers, Shirley Williams; 15. Maggie;
16. Horse

QUIZ 39

1. Shetlands; 2. A spider; 3. Clavicle; 4. Federal Bureau of Investigation;
5. FA Cup Final; 6. Three; 7. His hat; 8. Jane Torvill and Christopher
Dean's; 9. Philippines; 10. *Victory*; 11. Jaguar; 12. Cabbage Patch Kids;
13. New York; 14. John Fitzgerald Kennedy; 15. Kilt; 16. Miguel de
Cervantes

QUIZ 40

1. Germany; 2. Ark; 3. John Sullivan; 4. Neuritis; 5. Richard Branson;
6. Kaa; 7. Emperor Hirohito; 8. The Troubadour; 9. Two; 10. Great Wall of
China; 11. Topaz; 12. Lumberjack; 13. 'Endymion' by John Keats;
14. Muscles; 15. The Pennines; 16. 18

QUIZ 41

1. Vladimir Putin; 2. Snowy; 3. 1000; 4. The Singing Nun; 5. Ghana;
6. Knave of Hearts; 7. Red; 8. Lionel Bart; 9. pH scale; 10. Angela Rippon;
11. Very Important Person; 12. *Gone With the Wind*; 13. Robert Plant;
14. Glenister; 15. Juno; 16. Kookaburra

QUIZ 42

1. Captain Hook; 2. Mauna Loa (Hawaii); 3. Joel and Ethan; 4. Two;
5. Hundred Acre Wood; 6. Sweden; 7. Pullet; 8. 12; 9. 'To a Skylark' by
Percy Bysshe Shelley; 10. All Blacks; 11. Rudolf Nureyev; 12. 14mph;
13. Sir Paul McCartney; 14. Pectoral; 15. Barack; 16. Idi Amin

QUIZ 43

1. M; 2. Night-gown; 3. Whooping cough; 4. Margaret Thatcher Day;
5. Red; 6. Tabitha Twitchit; 7. 'Raindrops Keep Falling On My Head';
8. Dr Rowan Williams; 9. Castor and Pollux; 10. Pancakes; 11. James II;
12. Marchioness; 13. Istanbul; 14. Jesus; 15. The Ashes; 16. Symbionese
Liberation Army

QUIZ 44

1. Lions; 2. Zac Efron; 3. 13/20; 4. Hardy; 5. Penguin; 6. 21; 7. 400m
hurdles; 8. Test-tube baby; 9. 'When A Child Is Born'; 10. Lincoln;
11. One (Sedan chair); 12. *Blake's 7*; 13. Baseball; 14. Sir Terry Pratchett;
15. Oxford; 16. Moldova

QUIZ 45

1. Hull; 2. His cow; 3. 'Of last month'; 4. 1997; 5. Austen; 6. Prince Philip;
7. 102; 8. Soft or softly; 9. Edward Heath; 10. Stern; 11. *Hamlet*; 12. The
five continents; 13. On the ground; 14. Reginald; 15. Trees; 16. La Niña

QUIZ 46

1. A man; 2. Netherlands; 3. Mariah Carey; 4. Mars; 5. Seven; 6. Finch;
7. Diagonal cross; 8. Buddhism; 9. Marti Pellow; 10. Dec;
11. Worcestershire; 12. Tony Hancock; 13. Kelly Holmes; 14. Cycling;
15. Skoda; 16. Dustin Hoffman

QUIZ 47

1. Genuine; 2. Augustus Gloop; 3. Aneurysm; 4. Jenny Lind; 5. Ernesto;
6. Dronkeys; 7. Clothes (tailor); 8. General Franco; 9. New York; 10. Duke
and Duchess of Cambridge; 11. Istanbul; 12. One of the four World
Elephants; 13. Sir Arthur Sullivan; 14. *The Left Handed Gun*; 15. Dean;
16. California

QUIZ 48

1. Thumper; 2. Ca; 3. Edward Jenner; 4. Eight; 5. Roost; 6. 1941; 7. James; 8. Ava Gardner; 9. Gordon Durie's; 10. House-elf; 11. *Jeans*; 12. Bullet trains; 13. To overpraise; 14. *Hard Times*; 15. Green; 16. Anthony McPartlin and Declan Donnelly

QUIZ 49

1. Geography; 2. Unicorn; 3. Graham and Damon Hill; 4. Anchovies and eggs on toast; 5. General John Pershing; 6. Ten; 7. Lord Louis Mountbatten; 8. The Boers; 9. Albert Bridge; 10. Ireland; 11. Red; 12. Roger Vadim; 13. Hinduism; 14. Morpheus; 15. Five; 16. Ceres (1801)

QUIZ 50

1. Thrice; 2. Los Alamos; 3. Kiev; 4. 10ft (3.05m); 5. The Runaway Train; 6. Sergei Eisenstein; 7. Guitar; 8. Kitty; 9. Automobile Association; 10. Florence Nightingale; 11. Glenn Miller's; 12. 63; 13. Bass tuba; 14. *Blue Peter*; 15. Captain Edward Smith; 16. His fingerprint

QUIZ 51

1. Two; 2. 18th; 3. Oak; 4. 90°; 5. Windsor; 6. Ian Ogilvy; 7. Norfolk; 8. Frankie Dettori; 9. Field Marshal Douglas Haig; 10. Trafalgar Square; 11. Prince Andrew; 12. Sheffield; 13. USA; 14. No 6; 15. Himalayas; 16. Thomas Mann

QUIZ 52

1. Edward VII; 2. Tadpoles; 3. F Scott Fitzgerald; 4. 'Dig for Victory'; 5. Australia; 6. Five; 7. 1987; 8. Tribe of Native Americans; 9. Silverside; 10. Low ceilings/low clouds; 11. Batman and Robin; 12. 18th; 13. Toulouse; 14. Harold Macmillan; 15. Loch; 16. John Deacon

QUIZ 53

1. Charleston; 2. Ten thousand; 3. Clowder; 4. *Twelfth Night*; 5. Wren;

6. 007; 7. None; 8. Bay; 9. Jeff; 10. Rome; 11. Terry Malloy; 12. Seven;
13. Radio Caroline; 14. Southpaw; 15. Kiwi; 16. Jane Seymour

QUIZ 54

1. Hampden Park; 2. Buckingham Palace; 3. Slapstick; 4. Canada's;
5. 1616; 6. 18; 7. Pineapple; 8. Johnny Ray; 9. Apollo's; 10. Sir Christopher
Wren; 11. Montreux; 12. Frederick Delius; 13. Bolivia and Peru;
14. Kangaroo court; 15. Mars; 16. Greece's

QUIZ 55

1. One; 2. Bear Grylls; 3. Peter Blake; 4. Zoologist; 5. Sherlock Holmes;
6. Sex Pistols; 7. Charles river; 8. Horses; 9. 1908; 10. William
Shakespeare; 11. Dodo; 12. Birch tree; 13. Peter Pan; 14. Rome;
15. Global Positioning System; 16. Enrico Caruso

QUIZ 56

1. Abanazar; 2. Jason; 3. Robert Ludlum; 4. Poodle; 5. Lord Salisbury;
6. Beefeaters; 7. 1950; 8. Edward III; 9. Adolf Hitler; 10. Chelsea's;
11. Susan; 12. Johnny Cash; 13. George Orwell; 14. Pierce Brosnan;
15. Apple; 16. Steve Biko

QUIZ 57

1. 'All the king's horses and all the king's men'; 2. Michael Jackson's;
3. Australia's; 4. Tracey Emin; 5. Buffalo Bill; 6. Apple; 7. Katrina;
8. Venezuela (Venice); 9. Rook; 10. 'A partridge in a pear tree'; 11. RAM
(Random Access Memory); 12. *Spice World*; 13. Michael Crichton;
14. Archer; 15. The White House; 16. Blue

QUIZ 58

1. Thor; 2. Sugar; 3. Horse; 4. Sam Weller; 5. Rawplug; 6. Mile; 7. James II;
8. Sandy Lyle; 9. Chris Columbus; 10. Christian Dior; 11. J; 12. Sir Richard
Hadlee; 13. Essex; 14. Vendée; 15. United Nations; 16. Flamingo

QUIZ 59

1. Estevez; 2. The Cowardly Lion, the Scarecrow and the Tin Man;
3. Drey; 4. 12; 5. John Wesley; 6. Highwayman; 7. 1994; 8. St Joseph;
9. F W Woolworth; 10. Nickname; 11. Old King Cole; 12. Australia;
13. Sparkling; 14. Norwegian; 15. Cuckoo; 16. Engineering and
economics

QUIZ 60

1. Planets; 2. Joel Garner; 3. 180°; 4. Hercules; 5. Dublin; 6. Switzerland;
7. Robert Graves; 8. Derek Jacobi; 9. Europe and Asia; 10. Timothy;
11. Rowing; 12. Guilder; 13. Cindy Crawford; 14. Sheep; 15. Prince
Edward; 16. Candle-snuffer

QUIZ 61

1. Mumble; 2. *Romeo and Juliet*; 3. Dave Beasant (for Wimbledon v
Liverpool, 1988); 4. Moraine; 5. Obi-Wan-Kenobi; 6. *Tom Jones*;
7. The Pips; 8. Oliver Reed; 9. Vet; 10. 1170; 11. Jerome Kern and Oscar
Hammerstein; 12. *Schindler's Ark*; 13. Thomas Keneally; 14. Jumbo jet;
15. Jim Ryun; 16. Isoceles

QUIZ 62

1. Aunt Sally; 2. Types of cheese; 3. Jupiter; 4. American War of
Independence; 5. 'White bread and butter'; 6. *Still Life*; 7. Caste mark
worn by Hindu women; 8. Tashkent; 9. Adam Smith; 10. Coalminer;
11. Fencing; 12. Tuberculosis; 13. The Bee Gees; 14. Jane Lynch;
15. Panama Canal; 16. *Picture Post*

QUIZ 63

1. O; 2. 12; 3. Antisocial Behaviour Order; 4. Heinrich Himmler; 5. Eight;
6. Zulu War; 7. Stamen; 8. Noel Coward; 9. Bird of prey; 10. Nuclear
energy; 11. Britney Spears; 12. 17th; 13. Green jacket; 14. The owl and
the pussycat; 15. Britain; 16. M50

QUIZ 64

1. Old Mother Hubbard; 2. Alpha; 3. Silver; 4. Geraldine James; 5. Pacific; 6. Woodwind; 7. Washington; 8. Mt Everest; 9. Mother Teresa; 10. Long John Silver's; 11. Small hill; 12. New Zealand; 13. San Andreas; 14. Vikram Seth; 15. Four; 16. *Henry V*

QUIZ 65

1. Girl; 2. 16; 3. Ben Cross; 4. Grampians; 5. David Duval; 6. Rugby School; 7. Yemen; 8. Gulags; 9. Mars; 10. Diamond; 11. Gerhard Schroeder; 12. Paddington Bear; 13. 'Thou shalt not steal'; 14. Alderney; 15. Rugby; 16. Bright blue or violet

QUIZ 66

1. Eggbert; 2. *Hannah Montana*; 3. Leonardo da Vinci; 4. *La Gioconda*; 5. Three; 6. Cross of Lorraine; 7. Taff; 8. Velocipede; 9. Abraham Lincoln; 10. The Great Barrier Reef; 11. *Adios*; 12. Laughing gas; 13. Salt Lake City; 14. Balmoral Castle; 15. Backgammon; 16. *A Star is Born*

QUIZ 67

1. Francis; 2. Rosie and Poppy; 3. 23rd April; 4. Jawaharial Nehru; 5. Chrysalis; 6. Bell; 7. Weeping Willow; 8. Sex testing; 9. Forum; 10. 62; 11. Mannitol; 12. Sea bird; 13. 2003; 14. Iberian; 15. Air Force One; 16. *For Your Eyes Only*

QUIZ 68

1. German measles; 2. Ravens; 3. George Bernard Shaw; 4. Samosa; 5. Bossa Nova; 6. Because it is 'Very Hungry'; 7. Seven; 8. 1982; 9. Flageolet; 10. DW; 11. Hydrogen; 12. England and Scotland; 13. Mother-of-pearl; 14. *Escargot*; 15. Wolfgang Amadeus Mozart's; 16. Alan Bennett

QUIZ 69

1. William Shakespeare; 2. *Young Dracula*; 3. Harp; 4. Tony Curtis';
5. Pimply Paul's and Prissy Polly's; 6. Peter Wright's; 7. Chicago; 8. Jersey;
9. Andrew Flintoff; 10. Prince Rupert; 11. Fluorine; 12. Thirteen;
13. Buffalo milk; 14. Mt Logan; 15. Albie; 16. Duke of Wellington

QUIZ 70

1. Ring of Fire; 2. White; 3. Korean War; 4. MASSACHUSETTS; 5. Clive
Sinclair; 6. Robert E Lee's; 7. JU(juice); 8. 1875; 9. Beagle; 10. Its smile;
11. *The Satanic Verses*; 12. Best man; 13. 17th; 14. *Funny Girl*; 15. Adder
(or Viper); 16. African

QUIZ 71

1. Shirley; 2. Condor; 3. RESTAURATEUR; 4. *The White Ribbon*; 5. Tigris and
Euphrates; 6. 200; 7. Giuseppe Verdi; 8. Henry James and Jack London;
9. William Adama; 10. Blunt; 11. Astronomer Royal; 12. Separating
strands of old rope; 13. Uruguay; 14. 360°; 15. Berne; 16. Adrian IV

QUIZ 72

1. Two shillings; 2. Wendy; 3. Adam West; 4. Coolidge; 5. *Stormbreaker*;
6. Schumacher; 7. Oxen; 8. Eyrie; 9. Steam engines; 10. South America;
11. Blue whale; 12. 22; 13. Battle of Edgehill; 14. Margaret Drabble;
15. Cairo; 16. Loose-fitting shirt or jacket

QUIZ 73

1. Republican; 2. Abby Cadabby; 3. Petra the dog; 4. Singapura; 5. Marco
Polo; 6. John Dos Passos; 7. TUMBLE; 8. Charles Bronson; 9. Zola Budd;
10. Stepmother; 11. 1894; 12. Bouvier; 13. Ontario; 14. Necessity;
15. Three; 16. Sweden's

QUIZ 74

1. Helicopter; 2. England; 3. *Hair*; 4. Chan's Megastick (stick insect);
5. GIANT; 6. Colorado; 7. Eight; 8. Niki Lauda; 9. Obelix; 10. David
Beckham; 11. New Mexico; 12. Cricket; 13. President François Duvalier
of Haiti; 14. A washer woman; 15. Sally Ride; 16. St Stephen's Day

QUIZ 75

1. Rainfall; 2. 366; 3. The Lake Poets; 4. Divide by eight and multiply by
five; 5. Mozart; 6. Mammal; 7. Commander 'Buster' Crabb; 8. Richard
Nixon; 9. Boston Tea Party; 10. A vampire; 11. Indiana; 12. Chatter;
13. Salatini (pastry snacks); 14. Cook County General; 15. Elizabeth I;
16. Elephant dung

QUIZ 76

1. Curds and whey; 2. 150; 3. *La Marseillaise*; 4. Another 40 days of rain;
5. Snow; 6. David Lloyd George; 7. Nanki-Poo; 8. Randolph Scott's;
9. Calais; 10. Lord Baden-Powell; 11. Shouting at teammates; 12. 1988;
13. Santo Domingo; 14. Marylebone Cricket Club; 15. Alexander III;
16. *Lolita*

QUIZ 77

1. A kiss; 2. Modulate and Demodulate; 3. Denmark; 4. *Ville*;
5. Photography; 6. Bess; 7. Versailles; 8. 729; 9. Iceland; 10. Venus;
11. Mill; 12. Governor of New York; 13. Peter Cushing; 14. Plymouth;
15. Snow; 16. Port Moresby

QUIZ 78

1. Newt; 2. Germany; 3. Thunderfly; 4. Westminster Abbey; 5. Jockey;
6. John Singer Sargent; 7. Figaro; 8. Mel Smith; 9. Wagon; 10. Sir Paul
McCartney; 11. 1966; 12. Cambria; 13. Simón Bolivar; 14. Bay City
Rollers'; 15. British Broadcasting Corporation; 16. Strawweight

QUIZ 79

1. Po; 2. Mexico; 3. Hades; 4. Painkiller; 5. Horse; 6. Belfast; 7. Napa Valley; 8. *Frankenstein*; 9. Cheviots; 10. St Andrew; 11. Arizona; 12. Lenin; 13. 14th July; 14. Calf; 15. Bread; 16. Vienna

QUIZ 80

1. Rowlf; 2. *Confessions of a Dangerous Mind*; 3. Tim Canterbury; 4. Flotsam; 5. Mary Baker Eddy; 6. Harold; 7. *Pollo*; 8. Missouri; 9. Manchester; 10. Houses of Parliament; 11. Kelt; 12. Australia and New Zealand; 13. Whirlpool; 14. Lyndon Baines Johnson; 15. Diver; 16. *Morning Cloud*

QUIZ 81

1. Gulliver (in *Gulliver's Travels*); 2. Dance; 3. Bass; 4. Wolf; 5. SL (slice) 6. 3pm; 7. Jelly; 8. Regent's Park; 9. McKinley High; 10. Marion Stein; 11. Fletcher Christian; 12. 1977; 13. Dixie Dean; 14. Electricity; 15. *The Dandy*; 16. Queen Sofia

QUIZ 82

1. The Snowman; 2. 0.3; 3. Gamma; 4. H E Bates; 5. Sausage; 6. Gold Coast (Ghana); 7. International Monetary Fund; 8. 1987; 9. Elizabeth Swann; 10. Life; 11. Stephanie Meyer; 12. Diaspora; 13. San Francisco; 14. King Alfred; 15. Ten; 16. Leith

QUIZ 83

1. Guy the gorilla; 2. Hot chocolate; 3. 1942; 4. Bushy Park; 5. Cricket; 6. Tambourine; 7. Sean Connery; 8. Jetsam; 9. Nancy Reagan's; 10. Dingo; 11. 1954; 12. X-ray; 13. Alfred Tennyson; 14. Lorient; 15. Adam and Eve; 16. Grandson

QUIZ 84

1. Seamus Heaney; 2. Butterfly; 3. Islam; 4. Sir Thomas Fairfax;

5. Dr Klaus Fuchs; 6. Equator; 7. Before; 8. Wake; 9. Furness; 10. Elves;
11. Elephant's Memory; 12. Ecuador; 13. Tun; 14. Maud Watson;
15. HIPPOPOTAMUS; 16. Mist

QUIZ 85

1. Two; 2. Pinchy; 3. Austria; 4. *The Long Good Friday*; 5. GR (grape);
6. Moose; 7. *Coup d'état*; 8. Barents Sea; 9. Genesis; 10. Julia Donaldson;
11. Komodo dragon; 12. Psittacosis; 13. James I of England; 14. Salford
(Lancs); 15. Iceland; 16. Craig Stadler

QUIZ 86

1. Baloo; 2. Red and white; 3. St George's Hall; 4. Will Young; 5. Never
Never Land; 6. General Norman Schwarzkopf; 7. King of the Fairies;
8. Dragonfly; 9. Convolvulus; 10. Charles I; 11. Hampton Roads; 12. Japan;
13. Summers; 14. Cheetah; 15. Zouch; 16. Raleigh

QUIZ 87

1. Hill; 2. Seven; 3. Kim Basinger; 4. 3ft (0.914m); 5. The BFG; 6. Loft;
7. Samoa; 8. Sheep; 9. Michael Jackson; 10. Blackthorn; 11. Trygve Lie;
12. Norwegian; 13. *North*; 14. Shuttlecock; 15. Marzipan; 16. Felixstowe

QUIZ 88

1. Ayatollah Khomeini; 2. Hat; 3. Wisconsin; 4. Over two million; 5. Bob
Willis; 6. Tiger; 7. Joseph Stalin's; 8. By the fact itself; 9. The Queen's;
10. Roman Polanski; 11. Puppy; 12. Milhous; 13. John Lloyd; 14. Dunedin;
15. Autobiography; 16. Glandular fever

QUIZ 89

1. Vine; 2. *Stadt*; 3. Quentin Blake; 4. Bridgwater; 5. *The Cat in a Hat*;
6. Reflex; 7. Gough Whitlam; 8. Bath; 9. Elephant; 10. Emily Dickinson;
11. Mrs Corazon Aquino; 12. Quinine; 13. 50; 14. Geoffrey Boycott;
15. Jared Harris; 16. Pink Floyd

QUIZ 90

1. Big Friendly Giant; 2. Crimean War; 3. Anne Fine; 4. Darts;
5. Edinburgh; 6. Botswana; 7. Marty Wilde; 8. James Buchanan;
9. Encyclopedia; 10. Bertrand Russell; 11. Christiaan Barnard; 12. West Ham; 13. Shalott; 14. St Bernard; 15. Otto von Bismarck; 16. Colin Milburn

QUIZ 91

1. General Gordon; 2. Birds; 3. Boulting; 4. Mumps; 5. Charles Darnley;
6. Safari; 7. George Bernard Shaw; 8. Blue stocking; 9. 1958;
10. Springfield Elementary (*The Simpsons*); 11. Wimbledon; 12. Stephen;
13. The Moon; 14. The Quarrymen; 15. Chequered; 16. Bertrand Russell

QUIZ 92

1. Jupiter; 2. GR(growl); 3. Fenner's; 4. Henry Wadsworth Longfellow;
5. Snagglepuss'; 6. Tiger (*The Tiger Who Came For Tea*); 7. VW Golf;
8. Contour lines; 9. 1963; 10. Irish Sea; 11. Vaporetto; 12. Chickpeas;
13. Special Air Service; 14. To keep the flies away; 15. The artist L S Lowry; 16. George Santayana

QUIZ 93

1. Fox, Owl and Snake; 2. Oscar Wilde's; 3. 'Living Doll'; 4. Ronald Reagan;
5. Wendy, John and Michael; 6. Ice skating (jumps); 7. Castle;
8. Vitamin C; 9. Santa; 10. Dr Julius Nyerere; 11. Italy; 12. Peeping Tom;
13. 24; 14. Afghanistan; 15. *Uncle Tom's Cabin*; 16. Harriet Beecher Stowe

QUIZ 94

1. Oliver Goldsmith; 2. TALE; 3. Chlorophyll; 4. Manx cat; 5. Rabies;
6. The planned invasion of Britain; 7. Dromedary; 8. Table tennis; 9. Lee Marvin; 10. Clay; 11. Straits of Florida; 12. Robin; 13. Herbert Morrison and John Anderson; 14. Frequency Modulated; 15. Ace; 16. Three

QUIZ 95

1. On Her Majesty's Service; 2. Dr Kwame Nkrumah; 3. Laying down the keel; 4. Glasgow; 5. Lion; 6. The Queen; 7. Paul; 8. *The Archers*; 9. 'With regards to'; 10. St Valentine's Day; 11. Blacksmith; 12. Bessie Smith; 13. Arrows; 14. San Francisco; 15. Ten; 16. 'A Day of Infamy' (Pearl Harbour)

QUIZ 96

1. Jaguar; 2. By squeezing the life out of it; 3. Mycroft; 4. *The Ipcress File*; 5. Fozzie Bear; 6. Mega; 7. The Crickets; 8. Andre Agassi; 9. V-J Day; 10. Batman and Robin; 11. Chipping; 12. Sanatorium; 13. North Pole; 14. Stan Laurel making things difficult for Oliver Hardy; 15. Two more grow in its place; 16. F W de Klerk

QUIZ 97

1. Nails; 2. Benjamin Britten; 3. Henry I; 4. *Lorna Doone*; 5. Contents; 6. Ford Model T; 7. Brain; 8. Harlem; 9. Nigel Bruce; 10. Flea; 11. Seoul; 12. Camel; 13. Cranwell; 14. New Mexico; 15. Head; 16. Fra Angelico

QUIZ 98

1. Facsimile; 2. Italy; 3. A graph; 4. Rhinitis; 5. Erich Honecker; 6. Faroes; 7. Pumpkin; 8. Ludovico Einaudi's; 9. Ben Bradlee; 10. Derbyshire; 11. Santa's Little Helper; 12. Eliza Acton; 13. The Dreamtime; 14. Sonja Henie; 15. Australia; 16. Amphitrite

QUIZ 99

1. Mercury; 2. Llama; 3. *Little Big Man*; 4. Feet; 5. Katie Holmes; 6. Union Jack; 7. Nick Leeson; 8. Adidas; 9. Alicia Keys'; 10. Vienna; 11. Arsenal; 12. 1911; 13. *Modesty Blaise*; 14. Iago; 15. The Queen; 16. Malcolm Muggeridge

QUIZ 100

1. Manchester; 2. Pin; 3. Cupid; 4. Alaska; 5. Sirius; 6. Tunisia; 7. The Queen's coronation; 8. Alexander McQueen; 9. Campaign for Nuclear Disarmament; 10. Paul Simon; 11. Ant; 12. 1951; 13. William Butler; 14. 'The Lake Isle of Innisfree'; 15. Amphibians; 16. Glamorgan

QUIZ 101

1. Pigeons; 2. Daniel Ortega; 3. Albania; 4. Gertrude Stein; 5. Empire State Building; 6. Drums; 7. Nevada; 8. *The Voyage Home*; 9. Electronic; 10. Catkins; 11. Camden Town Group; 12. Yellow ('Mellow Yellow'); 13. Chaim Weizmann; 14. Angling; 15. 22; 16. Cow

QUIZ 102

1. Automatic pilot system; 2. Zorro; 3. Nipper; 4. *Macbeth*; 5. Billfold; 6. Three; 7. Joel Chandler Harris; 8. Roxy Music; 9. Archbishop Desmond Tutu; 10. Stan Laurel; 11. Basil; 12. Letitia Dean; 13. Guitar; 14. West Indies; 15. Hare; 16. Pacific

QUIZ 103

1. Red and white; 2. Four; 3. *Dead Man Walking*; 4. Victoria; 5. 'The Tent'; 6. Good luck; 7. Essex; 8. C S Forester; 9. Italy; 10. Ferry; 11. Commander Timothy Laurence; 12. Donald Dewar; 13. Bus driver; 14. Mickey Mouse; 15. Dance; 16. 1995

QUIZ 104

1. Six; 2. An essential condition or requirement; 3. King John; 4. Guy Ritchie; 5. Spine; 6. The Thunderbird; 7. Caspian Sea; 8. Mosquito; 9. Bamboo; 10. Elmore Leonard; 11. Altimeter; 12. Perry Como; 13. Horseradish; 14. Stomach; 15. Goat; 16. Earth Day

QUIZ 105

1. The Ugly Sisters; 2. Malaria; 3. Lake Eyre; 4. *Sense and Sensibility*;
5. Green Cross Code; 6. Jenny Shipley; 7. Sonic boom; 8. Viennese Waltz;
9. Lee Adama; 10. Australian aboriginal musical instrument; 11. *Major Barbara*; 12. Plum; 13. Manzanares; 14. One hour; 15. Keep; 16. Marcus Bentley

QUIZ 106

1. Board; 2. Penny Blacks; 3. Monkey; 4. R J Mitchell; 5. Cutlery; 6. Dr Thomas Arnold; 7. Heathrow Airport; 8. They all married Rita Hayworth; 9. Crufts'; 10. PHARAOHS; 11. Period; 12. *Rainbow Warrior*; 13. Beavis and Butt-head; 14. Derek Randall's; 15. Fish; 16. Jennifer Grey

QUIZ 107

1. Pricking her finger on a spinning wheel; 2. Loch Ness; 3. Speed of sound; 4. 1910; 5. Blue; 6. Umbilical chord; 7. Pilgrimage; 8. 50;
9. Dictionary; 10. John Boynton; 11. *The Good Companions*; 12. *Neighbours*; 13. Cristiano Ronaldo; 14. Three French hens; 15. William Booth;
16. Peter Ustinov

QUIZ 108

1. The fireman; 2. Duck-billed platypus; 3. Megabyte; 4. Mini Cooper;
5. The Pope; 6. Royal Society for the Prevention of Cruelty to Animals;
7. Rotorua; 8. 59; 9. Five (in *Anna of the Five Towns*); 10. Index; 11. 1907;
12. 'Stranger in Paradise'; 13. Tambourine; 14. Seven; 15. *Rage*;
16. Microchip

QUIZ 109

1. A pig; 2. W S Gilbert; 3. 1979; 4. Johnny Mercer; 5. Blood; 6. Himself;
7. Amazon; 8. Toledo; 9. Leslie Howard; 10. George Bernard Shaw;
11. Ostrich; 12. Tortoise; 13. Chicago; 14. Edelweiss; 15. The Cenotaph;
16. UEFA Cup

QUIZ 110

1. 100; 2. Red and white stripes; 3. Keiko the whale; 4. River Jordan;
5. Quakers; 6. Beaker; 7. Sean Connery; 8. China; 9. He tore his Achilles
tendon; 10. Galley; 11. Sarah Brightman and Michael Crawford;
12. Tallinn; 13. Peterborough United; 14. The Moon; 15. Hawaii; 16. Ryde

QUIZ 111

1. Nelson; 2. Goofy; 3. Humber; 4. 1928; 5. Muddy Waters; 6. A rainbow;
7. Eight years; 8. Alan Ayckbourn; 9. Tofu; 10. Ice cream sundae;
11. Fourth Thursday in November; 12. Kent; 13. Maria Callas; 14. Wolves;
15. Peter Krause; 16. 1974

QUIZ 112

1. A runcible spoon; 2. Anna Paquin; 3. Strong winds; 4. Edward VIII;
5. BELGIUM; 6. By solidified lava; 7. Spanish; 8. Leona Lewis; 9. Major;
10. John Smit; 11. Puerto Rico; 12. Danube; 13. Sundance Kid; 14. Al
Pacino; 15. Escalator; 16. David Frost

QUIZ 113

1. Piglet; 2. Munich; 3. Glebe; 4. Pope John XXIII; 5. A dolphin;
6. Buddhism; 7. Ryan; 8. Iris; 9. Juno; 10. Rome; 11. Tree; 12. Draconian;
13. Northamptonshire; 14. Edinburgh; 15. Canberra; 16. Irish

QUIZ 114

1. Air; 2. Drum; 3. Oval Office; 4. John Milton; 5. Cactus; 6. City; 7. 101;
8. *Parachutes*; 9. Tom and Jerry; 10. Edward Heath; 11. Nat Turner;
12. William Styron (*The Confessions of Nat Turner*); 13. Cornwall;
14. Thistle; 15. Ewan McGregor; 16. Japan

QUIZ 115

1. 80; 2. Jack in 'Jack and Jill'; 3. East; 4. Eric Clapton; 5. Edward; 6. Save
Our Souls; 7. Five; 8. Swiss Guard; 9. Five; 10. Cambridge; 11. Crazy bone;

12. Japanese; 13. Fall of wicket; 14. General Noriega (Panama);
15. Trident; 16. Legolas Greenleaf

QUIZ 116

1. The Grinch's; 2. *The Shootist*; 3. Topaz; 4. Mesa; 5. Unicycle;
6. Süleyman; 7. Justin Timberlake; 8. St Etheldreda; 9. Gambia; 10. Quads
(quadruplets); 11. Muriel; 12. Architect; 13. George Eastman; 14. *The
Thieving Magpie*; 15. Rossini; 16. 50

QUIZ 117

1. Hamlet (in the play of the same name); 2. The Easy Crew;
3. Mongoose; 4. Albatross; 5. Mt Everest; 6. Kremlin; 7. 12; 8. Dubai;
9. Deer; 10. Spotted; 11. Pink; 12. Michael Collins; 13. Trade war;
14. Shane Warne; 15. Small peninsula; 16. Kenneth Branagh

QUIZ 118

1. Denim; 2. Team of Tiddlers; 3. Amsterdam; 4. Robson and Jerome;
5. The Bachelors; 6. Milk; 7. Charles II; 8. Six; 9. Christine Truman;
10. Giant Condor; 11. 1957; 12. Merchant seaman; 13. Lake Tanganyika;
14. It's smell; 15. Lily; 16. Fairy

QUIZ 119

1. Fox; 2. Royal Flying Corps; 3. Ethiopia; 4. Katie Melua; 5. 12 seconds;
6. ⌐ ⌐ 'N' Avenue; 7. Leslie Thomas; 8. Shelley Rudman (skeleton); 9. Mick
McManus; 10. East; 11. William I; 12. In hands; 13. Belgium, Luxembourg
and the Netherlands; 14. Cat; 15. Brussels sprout; 16. Aldermaston

QUIZ 120

1. Birmingham; 2. June; 3. White Stripes; 4. Na; 5. Libya; 6. Sam Torrance;
7. Ed; 8. Seikan Tunnel; 9. Air Chief Marshal Arthur Harris; 10. Alan
Simpson and Ray Galton; 11. Bow and arrow; 12. *Fedora*; 13. John
Aubrey's; 14. Kipper; 15. Wellington (New Zealand); 16. Thor Heyerdahl

QUIZ 121

1. Ceres; 2. Red; 3. Calculating machine; 4. Lady Gaga's; 5. Black Sea;
6. Mildred Hubble's; 7. Carl Bernstein and Bob Woodward; 8. Brendan
Behan; 9. Melton Mowbray; 10. Holland; 11. Ireland; 12. Micky Dolenz;
13. Lotus; 14. David Peace's; 15. An easel; 16. Ospreys

QUIZ 122

1. None; 2. Kangaroos; 3. 46; 4. God; 5. Australia; 6. Jordan; 7. Christopher
Fry; 8. Parliament; 9. Seven; 10. Spook; 11. Flying doctor service;
12. Mediterranean Sea; 13. Pot of gold; 14. Badger; 15. Bonnie Prince
Charlie (Charles Edward Stuart the 'Young Pretender'); 16. Dance

QUIZ 123

1. Aintree; 2. Monks; 3. Volga; 4. Weightlifting; 5. Dr Michael Ramsey;
6. Citrus; 7. William and Mary; 8. George; 9. Owl; 10. Trombone; 11. Joe
Mercer; 12. Radio Corporation of America; 13. 1944; 14. Fish; 15. Molly;
16. In taxis

QUIZ 124

1. Madison Avenue; 2. 12; 3. France; 4. Goldie the eagle; 5. *Victor Victoria*;
6. Igloo; 7. Le Corbusier; 8. Cavity or recess; 9. Catalonia; 10. Nut;
11. Janus; 12. Louis XVI; 13. Gross Domestic Product; 14. Elvis Costello;
15. *David Copperfield*; 16. Double agent Eddie Chapman

QUIZ 125

1. Mouse; 2. Winds; 3. Green with red spots; 4. Sandringham House;
5. Sergio Garcia; 6. Surrealism; 7. Dover; 8. Athens; 9. 'The Song of
Hiawatha' by H W Longfellow; 10. Florenz Ziegfeld's; 11. An astronaut;
12. Michael Caine; 13. John Glenn; 14. Carl Wilson; 15. Spoke; 16. White

QUIZ 126

1. Wings; 2. Migrate; 3. Sheffield; 4. Mother Teresa; 5. Archbishop
Geoffrey Fisher; 6. Yellow; 7. Lucy Davis; 8. Supreme Court; 9. Romania;
10. Cheddar; 11. Spencer; 12. Anne of Cleves; 13. Bobby Charlton;
14. A cow; 15. 78; 16. *Abbey Road*

QUIZ 127

1. On your head; 2. Pasta; 3. Marcello Mastroianni; 4. South Africa;
5. One penny; 6. Teifi; 7. Type of rock; 8. Ted Dexter; 9. Meat; 10. Round
Table; 11. Duff; 12. 'A Visit from St Nicholas'; 13. Minoan; 14. Jersey;
15. Noiseless; 16. 22

QUIZ 128

1. Knighthood; 2. Do It Yourself; 3. Julia Ward Howe; 4. Charlie Parker;
5. On the toes; 6. Bait; 7. Bunter; 8. Colin Meads; 9. Burt Kwouk;
10. Bashful; 11. Lisbon; 12. Chesterfield; 13. Sears; 14. Prince Bira;
15. New Year's Eve; 16. *The Magnificent Seven*

QUIZ 129

1. Fat free; 2. No 6; 3. Montgolfier brothers; 4. Cigarette advertising;
5. St George's; 6. Stamps; 7. Honoré de Balzac; 8. Georgia; 9. June Carter;
10. New York; 11. Excessive fondness for one's wife; 12. Diametric;
13. Andrew Morton; 14. Grass; 15. Four; 16. Shinto

QUIZ 130

1. Henry Williamson; 2. Dordogne and Garonne; 3. Sage; 4. 1973;
5. Bermuda; 6. Paddy field; 7. £5; 8. Pierce; 9. *The Deer Hunter*;
10. Chocolate; 11. Sgt major Williams; 12. Canary Wharf Tower;
13. Claude Debussy; 14. Australia; 15. Bristol; 16. Archibald Leach

QUIZ 131

1. Bobby Robson; 2. Pontypandy; 3. Knowledge; 4. Germany; 5. 1963;
6. Frédéric Chopin; 7. Bat; 8. Queen Anne; 9. Dahlia; 10. Middlesex;
11. Capitol Hill; 12. A lighthouse (one of the Seven Wonders of the
Ancient World); 13. Violin; 14. Billy Bunter; 15. Bridge; 16. Left

QUIZ 132

1. Blue; 2. William Shakespeare; 3. River Danube; 4. Maroon 5; 5. 1916;
6. Nine; 7. Frances Edmonds; 8. Edelweiss; 9. Bring Your Own; 10. 21;
11. Roland Joffé; 12. 1947; 13. Camelot; 14. Coven; 15. Maoris; 16. Sir
Michael Tippett

QUIZ 133

1. Utah; 2. Cooking; 3. Shelagh Delaney; 4. 1666; 5. Prince Andrew;
6. The guard; 7. Nuremberg; 8. Synod; 9. Derek Bell; 10. St Paul's;
11. Nigeria's; 12. Fiefdom; 13. *Zulu Dawn*; 14. 3600; 15. Plum blossom;
16. White Volta (Red Volta, Black Volta)

QUIZ 134

1. 31st; 2. On his head; 3. Napoleon Bonaparte's; 4. 'The Party of Wales';
5. D H Lawrence; 6. Perks; 7. Etienne; 8. Poinsettia; 9. Curaçao; 10. Right;
11. Dennis and Hannah Waterman; 12. National Union of Journalists;
13. Alan Turing; 14. Timbaland; 15. Hats; 16. Potomac and Shenandoah

QUIZ 135

1. Leveret; 2. Island of Sodor; 3. Marseille; 4. John Frankenheimer;
5. Britain, France and Israel; 6. LEMON; 7. George Grundy; 8. By whistle
or pipe; 9. Montmartre; 10. 240; 11. Brandon Flowers; 12. Russia;
13. Solidarity; 14. Elvis Cridlington; 15. Denis Law; 16. Jane

QUIZ 136

1. Florist; 2. *Quod vide* (which see); 3. Woodstock; 4. Caper; 5. *The Informant!*; 6. Ice breaker; 7. The groom; 8. Flying; 9. Alfred Dreyfus; 10. Isle of Thanet; 11. Boasting about your talents or achievements; 12. Nine; 13. Circular; 14. Eight; 15. Red; 16. Arthur Milton

QUIZ 137

1. Kermit the Frog; 2. An Indian stringed instrument; 3. Leela; 4. Charles Mackintosh's (the inventor); 5. Sailor; 6. American Civil War; 7. Fruit; 8. *The Goon Show*; 9. By a bomb; 10. Pips; 11. 'English Bob'; 12. Rock column (in the Orkneys); 13. Cream cakes; 14. Salman Rushdie; 15. Mersey; 16. Rangers

QUIZ 138

1. Eva Braun; 2. Chewbacca; 3. Ashmolean (Oxford); 4. Jade Ewen; 5. Louisiana; 6. Buzzard; 7. The bank; 8. *Cinderella*; 9. Milan; 10. Greyhound; 11. Henry VI; 12. Madrid; 13. Amy Irving; 14. *Blücher*; 15. Reindeer; 16. Ice cream

QUIZ 139

1. Golf; 2. Cucumber; 3. Sicily; 4. Tinker; 5. Georgia; 6. The Troll; 7. Jane Wyman; 8. Mt McKinley; 9. Yorkshire's; 10. Two goldfish; 11. Croatia; 12. *Grease*; 13. Ernest Simpson; 14. Seven; 15. Lucifer; 16. *Be Cool*

QUIZ 140

1. *The Pickwick Papers*; 2. The Furious Five (in *Kung Fu Panda*); 3. Right; 4. Fremantle; 5. 1896; 6. Knots; 7. Darts; 8. Clementine; 9. Guildford; 10. Kentucky Fried Chicken; 11. Reliquary; 12. No 5; 13. R S Surtees; 14. Doc; 15. Fifteen; 16. King's Lynn

QUIZ 141

1. Hudson; 2. Nothing; 3. Bud or budding; 4. Emile Zola; 5. He operates the roundabout; 6. Throwing the hammer; 7. Black Eyed Peas; 8. Ten; 9. Drone; 10. Eros; 11. TGV; 12. Pectin; 13. Stork; 14. Henry Cooper; 15. Molten lava; 16. Arctic, Atlantic, Pacific

QUIZ 142

1. Lavender; 2. The Zimmers'; 3. Alexandra; 4. California; 5. Gondola; 6. Finch; 7. Greyfriars; 8. Gary Lineker; 9. 'The Emperor'; 10. Bishop's; 11. Alexandra Palace; 12. 1785; 13. John; 14. Liberty Island; 15. 12; 16. Nancy Astor

QUIZ 143

1. Chips; 2. Hatter; 3. Shropshire; 4. German; 5. Puss in Boots; 6. 1620; 7. Their wings; 8. Frank and Nancy Sinatra; 9. Chelsea; 10. Cornwall; 11. Penne; 12. Belgian; 13. Judo uniform; 14. Waterloo; 15. Type of clay; 16. Paul Simon

QUIZ 144

1. St Patrick's; 2. Phil and Lil; 3. *Rex*; 4. France; 5. Cumberland; 6. Missing animals; 7. 1791; 8. WD-40; 9. Long jump; 10. Submarine; 11. Sardi's; 12. Fumarole; 13. Lana Turner; 14. Cavalry; 15. Small waves; 16. Lifejacket

QUIZ 145

1. Eight; 2. Chimney sweep; 3. *Flamingo*; 4. Archbishop Makarios; 5. Rory O'Connor; 6. Yellow; 7. Nicaragua; 8. Gourmet; 9. Head to head; 10. 64; 11. *Nabucco*; 12. Carol Beer's; 13. Moth; 14. *Casablanca*; 15. Consonants; 16. Alan Titchmarsh's

QUIZ 146

1. Hastings; 2. Acorn; 3. Ken Kesey; 4. Oklahoma; 5. The Verve; 6. Green

Goblin; 7. 1929; 8. Welsh; 9. Leicester; 10. Silk; 11. 'All Shook Up';
12. Pol Pot; 13. Individual Savings Account; 14. Darjeeling; 15. Yellow;
16. London Eye

QUIZ 147

1. Vulcan; 2. Michael Bond; 3. Fossils; 4. Edinburgh; 5. National anthem
6. Thrace; 7. Aachen; 8. Durban; 9. 'Sea-Fever' by John Masefield;
10. Joust; 11. Ethan Hawke; 12. Kent; 13. Saxophone; 14. Robin
Maugham's; 15. Polo; 16. The Temptations

QUIZ 148

1. Veterinary surgeon; 2. The Hague; 3. Double decker; 4. *Madame
Butterfly*; 5. Paul McCartney and Wings; 6. Boot Hill; 7. Switzerland;
8. Bruce Forsyth; 9. 6300; 10. Geoffrey of Monmouth; 11. Union des
Associations Européennes de Football; 12. Bullseye; 13. Queen Victoria;
14. Suva; 15. Every two years; 16. Six

QUIZ 149

1. Cowboy; 2. James Callaghan; 3. Philippines; 4. Evelyn Glennie;
5. Hamper; 6. Lighthouse Family's; 7. Local Defence Volunteers;
8. Melbourne; 9. Friar Tuck; 10. Grendel; 11. Blind side; 12. Sherlock
Holmes; 13. 17 (and 75 days); 14. Launch; 15. Wellington; 16. Admiral
Wilhelm Canaris

QUIZ 150

1. Angelina (Ballerina) Mouseling's; 2. Land of silver; 3. Snoop Dogg;
4. *News of the World*; 5. Banana; 6. Louis-Philippe; 7. New York City
Subway; 8. *Doctor in the House*; 9. 21; 10. French windows; 11. Nine Elms,
Battersea; 12. 1st March; 13. Edmond Rostand; 14. 'Daffodils' by William
Wordsworth; 15. Red Indian chiefs; 16. Each captained 31 times

QUIZ 151

1. Oil or water on the track; 2. Oval shape; 3. Because his real name is unpronounceable; 4. Sr; 5. West; 6. Jack the Ripper's; 7. Poppy; 8. Nightingale; 9. Blue cornflower; 10. Rossini; 11. Oklahoma; 12. Machine gun; 13. Bourgeois; 14. Will Champion; 15. Darth Vader; 16. Lot's wife

QUIZ 152

1. Georgia; 2. Mr Chatterbox; 3. Elba; 4. Rice; 5. Horses; 6. Warrior; 7. Isle of Wight; 8. Joshua; 9. Robert Brown; 10. Victoria; 11. North; 12. Myanmar (Burma); 13. *The Andy Williams Show*; 14. Lawn croquet; 15. Swiss Alps; 16. Sheep

QUIZ 153

1. Intelligence Quotient; 2. In his cheeks; 3. Plants; 4. Velvet Brown; 5. Light signals; 6. Red Indians (Native Americans); 7. Elbe; 8. *The Observer*; 9. Everyman's Library; 10. Big Babies; 11. Cornish Cave; 12. Tower of London; 13. Snoopy; 14. Peter Shaffer; 15. Rodent; 16. Abu Dhabi

QUIZ 154

1. Little Miss Late; 2. Argentina; 3. Rex Harrison; 4. Catherine of Aragon; 5. Matriarch; 6. True; 7. 1713; 8. The Barron Knights; 9. Sir Edward Grey, British foreign secretary (1914); 10. Catnap; 11. Prometheus; 12. Dr Hewlett Johnson; 13. John Hannah; 14. Mary Portas; 15. Suez; 16. Rick Wakeman

QUIZ 155

1. Phone booth; 2. Whistle; 3. A cheese; 4. *Bleak House*; 5. Jean Borotra; 6. Canada; 7. Henrik Ibsen; 8. Right to left; 9. Celtic; 10. Rocket; 11. The dark; 12. Ronan Keating; 13. Indian Ocean; 14. Excisemen; 15. Kit; 16. French

QUIZ 156

1. Mare; 2. Registrar; 3. News agency; 4. Nebuchadnezzar; 5. GALE;
6. Dorothy Wordsworth; 7. Mungo; 8. Stormy Petrels; 9. Iran; 10. Nev;
11. Charlton Athletic's; 12. Egyptian; 13. Japan; 14. Anthony Burgess;
15. Nut; 16. Scotland

QUIZ 157

1. Playing the piano; 2. Odysseus (or Ulysses); 3. *Prisoner of Azkaban*;
4. *Grease*; 5. Mr Funny; 6. Sponges; 7. Harvey Smith; 8. Theodore
Roosevelt; 9. The *Abwehr*; 10. Hawaii; 11. Danny Boyle; 12. Munster's;
13. South Dakota; 14. Euros; 15. The Netherlands; 16. 'Ferry 'Cross The
Mersey'

QUIZ 158

1. Rose Tyler; 2. Dorset; 3. Italian; 4. 36; 5. Medical; 6. Mr Mistoffelees;
7. *Beautiful World*; 8. Oliver; 9. Tony Williams; 10. Three times; 11. Japan;
12. Bessie; 13. Larry King; 14. Midshipman; 15. Seven; 16. Pink

QUIZ 159

1. Helen of Troy's; 2. 24; 3. Ambidextrous; 4. Sergei Diaghilev; 5. 'In the
beginning'; 6. Dodie Smith; 7. *Ears*; 8. Areas of land reclaimed from the
sea; 9. Archery; 10. Earl Mountbatten; 11. Galapagos Islands; 12. 17th;
13. 69; 14. Stefan Gates; 15. 1916; 16. John Lennon

QUIZ 160

1. J M Coetzee; 2. America; 3. Cyber crime; 4. 'Its beak holds more than
its belly can'; 5. Topeka; 6. The Mounties (Royal Canadian Mounted
Police); 7. Orville and Wilbur; 8. Mr Sneeze; 9. Oxford; 10. Blubber;
11. Niccolò Machiavelli; 12. Red herring; 13. Deuteronomy; 14. Daily;
15. Bob Champion; 16. In the middle of a road

QUIZ 161

1. In a roof; 2. On a cold and frosty morning; 3. 'A Hard Day's Night';
4. Wales; 5. William Boyd; 6. Clownfish; 7. 20,000; 8. Wilton; 9. Arethusa;
10. Australia; 11. Eye; 12. Richard Nixon; 13. Architecture; 14. Stag;
15. Cagliari; 16. Four

QUIZ 162

1. George Harrison's; 2. Monkey; 3. Sport Utility Vehicle; 4. *Life In Cartoon Motion*; 5. CASH; 6. Mortarboard; 7. Leicestershire; 8. Turtle; 9. Opticians;
10. No choice; 11. Charles Laughton; 12. Perjury; 13. Limestone;
14. Aurora; 15. Apple; 16. 'Friend of a friend'

QUIZ 163

1. Zac Effron; 2. 32; 3. Cuckoo; 4. The Jolly Swagman (Waltzing Matilda);
5. Arquette; 6. Spain; 7. 'Anyone Who Had A Heart'; 8. Butterflies;
9. Dutch barn; 10. Three; 11. The Godfather; 12. Beak; 13. Mel, Josh and
Lucy Barker; 14. Jordan; 15. Warsaw; 16. Diego Maradona talking about
Carlos Tevez

QUIZ 164

1. Spain; 2. Horse racing; 3. Longshoreman; 4. Blue; 5. Jay-Z; 6. String;
7. Little Miss Twins; 8. Cologne Cathedral; 9. Cpl 'Radar' O'Reilly;
10. 1962; 11. Snakes; 12. Ronnie Biggs; 13. *Little Women*; 14. 100;
15. Dutch elm; 16. Dugong

QUIZ 165

1. Cello; 2. King Canute; 3. The Queen; 4. Steve Davis; 5. Bull; 6. New
York; 7. His 'Wings'; 8. Perambulator; 9. Antelope; 10. 30; 11. John
Dillinger; 12. Glasgow; 13. Aberdeen; 14. Venezuela; 15. Australia;
16. Beetle

QUIZ 166

1. Hammer Films; 2. Metre; 3. Chicago; 4. Ron Grainer; 5. Rouen;
6. Wasps; 7. Draughts; 8. France; 9. Kinshasa (Zaire); 10. Colón; 11. Kitten;
12. Dust and smoke particles; 13. Barnacle; 14. *Nicholas Nickleby*;
15. Corn; 16. Partisan

QUIZ 167

1. Cruella de Vil; 2. Hoof and mouth; 3. Geronimo's; 4. Auk; 5. Apple;
6. Istanbul; 7. Needle; 8. John Adams and Thomas Jefferson; 9. Newark;
10. 'Monster Mash'; 11. Singing Chipmunks; 12. Canadian; 13. Beijing's
Olympic stadium; 14. J D Salinger; 15. The Dumping Ground;
16. *M*A*S*H*

QUIZ 168

1. Clark Gable's; 2. Thumbelina; 3. Yemen; 4. Daub; 5. Long johns;
6. Bowls; 7. An idiot; 8. Grand Union; 9. Left; 10. Brown; 11. Odette
Sansom; 12. Bathypelagic; 13. Phil Hill; 14. Ford's Theatre, Washington
DC; 15. New York's; 16. Karl Marx's

QUIZ 169

1. Mr Bounce; 2. Marion Cotillard; 3. MDCLXVI; 4. Cricket; 5. Draupnir;
6. Donizetti; 7. D W Griffith; 8. George VI (as Duke of York); 9. Moat;
10. William Faulkner; 11. Electric eel; 12. Suez; 13. Coal; 14. France's;
15. Thomas à Kempis; 16. Malta

QUIZ 170

1. *Viva la Vida*; 2. Wolf; 3. Strawberry Fields; 4. Portraits; 5. Fertilizer;
6. Ninky Nonk; 7. Leona Lewis'; 8. Palaeolithic; 9. Peter O'Sullivan;
10. Italy; 11. Golden Lion; 12. René Goscinny; 13. Hermit crabs;
14. Joseph; 15. Charles III; 16. Akmal

QUIZ 171

1. Mickey; 2. Scotland; 3. Aubergine; 4. Cape Town; 5. Rock; 6. St Thomas More; 7. Acrobat (Jules Léotard); 8. Butterfly; 9. Ronald Reagan; 10. Right; 11. Polo; 12. San Diego; 13. *Columbia*; 14. Oliver Stone; 15. Michael Jackson; 16. Gardening

QUIZ 172

1. Martin Johnson; 2. Ivory; 3. George Harrison; 4. Cu; 5. 1964; 6. Apple; 7. Gorillas; 8. Lake Baikal; 9. World War I; 10. Stoat; 11. Volkswagen; 12. Emil Jannings; 13. Duck; 14. Margaret Thatcher; 15. Baghdad; 16. His son Felix Francis

QUIZ 173

1. What you see is what you get; 2. Goldilocks; 3. Brentwood; 4. George Eliot; 5. *The Last Emperor*; 6. Panda; 7. Las Malvinas; 8. Margaret Thatcher; 9. Texas; 10. Roman Catholicism; 11. East; 12. Cutting tool; 13. 63 (and seven months); 14. Goat; 15. Grape; 16. Martin Luther King Jr Day

QUIZ 174

1. 100; 2. Swarm; 3. Rory McIlroy; 4. Vitamin C; 5. LOT; 6. Lord Chancellor; 7. Rugby; 8. Horatia; 9. Kieran Prendiville; 10. Busby Berkeley; 11. Sugar; 12. Western; 13. Avocet; 14. Hecuba; 15. North Pole; 16. 'Baby Face' Nelson

QUIZ 175

1. Boomerang; 2. Officer Cadet Wales; 3. Fungi; 4. Robbie Fowler; 5. Five; 6. 1921; 7. Richard Mulligan; 8. Sea Potato; 9. *The Adventures of Pinocchio*; 10. Water; 11. Esperanto; 12. International Red Cross; 13. *The Two Towers*; 14. 'Eastern kingdom'; 15. Howdy; 16. Tic-Tac

QUIZ 176

1. Blue; 2. Bedouin; 3. Acetic acid; 4. Eva Perón (*Evita*); 5. William Shakespeare; 6. 46; 7. 50; 8. Flora; 9. Sepang; 10. Kenya; 11. Queen of Hearts; 12. 1989; 13. Duffy's; 14. Miguel; 15. Sheriff; 16. James I

QUIZ 177

1. Method acting; 2. No 18; 3. Hengist and Horsa; 4. Before the war; 5. John Reid; 6. Albert Einstein; 7. Henry; 8. Ernie (Benny Hill); 9. Petrarch; 10. Howard Jacobson; 11. Royal Wootton Bassett; 12. Nigel Mansell; 13. Tamil Tigers; 14. Princess Grace of Monaco; 15. Portcullis; 16. Julie Andrews

QUIZ 178

1. Natasha Bedingfield; 2. Bone; 3. It's frozen before the game; 4. Lady; 5. Stanley (Falkland Islands); 6. Pancake; 7. Paul; 8. 1985; 9. Lancet; 10. Edward Lear; 11. *Blake's 7*; 12. Crane; 13. Decibel; 14. Thirteen; 15. Master-at-arms Claggart; 16. Melbourne Cricket Ground

QUIZ 179

1. Long winded; 2. Kos (Cos lettuce); 3. Joseph; 4. Barre; 5. Magistrate; 6. Hammer and Sickle; 7. Henley; 8. Narcissus; 9. *Neun*; 10. 289; 11. China; 12. Ship-to-shore telegraph; 13. Reich Marshal; 14. Una Stubbs; 15. *The Curse of the Were-Rabbit*; 16. Alain Prost

QUIZ 180

1. John Travolta; 2. Batman's; 3. Ash Wednesday; 4. Marquis of Bath's; 5. Gruyère; 6. Saturn; 7. *From Here to Eternity*; 8. 29th September; 9. W C Fields'; 10. White; 11. Tanzania; 12. Marshal Pétain; 13. John McCain; 14. Kabul; 15. Mark Webber; 16. Tractors

QUIZ 181

1. Little Miss Somersault; 2. As a matter of fact; 3. Frank Richards;
4. Donkey or ass; 5. Net; 6. Tap; 7. Henrietta Maria; 8. Destiny; 9. Turin;
10. Palm Sunday; 11. Quebec; 12. Annie Lennox's; 13. Rand; 14. Croesus;
15. Albus Dumbledore; 16. The Orkneys

QUIZ 182

1. Walker; 2. Remy; 3. When horse riding; 4. Oahu; 5. King Arthur;
6. Romulus and Remus; 7. John Williams; 8. 50°F; 9. Because he tells lies;
10. Ralph Vaughan Williams; 11. Edith Cavell; 12. Nick Farr-Jones;
13. Danish krone; 14. Germany; 15. Captain Charles Upham (NZ);
16. *The Ladykillers*

QUIZ 183

1. *The Owl Service* by Alan Garner; 2. Alex the Lion; 3. Melbourne Cricket
Ground; 4. Wine; 5. Lord Palmerston; 6. 18; 7. Robson Green and Jerome
Flynn's; 8. Yellow; 9. Dance; 10. Cornwall; 11. Electrical resistance;
12. Beetle; 13. Hyde Park; 14. Matthew, Mark, Luke and John; 15. Belt;
16. Jimmy Savile

QUIZ 184

1. Elephant; 2. Hugh Scully; 3. Coventry; 4. Bellhop; 5. Four; 6. Burial
mound; 7. Durham; 8. Virgin birth; 9. Brandenburg; 10. The Midlands;
11. Arizona, Nevada, Oregon; 12. Yin; 13. Tuscany; 14. François 'Baby Doc'
Duvalier; 15. Subtract; 16. 'Without You'

QUIZ 185

1. Royal Shakespeare Company; 2. Tongue twister; 3. 2nd February;
4. Fry's Turkish Delight; 5. Vermont; 6. Foal; 7. General Sikorski; 8. To
make obscure or unintelligible; 9. Charles Lindbergh; 10. Box; 11. 1989;
12. *The Magic Flute*; 13. Abyssinia; 14. Non-flying insect; 15. *Treasure
Island*; 16. James Blunt

QUIZ 186

1. *Répondez s'il vous plait*; 2. 121; 3. A mouse (Stuart Little); 4. Thomas Mann's; 5. Prison; 6. Willow; 7. Stalemate; 8. Captain Matthew Webb; 9. Anti-cyclone; 10. Seven; 11. Wayne Rooney; 12. Gwyneth Paltrow; 13. Traitors Gate; 14. Memory data storage device; 15. Cardiff; 16. *The Producers*

QUIZ 187

1. Mecca; 2. Leprechaun; 3. Five; 4. The Wash; 5. Beefeaters; 6. Wellington boot; 7. Jester; 8. Israel's (Star of David); 9. Midge; 10. Dances; 11. Oars; 12. Scout; 13. Circe; 14. Six; 15. To deny; 16. The Barretts

QUIZ 188

1. Lionel Shriver; 2. E; 3. Pat Phoenix; 4. 'On his Blindness' by John Milton; 5. Jenny Frost; 6. Southern hemisphere; 7. Tearful; 8. Strength of earthquakes; 9. St David's; 10. Deer; 11. Pamplona; 12. Eye; 13. George Foreman; 14. Slow vehicle on track; 15. Choreographer; 16. The Great Plague

QUIZ 189

1. Bow Street Runner; 2. *The Wind in the Willows*; 3. Tokyo; 4. Salamis; 5. St Columba; 6. Hole in one; 7. Madame Tussaud's; 8. Oliver Postgate; 9. Order of the Thistle; 10. New Zealand; 11. Mother and Father; 12. Florence Nightingale; 13. A word and picture puzzle; 14. 'Break a leg!'; 15. Twelfth Man; 16. Ordnance Survey

QUIZ 190

1. Gloria; 2. H; 3. Geoffrey Chaucer; 4. Clara Bow; 5. Kiki; 6. *Adios*; 7. Jerome Robbins; 8. Trumpet; 9. Robert Menzies; 10. Sloth; 11. Multiply its length by its width; 12. Léo Delibes; 13. *David Copperfield*; 14. Small stream; 15. Scilly Isles; 16. My fault

QUIZ 191

1. Wilbur; 2. Beirut; 3. Massachusetts; 4. Berlin; 5. Junk; 6. Three;
7. Ceilidh; 8. Whisky; 9. Spores; 10. British Telecom; 11. Silo;
12. Carradine; 13. The Golden Tablet of Pharaoh Akhmenrah; 14. Coral
Sea; 15. Barbarians; 16. Montagues and Capulets

QUIZ 192

1. New Delhi; 2. Mr Wrong; 3. Greco-Roman; 4. Jules Rimet Trophy;
5. Four; 6. Suit; 7. Michael Heseltine; 8. Jump jet; 9. Empty orchestra;
10. Yeast; 11. 'Killing In The Name' (Rage Against the Machine);
12. Windmill; 13. *Gone With the Wind*; 14. Boxer; 15. Badminton;
16. Antarctica

QUIZ 193

1. The Prodigy; 2. Budge; 3. Lych gate; 4. Theodore Roosevelt; 5. Nenya
'The Ring of Water'; 6. 0.17; 7. Appearing or found everywhere;
8. Jane Tennison; 9. Brian Johnston; 10. Bread; 11. Two; 12. Veal;
13. Cadillac (Antoine de Cadillac); 14. Sir Ian Botham; 15. Negative;
16. Rob Roy

QUIZ 194

1. The Big Shots; 2. Leicester City; 3. Sea sickness; 4. John le Carré;
5. Eagle; 6. Bertie; 7. 'Wales forever'; 8. Gerald Ford; 9. Gaelic; 10. Both
teams sank; 11. ¼; 12. St Lawrence; 13. 0049; 14. Lemurs; 15. James I;
16. In fashion

QUIZ 195

1. Democrat; 2. The Penguin (in *Batman*); 3. Pink's; 4. 1938; 5. Bungalow;
6. Yang; 7. Classification of fingerprints; 8. President Harry Truman;
9. New growth; 10. Fruit; 11. Madonna's; 12. Escamillo; 13. Yellow;
14. The Simpsons'; 15. 'By the Sleepy Lagoon' (Eric Coates); 16. Those
who are friends

QUIZ 196

1. Victoria Wood; 2. Black Ferns; 3. Gingerbread Man; 4. Ford; 5. Beech;
6. USA (1935); 7. Wilfred Hyde-White; 8. Leon Trotsky; 9. *Digital Fortress*;
10. A large city, often the capital; 11. Ian Smith; 12. 12; 13. Master of
the Rolls; 14. William Gilbert; 15. William V; 16. Elizabeth I

QUIZ 197

1. The Cardinal's; 2. Steal; 3. Antonio Canova; 4. Break; 5. Brazil; 6. 1707;
7. Richard Wagner; 8. House of Representatives; 9. Vonetta Flowers
(bobsled, 2002); 10. The eleventh hour; 11. Hera; 12. Chihuahua;
13. 1900; 14. India; 15. M4; 16. Davy Jones

QUIZ 198

1. King Minos; 2. Gloucester; 3. Proscenium arch; 4. Woodrow Wilson;
5. 648; 6. 1906; 7. 9pm; 8. Robert Mitchum; 9. John Fletcher; 10. John
Brown's; 11. Bud Taste; 12. Pride; 13. Ernest Hemingway; 14. South
Africa; 15. A fungus; 16. Concealed ditch

QUIZ 199

1. *Little Men*; 2. An illegal immigrant koala; 3. *Matilda*; 4. Soles of the
feet; 5. Mir; 6. Northumberland; 7. George Stevenson; 8. London,
Midland and Scottish; 9. Mary Shelley; 10. Caber; 11. Emily Howard
(David Walliams); 12. The Althing in Iceland; 13. Deer; 14. Pudding-
stone; 15. Intentional; 16. Ryan Sidebottom

QUIZ 200

1. The cat; 2. Sir Walter Scott; 3. Mercury; 4. Benito Mussolini; 5. Kiln;
6. Dustman; 7. *The A Team*; 8. Zagreb; 9. Wessex; 10. Queen Victoria;
11. Three golden balls; 12. Rod Steiger; 13. General Medical Council;
14. Causton; 15. Hound of the Baskervilles; 16. Diaper

QUIZ 201

1. Queen of Sheba's; 2. Ali G's (Sacha Baron Cohen); 3. Mr Tinkles; 4. Brevity; 5. Hippocrates; 6. Dune; 7. Thomas Jefferson; 8. Robbie Williams; 9. Blair Waldorf; 10. RIDER; 11. Ernest Hemingway; 12. John Donne ('Meditation XVII'); 13. Sebastian Coe; 14. Magic (in *Harry Potter*); 15. Argentina; 16. Knot

QUIZ 202

1. 70; 2. Madonna; 3. Aquarius; 4. Australia; 5. Pussycat Dolls; 6. Blood; 7. John Barrowman; 8. Victor Hugo's; 9. Heraldry; 10. Anne Boleyn; 11. Basketball; 12. Cabot; 13. Crimea; 14. Immigration; 15. Captain Darling; 16. Rabbi

QUIZ 203

1. London School of Economics; 2. 20; 3. *The Da Vinci Code*; 4. Joshua Reynolds; 5. Counting; 6. Wimbledon; 7. Reticulated python; 8. Cherry; 9. Anarchy; 10. Cricket; 11. The ocean depths; 12. Eric Morecombe's; 13. Skull; 14. Two; 15. Boer War; 16. An early form of hand gun

QUIZ 204

1. Wensleydale; 2. 0°C; 3. Austria; 4. Anthony Horowitz; 5. Jacques Villeneuve; 6. 18; 7. Battle of Mons; 8. State Department; 9. Isle of Wight; 10. Tasmania; 11. Vincenzo Bellini; 12. Ceylon; 13. Donkey or ass; 14. Vera Lynn; 15. Ranch; 16. All have won *I'm a Celebrity...Get Me Out of Here!*

QUIZ 205

1. Anne of Cleves; 2. Bitzer; 3. 10cm (4in); 4. Suicide with a cyanide capsule; 5. Bloody Mary; 6. Plough; 7. London; 8. The Kiwis; 9. David Lloyd George; 10. Jacqueline Wilson; 11. The study of regional

geography; 12. Abominable Snowman; 13. David White; 14. Mexico;
15. Saunders; 16. Sir Paul McCartney

QUIZ 206

1. Little Miss Brainy; 2. 1000; 3. *Inn of the Sixth Happiness*; 4. Allsopp and
Spencer; 5. Ali Baba; 6. Acid; 7. William Joyce; 8. 1977; 9. Great Auk;
10. Discus thrower; 11. Dr Samuel Johnson's; 12. Chat; 13. John Webster;
14. Given as a favour; 15. Minor; 16. Renault Clio

QUIZ 207

1. The Grinch; 2. Bonn; 3. Charles Frazier's; 4. Robbie Williams';
5. Thomas Edward; 6. Rice Krispies; 7. Arroyo; 8. Pan; 9. Royston Vasey;
10. Horn; 11. *Ulysses*; 12. Timber; 13. Bread; 14. Broom; 15. Pacific Ocean;
16. *Romeo and Juliet*

QUIZ 208

1. Family trees; 2. Jellystone Park; 3. Strasbourg; 4. 1024; 5. Dove;
6. 90 minutes; 7. Genesis; 8. Czechoslovakia; 9. Stonehenge;
10. Amsterdam; 11. William Bligh; 12. Nephew; 13. Allan Border;
14. British Petroleum; 15. Third degree; 16. Wigan

QUIZ 209

1. Deciduous; 2. Fat Sam's; 3. James Blunt; 4. 1799; 5. Weaving; 6. Athos;
7. House of Commons; 8. Arthur Scargill; 9. Red; 10. Staffa; 11. Oliver;
12. 1897; 13. Barbados; 14. On a stone; 15. Reno; 16. No man

QUIZ 210

1. Dock leaves; 2. Beagle; 3. 1852; 4. Picardy; 5. Jellyfish; 6. *M*A*S*H*;
7. Dennis Hopper; 8. Dylan Thomas; 9. Hedgehog; 10. Wader; 11. 44th;
12. Bobby Fischer; 13. Brian Wilde; 14. 80 minutes; 15. Wanganui;
16. Taste

QUIZ 211

1. Fireman Sam; 2. William Wallace; 3. Organs of smell; 4. Iran; 5. Horse Guards Parade; 6. 1912; 7. Solomon; 8. 12; 9. Sting; 10. Painter; 11. Dunnet Head; 12. *Red Dwarf*; 13. New Street; 14. Richard; 15. Master; 16. Samuel Pepys

QUIZ 212

1. Diana Vickers; 2. Battle of Britain; 3. *Avatar*; 4. Captain Flint; 5. Ellipsis; 6. Beginning; 7. Elizabeth I; 8. *The Commitments*; 9. Cartilage; 10. Rocky the Rhode Island Red; 11. New Zealand; 12. Knot; 13. Clarinet; 14. Grass; 15. General Erwin Rommel; 16. Mickey Mouse (1932)

QUIZ 213

1. Grizabella; 2. Frankfurt; 3. Eminem; 4. South Australia; 5. None; 6. Eric Morecombe; 7. Knowing what to do or say; 8. Dundee United's; 9. Valentina Tereshkova; 10. Grand Cross of the Royal Victorian Order; 11. *Life of Pi*; 12. William II; 13. New York; 14. Katharine Hepburn and Spencer Tracy's; 15. White; 16. Ragetti

QUIZ 214

1. Late; 2. Boo-Boo Bear; 3. Hayley Mills; 4. May; 5. Ginger; 6. New Zealand; 7. X; 8. Henry IV; 9. Lumberjack; 10. Netiquette; 11. George Bush; 12. 2005; 13. Atlas Mountains; 14. Duck; 15. Portugal; 16. Ipswich Town's

QUIZ 215

1. Elizabeth I; 2. Moss; 3. Kate Thompson; 4. California; 5. Kenneth Branagh; 6. Venice; 7. Ronald Reagan; 8. Cheese; 9. Oxford; 10. Tracy Island; 11. Papa; 12. William Gladstone; 13. Tree; 14. Philosopher; 15. Hybrids; 16. Lady Gaga

QUIZ 216

1. Holly Golightly; 2. Sausage; 3. 12; 4. Ken Russell; 5. Louis XIV of France; 6. Sickle; 7. Slovakia; 8. Other birds; 9. Carr; 10. Caribbean Sea; 11. His then wife Sarah Lowndes; 12. Seven; 13. Orange; 14. Ben Elton; 15. Eight; 16. To exaggerate for effect

QUIZ 217

1. Man Friday; 2. Seve Ballesteros; 3. Denmark; 4. Rudolf Hess; 5. Dance; 6. Carnaby St; 7. *Doctor Zhivago*; 8. Maurice Jarre; 9. Asteroids; 10. Hundreds and thousands; 11. Judi Dench, Joan Plowright, Maggie Smith; 12. Brittany; 13. Dover Straits; 14. Bass; 15. Flixborough; 16. Billericay

QUIZ 218

1. Shia LaBeouf; 2. Great Dane; 3. Alan Shearer; 4. Ukulele; 5. 12; 6. Spy ring; 7. Saudi Arabia; 8. James S Fixx; 9. South Bank; 10. Pokemon; 11. 1942; 12. Inigo Jones; 13. George IV; 14. Dundee; 15. Mountain; 16. 104°F

QUIZ 219

1. Ireland; 2. Labradoodle; 3. Bristol Rovers; 4. David Furnish; 5. Passepartout; 6. The USA's; 7. Pickpocket; 8. James Fenimore Cooper; 9. Calcium; 10. Greendale; 11. Thermodynamic temperature; 12. Spanish; 13. Potomac; 14. Davenport; 15. Blog; 16. Colin Farrell

QUIZ 220

1. Cursor; 2. Talk show stardom (*Hacker Time*); 3. Rory Williams; 4. Italian dumplings; 5. Noughts and Crosses; 6. Flute; 7. *Love Story*; 8. Hainburg (Austria); 9. Middle Earth; 10. A woman's; 11. Paris; 12. Lace; 13. One; 14. Dodgem; 15. Venus Williams; 16. Video jockey

QUIZ 221

1. Inventing things; 2. 57; 3. US Masters; 4. Sidonie; 5. Caterpillar; 6. 31st July; 7. Jeb; 8. Women's Land Army; 9. Asunción; 10. Shifu; 11. *True Grit*; 12. Dance; 13. Willow; 14. London Marathon; 15. Five; 16. 'If' by Rudyard Kipling

QUIZ 222

1. Mrs Goggins; 2. Short sighted; 3. Clipper; 4. 'The young man' (in a poem in *Alice in Wonderland*); 5. Jumbo jet; 6. Abel Tasman; 7. 6th June 1944; 8. Harold Wilson; 9. Opponent; 10. Melvin Bragg's; 11. Botany; 12. Nürburgring; 13. Pink Floyd's; 14. Pevensey Bay; 15. Four; 16. Algeria, Morocco, Tunisia, Libya and Mauritania

QUIZ 223

1. Mother Goose; 2. *The Iron Man* by Ted Hughes; 3. Bishop; 4. Wolverine; 5. LANCE; 6. Vincent van Gogh; 7. Leona Lewis; 8. Andrew; 9. A drought; 10. Ruth Rendell; 11. Crampons; 12. Jerboa; 13. Graphite; 14. Bill Clinton; 15. Eight; 16. Alaska Standard Time

QUIZ 224

1. Kara Tointon; 2. *Alvin and the Chipmunks*; 3. Clay; 4. Alan Parker; 5. Extra-Sensory Perception; 6. Blackbeard; 7. Beirut; 8. 1841; 9. Michael Campbell; 10. Lewis Carroll; 11. Earl Spencer; 12. Barnes Wallis; 13. Salisbury; 14. Footwear; 15. Peter Nichols; 16. John Cazale

QUIZ 225

1. Little Miss Tiny; 2. Please Turn Over; 3. 540; 4. Spinner's End; 5. Feet; 6. Worcestershire; 7. Yasser Arafat; 8. Martin Amis'; 9. Cricket; 10. Volkswagen 'Beetle'; 11. Fernando Alonso; 12. Kerry Packer; 13. The Phoney War; 14. Leeds; 15. Chester; 16. Sexton Blake

QUIZ 226

1. The Empire; 2. Good; 3. 14; 4. James Blunt's; 5. *The Twits*; 6. Red-legged; 7. Coins; 8. Flower; 9. 24; 10. Nose; 11. Fabrics; 12. Weaver (loom); 13. Alexander Kerensky; 14. Elbow; 15. Water; 16. Jerry Lewis

QUIZ 227

1. The princess in 'The Frog Prince'; 2. Donny Osmond; 3. Legal; 4. Fungus; 5. Rosemary; 6. Henry; 7. Britt Ekland; 8. Stigma; 9. Jason Orange; 10. Sherpa Tenzing Norgay; 11. Michael Palin; 12. The Steppes; 13. Four; 14. Snake; 15. Gauteng; 16. Cambodia

QUIZ 228

1. Stroller; 2. Soft drink can; 3. Rowland Hill; 4. Giant sea monster; 5. Robin Knox-Johnston; 6. Muppet; 7. Leo; 8. Fiver's; 9. Buttercup; 10. A A Milne; 11. France and Spain; 12. Miss Lemon; 13. Trolley; 14. Sculptor; 15. Rwanda; 16. Anya Hindmarch

QUIZ 229

1. London; 2. Gromit's; 3. Pocahontas; 4. Jacques Tati; 5. 24; 6. Brett Lee; 7. Turkey; 8. Mars bar; 9. Sow; 10. John Stokes; 11. Addis Ababa; 12. George IV; 13. Forint; 14. Roddy Doyle; 15. Pylons; 16. The Hollies

QUIZ 230

1. A king; 2. Litter; 3. *Peer Gynt*; 4. England and France; 5. Dried fruit; 6. James Clavell; 7. Composer; 8. Gulf of Finland; 9. Mute swan; 10. Mediterranean Sea; 11. Nine; 12. Alabama; 13. Ox; 14. Lowestoft; 15. Chess; 16. Meryl Streep and Dustin Hoffman

QUIZ 231

1. Twelfth Night; 2. Joseph Haydn (No 92); 3. Baby eel; 4. Yellow River;
5. Mane; 6. Paul Young; 7. David Walliams; 8. Royal Variety Performance;
9. Henry V; 10. 'Nine ladies dancing'; 11. Coney; 12. Rembrandt;
13. Testing nerve gas; 14. Steve Backshall; 15. Firth of Forth; 16. 1919

QUIZ 232

1. Piglet; 2. Violoncello; 3. Crudités; 4. Marmara Sea; 5. Dog; 6. Drew
Barrymore's; 7. New York; 8. With good faith; 9. Endured;
10. Kookaburra; 11. Gene Kelly; 12. 1974; 13. Zambia; 14. Jude's;
15. Diving; 16. *The Beautiful Game*

QUIZ 233

1. William I; 2. Stockton to Darlington; 3. Elaine Paige; 4. Rowing;
5. Putting green; 6. Decathlon; 7. Mel Gibson; 8. Pumpkin pie; 9. Ballet;
10. Case; 11. Coal mines; 12. Empire; 13. Thomas Hardy; 14. Senegal;
15. Westminster Abbey; 16. *Manchester Guardian*

QUIZ 234

1. Central Intelligence Agency; 2. A Christmas pie; 3. All Souls; 4. Obelisk;
5. Sir Terry Pratchett; 6. Eyes; 7. Dalai Lama; 8. Tom Stoppard; 9. Trotters
Independent Traders; 10. Aquarium; 11. Duffy; 12. C (for *chaud*) and F
(for *froid*); 13. Dorothy Lamour; 14. Film studio; 15. Gerald Durrell;
16. Lawrence Durrell

QUIZ 235

1. Kaiser Chiefs; 2. Babe; 3. Czech; 4. Jimmy White; 5. Snake; 6. Dr Frasier
Crane's (*Frasier*); 7. Gum disease; 8. Rudolph Valentino; 9. Climbing plant;
10. The night sky; 11. Cello; 12. Squab; 13. Autocue; 14. Hampshire;
15. Troubadours; 16. Harry Truman

QUIZ 236

1. Zebra; 2. 1919; 3. Golden Gate; 4. Issac Pitman; 5. Wisdom teeth; 6. Appearing to be real or true; 7. Anthony Eden; 8. Ellis Island; 9. Mike Brearley; 10. Ewe; 11. Samuel Beckett; 12. Salem; 13. Rubeus Hagrid; 14. The Ancient Mariner (in S T Coleridge's poem); 15. Atlantic Ocean; 16. Lancashire

QUIZ 237

1. Nick Park; 2. Doc; 3. Catherine the Great; 4. *The Colour of Magic*; 5. The 'Gherkin'; 6. Roger Daltrey; 7. Four; 8. Bill Giles; 9. Hills; 10. Six; 11. Rabbit warren; 12. 15th; 13. Himalayas; 14. Lenny Bruce; 15. Chancellor of the Exchequer; 16. England

QUIZ 238

1. Mr Skinny; 2. Thames Estuary; 3. Turkey; 4. Lymeswold; 5. Shopping centre; 6. Churchill, Roosevelt, Stalin; 7. Law (honorary) 8. Beethoven's; 9. Blossom; 10. Computer languages; 11. Falsetto; 12. Stephen Daldry; 13. Trawler; 14. Straw; 15. The Joads; 16. £1.1m

QUIZ 239

1. Gretna Green; 2. Pidsley the Cat; 3. John Maynard Keynes; 4. Pig-like; 5. Violin; 6. Nine; 7. Julius Caesar; 8. 15th March; 9. Terracotta; 10. Garden; 11. Nigeria's; 12. Aspartame; 13. Barbie Doll; 14. Piano keys; 15. Birmingham; 16. 'Our thing'

QUIZ 240

1. Dogwarts; 2. Jonathan Swift; 3. Syria; 4. Dirk Bogarde; 5. Seven; 6. Fluffums; 7. Sandie Shaw; 8. Fat Tuesday; 9. 1948; 10. Pod; 11. Success; 12. David Beckham; 13. American Civil War; 14. At the state opening of Parliament; 15. Liverpool; 16. Cartoonist

QUIZ 241

1. Napoleon; 2. Douglas, Isle of Man; 3. Red Queen (in *Alice in Wonderland*); 4. Three; 5. Fanny Brice; 6. Sydney Smith; 7. Pod; 8. William Wordsworth; 9. Omega; 10. Greece; 11. Caligula; 12. Slade's; 13. Laurence Olivier; 14. Electric and Musical Industries; 15. A steeplejack; 16. Circumference

QUIZ 242

1. BAFTAs; 2. Butterfly; 3. Roger Moore; 4. Agent Orange; 5. Red Rum; 6. Paul Daniels; 7. Knickerbocker Glory; 8. Harold lloyd; 9. Julius Caesar; 10. The Pope; 11. Edith Wharton; 12. Head and hands; 13. Five; 14. The *Mary Rose*; 15. English Channel; 16. Honesty and uprightness

QUIZ 243

1. The plank; 2. Michael Flatley; 3. Zaire; 4. Cyrus the Great; 5. A *tandoor*; 6. 3pm; 7. W H Auden; 8. Apple; 9. Mars at night; 10. World Trade Center; 11. Yuri Gagarin; 12. Canaries; 13. Australia; 14. Words; 15. Heavy Goods Vehicle; 16. The aerial

QUIZ 244

1. Peter Sallis; 2. Collie; 3. Michael Fish in 1987; 4. Clergyman; 5. Edgar Rice Burroughs; 6. Wales'; 7. Venice; 8. Prosper Mérimée's; 9. Kitsch; 10. Daniel Craig; 11. Nobel Prize in Literature; 12. Greeks and Persians; 13. New Jersey; 14. Its shoes; 15. Plane crash, 1999; 16. Taipei 101

QUIZ 245

1. Athens; 2. Cinema; 3. Titania; 4. 1982; 5. Battle of Hastings; 6. Robert Burns; 7. *Martin Chuzzlewit*; 8. Jack Hobbs; 9. Smell; 10. Dandy; 11. Familiar; 12. Vinyl; 13. Olivia de Havilland; 14. Gibbon; 15. Nick Bracegirdle; 16. Michael Redgrave

QUIZ 246

1. Vulcan; 2. Princess Anne; 3. Canada; 4. His home, Giverny; 5. Loaf of bread; 6. *The China Syndrome*; 7. Tag Image File Format; 8. Dubbing; 9. *Prince Caspian*; 10. Yew; 11. Tchaikovsky's '1812 Overture'; 12. Crevasse; 13. None; 14. Chameleon; 15. Montreal; 16. *A Beautiful Mind*

QUIZ 247

1. Military Intelligence; 2. *Opera*; 3. 78; 4. Brian Close; 5. Crowds; 6. Chess; 7. Nero; 8. Hector Berlioz; 9. Herbivores; 10. Devonshire; 11. Crete; 12. Sir Humphry Davy; 13. Prince; 14. A duet; 15. Esau; 16. Zit

QUIZ 248

1. In May; 2. Squint; 3. Blind baking; 4. British Museum; 5. Two dogs and a cat; 6. *Charlotte's Web* by E B White; 7. She threw herself under the king's horse at the Derby; 8. *Birds of a Feather* (Pauline Quirke); 9. Percy Shelley; 10. Cheese; 11. Prince; 12. Beaver; 13. HMS *Dreadnought*; 14. Colorado beetle; 15. 'Indiana' Jones'; 16. Real

QUIZ 249

1. *Nation*; 2. *Pictionary*; 3. Muscovite; 4. Naive; 5. Ireland; 6. *Horrible Histories*; 7. Canteen; 8. Phil Collins; 9. Clement Atlee, who had become prime minister; 10. Tottenham Hotspur; 11. Ming; 12. Cleveland, Ohio; 13. Tony Greig; 14. Forked; 15. Anton Chekhov; 16. Dictionaries

QUIZ 250

1. Amber; 2. Andrea Levy's; 3. 10.8cm (4¼in); 4. *Fingal's Cave*; 5. Bird; 6. Shakin' Stevens; 7. Elizabeth I; 8. Draft Cards; 9. Lucian Freud; 10. Coins; 11. Murray Mint (ad slogan); 12. Snake; 13. Winston Churchill; 14. Australia; 15. Girls Aloud; 16. Blood pressure

QUIZ 251

1. Ennio Morricone; 2. Candyfloss; 3. Nadia Comaneci; 4. Belgian Congo;
5. Loo; 6. Iranian; 7. *Dramatis personae*; 8. Dennis Franz; 9. Roentgens;
10. Blackpool; 11. House Un-American Activities Committee;
12. Macedonia; 13. Flying boat; 14. Persia; 15. Victoria; 16. Hearth

QUIZ 252

1. Little boys; 2. Sistine Chapel; 3. Jeremy Irons; 4. Melanesia;
5. Kilometre; 6. Kemal Atatürk; 7. Flounder; 8. Noses; 9. Reform Club;
10. Belgium; 11. Maureen Connolly; 12. Diminuendo; 13. 14th;
14. Menuhin; 15. A constituency; 16. New Orleans

QUIZ 253

1. Wicked; 2. Greedy Graham; 3. Checks; 4. Four; 5. Paul Gauguin;
6. Retreat; 7. 39 (*The Thirty-Nine Steps*); 8. Connecticut; 9. 35th;
10. Thom Yorke; 11. Kind and generous; 12. *Macbeth*; 13. New Orleans;
14. Sandwiches; 15. Myanmar (Burma); 16. Ice cream

QUIZ 254

1. *The Rivals*; 2. Knesset; 3. Mayonnaise; 4. Fuzzypeg; 5. Corsage;
6. Because of his powerful drives; 7. Frome; 8. Bully-off; 9. The Ghost of
Christmas Yet to Come; 10. Richard III; 11. Huckleberry Finn; 12. *Kipps*;
13. Accelerated Freeze Drying; 14. White heather; 15. Middle ear;
16. Isle of Man

QUIZ 255

1. Patrick O'Brian; 2. Cats in *Cats*; 3. De-frocked; 4. Communist;
5. Pentecost; 6. The Grand Canal; 7. Very happy; 8. Solomon Islands;
9. Brazil; 10. *Pants*; 11. Sir Henry Wood; 12. Air-to-air missile; 13. Birds;
14. Boxing; 15. Matron Mama Morton; 16. Tupperware's

QUIZ 256

1. Hattifatteners; 2. A bull; 3. George Frederick Handel; 4. Charles Kingsley; 5. Belfast; 6. Beagle; 7. Madonna's; 8. Martin Luther; 9. Chinook; 10. Bookworm; 11. Skein; 12. V-1 flying bomb; 13. Lee Mead; 14. Pigeon post; 15. Copenhagen; 16. Salmon

QUIZ 257

1. Lara's; 2. Bram Stoker; 3. Barbary Macaque; 4. Hyde Park; 5. Tachograph; 6. Anton Ego; 7. Pre-Raphaelites; 8. High jump; 9. France; 10. Cat burglar; 11. Sir John Barbirolli; 12. Interflora's; 13. Munster; 14. Oslo; 15. Wabash; 16. Soft, flaky rock

QUIZ 258

1. Gustav Holst; 2. Standard Oil (enunciation of initials); 3. Toffee; 4. Aten; 5. Smörgasbord; 6. John Ridd; 7. 1829; 8. Tower of London; 9. Mohican; 10. Escudo; 11. Frankfurt; 12. Dax; 13. The Jolly Roger; 14. The Boxers; 15. Plucked; 16. *Punch*

QUIZ 259

1. Nancy Drew; 2. Manchester; 3. Blue; 4. Rabbit; 5. Cliff Richard's; 6. Spot the Dog's; 7. Cotton; 8. Prussia; 9. Brazil; 10. *Ben Hur*; 11. *Blue Peter*; 12. Longchamp; 13. America OnLine; 14. Toggles; 15. Jedi Master; 16. Father Brown

QUIZ 260

1. A type of dried fish; 2. Groynes; 3. Collie; 4. £1m ('The Million Pound Bank Note'); 5. Memory; 6. Atlantic City; 7. Lode; 8. Vienna; 9. Oysters; 10. Diva; 11. George; 12. Jules Verne; 13. Crystal set; 14. Comedian Vic Oliver; 15. Australia; 16. Del Boy in *Only Fools and Horses*

QUIZ 261

1. Mongrel; 2. 76 (in *The Music Man*); 3. Sir Robert Walpole; 4. *Cairo*;
5. Cat-o'-nine-tails; 6. A3; 7. Jane; 8. Cliffhanger; 9. Lionel Richie; 10. The
Mall; 11. *Othello*; 12. O; 13. The Queen; 14. 1615; 15. Finland; 16. Rod
Laver (1962, 1969)

QUIZ 262

1.Beethoven's; 2. Daisy; 3. Chivalry; 4. Rhode Island; 5. Underwood;
6. Merlin; 7. Lament; 8. Edinburgh; 9. Jacob and Wilhelm; 10. Leg;
11. Buff; 12. Czechoslovakia; 13. British Film Institute; 14. Harrogate;
15. BBC 3; 16. Noel Coward

QUIZ 263

1. Mr Plod; 2. 'The Good Ship Lollipop'; 3. Coldplay's; 4. Heifer;
5. Confucius; 6. The Polar Express; 7. Match officials; 8. Loggia;
9. Masters and servants in *Upstairs Downstairs*; 10. Chipmunks;
11. Denouement; 12. Memsahib; 13. Venice; 14. Indian Summer;
15. *Aida*; 16. Supertanker (Very Large Crude Carrier)

QUIZ 264

1. Werewolf; 2. Mr Topsy-Turvy; 3. Livia; 4. Swedish; 5. Bourse;
6. Springbok; 7. 102; 8. Greece; 9. Munich; 10. None; 11. L Frank Baum;
12. Zadok; 13. Hobo; 14. Dinosaur's; 15. Dancing; 16. Joyce

QUIZ 265

1. Transylvania; 2. Weaver; 3. Sue Cook and Nick Ross; 4. Land Rover;
5. Bird; 6. *Enigma*; 7. Nathan Astle; 8. 1845; 9. Warlock; 10. Alexandra
Burke ('Hallelujah'); 11. Alternative Investment Market; 12. Kirk Douglas';
13. Guy Crouchback; 14. Yoga; 15. Havana; 16. SuperTed

QUIZ 266

1. *Pinkalicious*; 2. Alice Cooper; 3. Alison Steadman; 4. *Pieds noirs*; 5. West; 6. Union Carbide; 7. Bones; 8. The sea; 9. *Prost*; 10. Six; 11. 'Ring-a-ring o'roses'; 12. Czechoslovakia; 13. USA; 14. 708; 15. Amateur; 16. Oriental gong

QUIZ 267

1. *Phantom of the Opera*; 2. Fly; 3. Porsche; 4. Lew Wallace; 5. The Three Musketeers; 6. National Assembly; 7. Franz Lehar; 8. Stuart Pearce; 9. Lobe; 10. David Dickinson; 11. John le Carré's; 12. *The Magnificent Seven Ride!*; 13. Moscow; 14. *Discovery*; 15. Pierre-Augustin Beaumarchais; 16. Pear shape

QUIZ 268

1. Sir Edwin Landseer; 2. Tail; 3. Glasshouse; 4. Jackie Collins; 5. *Julius Caesar*; 6. Love; 7. 37; 8. Inspector Lynley; 9. Wandering minstrel; 10. The Simpsons; 11. King Canute; 12. 'Pass slipped stitch over'; 13. George Brown; 14. Hot cross bun; 15. Sylvester Stallone; 16. Lamb of God

QUIZ 269

1. Maps; 2. Calf; 3. Saluki; 4. Cumberland sausage; 5. New Orleans; 6. The Animals; 7. Jelly babies; 8. *War Cry*; 9. Father Dougal McGuire; 10. Mouse; 11. Abattoir; 12. Renée Zellweger; 13. Toulon; 14. Belgium; 15. Oliver Cromwell; 16. Shooting

QUIZ 270

1. Chest of drawers; 2. Hans Holbein's; 3. 20 years; 4. Badminton Horse Trials; 5. *Octopussy*; 6. The Kingmaker; 7. Vegetarians; 8. Iris; 9. 77; 10. Sleigh bells; 11. Sunnis and Shiites; 12. Comic operetta; 13. Finnish; 14. Northumberland; 15. ITALY; 16. George V

QUIZ 271

1. H G Wells; 2. Ben & Jerry; 3. Doggerel; 4. Boston; 5. Emily Blunt; 6. Kid;
7. Berchtesgaden; 8. Parental guidance suggested; 9. William Blake's
'The Tiger'; 10. Propane; 11. Arsenal; 12. 'The Elephant Man';
13. Germany; 14. Chelsea; 15. Passport; 16. Praetorian Guard

QUIZ 272

1. Cauliflower; 2. Cubism; 3. Old Father Thames; 4. George Clooney;
5. Great-great-grandmother; 6. Clackmannanshire; 7. *The Old Curiosity
Shop*; 8. 15; 9. Daddy-long-legs; 10. Ten; 11. André Michelin;
12. Afrikaans; 13. 2005; 14. Ring; 15. Stun gun; 16. Grouse shooting
season

QUIZ 273

1. Richard III; 2. Brussels; 3. Wallaby; 4. Oulton Park; 5. Aloysius Parker;
6. Fencing; 7. Cupid; 8. Chalk; 9. Accountant; 10. Louis Blériot; 11. USA;
12. Charlton Heston; 13. Queen; 14. The Pentagon; 15. Sinn Fein;
16. David Campese

QUIZ 274

1. Madeline; 2. Duck; 3. Korean War; 4. Dublin; 5. Pup; 6. Mt St Helens;
7. +39; 8. Vincent van Gogh; 9. South Korea's; 10. *Test Match Special*;
11. Edie Falco; 12. Mediterranean and Atlantic; 13. Rivers; 14. William
Blake's; 15. Pass the buck; 16. A screaming skull

QUIZ 275

1. One o'clock; 2. Atomic bomb; 3. Carol Ann Duffy; 4. 4077th; 5. Cricket;
6. Madonna; 7. Beijing; 8. Supt Peter Boyd; 9. Stunt doubles; 10. Frog;
11. Mantilla; 12. Boxing; 13. Miranda; 14. To issue a challenge; 15. Hawaii;
16. Richard Wagner

QUIZ 276

1. Flock together; 2. Diaphragm; 3. John Wesley; 4. Paradise; 5. Merry-go-round; 6. 37°C; 7. Drums; 8. Flags; 9. Home run; 10. Chicago;
11. Nathanael West's; 12. Wall; 13. San Francisco; 14. Olive branch;
15. Technical knockout; 16. Whoopi Goldberg

QUIZ 277

1. Babylon; 2. Pours; 3. Beta; 4. *The Exorcist*; 5. German Shepherd;
6. Marge; 7. Two; 8. Sand or mud; 9. The sea; 10. Colony; 11. Sheep;
12. Samantha Stewart; 13. Graham Gooch; 14. Six; 15. Kernel; 16. Club foot

QUIZ 278

1. Nose; 2. 1993; 3. *Gulliver's Travels*; 4. Mark Waugh; 5. Navel;
6. Lutine Bell; 7. John C Reilly; 8. Uranus; 9. Claire Tomalin; 10. Backbone;
11. Quickstep; 12. Stag beetle; 13. *Digby*; 14. Bees; 15. Amis; 16. USS *Nautilus*

QUIZ 279

1. Marco Pierre White; 2. Sandals; 3. Keith Waterhouse; 4. Luton Town;
5. New Zealand; 6. David and Kenneth; 7. Scrum; 8. Eleanor of Aquitaine (Henry II and Louis VII); 9. Balletomane; 10. Benedictine; 11. Gosling;
12. Big end; 13. Frog-shaped; 14. Pollock; 15. Pie in the sky; 16. The number 10 to the power 100

QUIZ 280

1. Nutwood; 2. Patrick O'Brian; 3. Benazir Bhutto; 4. Japan; 5. Big Anthony; 6. Celtic and Glasgow Rangers; 7. Ballroom dance category;
8. Hammer; 9. Jonathan Demme; 10. KNEAD; 11. Pantone; 12. Falling;
13. Saturday; 14. James I; 15. Mobile phone; 16. Pablo Picasso

QUIZ 281

1. South Africa; 2. Pegasus; 3. Piglet; 4. Queen Boadicea; 5. Companion of Honour; 6. Male head of the household; 7. Betty Boothroyd; 8. Crazy Old Mother Goose; 9. High jump; 10. Perjury; 11. Hippopotamus; 12. Robert Herrick; 13. Frances de la Tour; 14. Marie Antoinette; 15. Engelbert Dollfuss; 16. GERMANY

QUIZ 282

1. A silly answer; 2. Fool's gold; 3. *Far from the Madding Crowd*; 4. Norman Hartnell; 5. Flannel; 6. Monza; 7. Nephew; 8. Norwich City; 9. Medicine man or witch doctor; 10. 12; 11. Eugénie; 12. Shirley Bassey; 13. James Cromwell; 14. One square at a time in any direction; 15. Jamaica; 16. Liza Minnelli

QUIZ 283

1. Pup; 2. Plastic; 3. Aspirin; 4. Horses; 5. Rotator; 6. Sierra Leone; 7. Fruit and veg; 8. Swine flu; 9. Criminal Investigation Department; 10. Harry Enfield; 11. Yodel; 12. 1920s; 13. Nostalgic; 14. Frontier; 15. Nunchuk; 16. Gareth Malone

QUIZ 284

1. 'The last day of September'; 2. Sedimentary; 3. Ned Sherrin; 4. Sancho Panza; 5. 'My son John'; 6. Philip Roth; 7. New Zealand; 8. James Goldsmith; 9. Discworld (Terry Pratchett); 10. César awards; 11. 'The Barefoot Contessa'; 12. Rudyard Kipling; 13. Chairman Mao Tse Tung's; 14. Sir John Betjeman; 15. Clough; 16. Ian Botham

QUIZ 285

1. King of the castle; 2. Calcium carbonate; 3. South Africa; 4. Baroness Thatcher of Kesteven; 5. Wilbur the pig; 6. West Ham's; 7. Lieutenant Gruber; 8. Héloïse; 9. Joe Orton; 10. Four; 11. Cat; 12. Lord Lucan; 13. W G Grace; 14. Lynn Barber's; 15. Vincent van Gogh; 16. Warren Buffett

QUIZ 286

1. Dublin; 2. Mike Denness; 3. Two; 4. Diamond shape; 5. Thomas Gainsborough; 6. Hobbits; 7. *Porridge*; 8. Villa Torlonia; 9. Molière's; 10. 80; 11. C J Cregg; 12. Stan Smith; 13. Lowering; 14. Jemaine Clement and Brett McKenzie; 15. Splint; 16. Barcelona's

QUIZ 287

1. Moggy Malone; 2. *Voyager 2*; 3. John Everett Millais; 4. The Saint; 5. Llama; 6. Three; 7. Hardening of the arteries; 8. Barmy Army; 9. Affleck; 10. A diamond ring; 11. Miller; 12. Sarajevo; 13. *Letter to Brezhnev*; 14. Albania; 15. STEAK; 16. E Nesbit

QUIZ 288

1. Basil Brush; 2. Alice in *Alice in Wonderland*; 3. Vocal sounds; 4. Victoria and Albert; 5. David Lloyd's; 6. Crook; 7. Tautology; 8. Coney Island; 9. Ford Anglia; 10. Jill; 11. Electric charge; 12. *Hamlet*; 13. Manchester; 14. Ellipsoid; 15. Polynesia; 16. The horse

QUIZ 289

1. Adam's; 2. Dame Laura Knight; 3. 960; 4. Hill; 5. Horse; 6. Under the skin; 7. Michael Keaton; 8. *The Voyage of the Dawn Treader*; 9. In the bath; 10. Waterproof hat; 11. Barcelona; 12. Thing; 13. Dow Jones; 14. Ethiopian; 15. Timon and Pumbaa; 16. John Clayton (Earl Greystoke)

QUIZ 290

1. And; 2. *The Nutcracker Suite*; 3. Julia Child; 4. 15th; 5. Anne; 6. Mister Wolf; 7. Snooker; 8. Paul Potts'; 9. 1919; 10. A big thaw; 11. Connie Fisher; 12. Steve Bucknor; 13. Small children; 14. In a Chinese restaurant; 15. Fred Flintstones'; 16. Charles II (1675)

QUIZ 291

1. Arabic numerals; 2. VW Beetle; 3. Alaska; 4. Spin doctor; 5. Oliver Twist; 6. Milly-Molly-Mandy; 7. White Persian; 8. 1694; 9. Giant Star Turtle; 10. Cricket; 11. 1933; 12. Romania; 13. Amy; 14. Wellington; 15. *A Single Man*; 16. Bart Simpson

QUIZ 292

1. *The Fantastic Mr Fox*; 2. 1997; 3. Bronchi; 4. Jude Fawley (in *Jude the Obscure*); 5. 72; 6. Stewart; 7. Tatum O'Neal; 8. Calcutta; 9. 12; 10. Little Jackie Paper; 11. Ireland; 12. Sexton Blake; 13. Terry Wogan's; 14. Fangs; 15. Georges Simenon; 16. Filly

QUIZ 293

1. Boat; 2. Paris; 3. Stephen Hawking; 4. Salt; 5. Norway; 6. John Tenniel; 7. Three; 8. Patrick Troughton; 9. Emily Brontë; 10. Dawn; 11. Richard Todd; 12. Absent without leave; 13. Debbie Reynolds; 14. Norfolk; 15. Two; 16. Napoleon Bonaparte

QUIZ 294

1. San Francisco's; 2. DINOSAUR; 3. 21; 4. Pendulum clock; 5. Sitting Bull; 6. Sheep; 7. Edward Rochester; 8. John Buchan; 9. Germaine Greer; 10. Curry; 11. Uncas; 12. Sir Trevor Brooking; 13. Black; 14. James Boswell; 15. A sheep; 16. Gyles Brandreth

QUIZ 295

1. John Keats; 2. Susan Boyle's (*I Dreamed A Dream*); 3. Uranus; 4. Poach; 5. Lady Catherine de Bourgh; 6. Big Nutbrown Hare; 7. Golf; 8. Ronald Reagan; 9. 36; 10. Colorado; 11. Sissy Spacek; 12. *Dombey and Son*; 13. Georges Pompidou; 14. Spines; 15. International Cricket Council; 16. Pogroms

QUIZ 296

1. Chopsticks; 2. George; 3. Robert Redford; 4. Australia; 5. Zadie Smith; 6. GRASSHOPPER; 7. James Corden and Ruth Jones; 8. Konstantin Chernenko; 9. Ten; 10. Venus; 11. Crystal Palace; 12. James J Corbett; 13. Nebuchadnezzar; 14. *The Crucible*; 15. Billy Mack; 16. The Wild Things in *Where the Wild Things Are*

QUIZ 297

1. *Charlie*; 2. Radium; 3. Six; 4. Aristophanes; 5. Damien Hirst's; 6. 1904; 7. Will Smith; 8. Ian Smith; 9. Tortoise; 10. England; 11. Mali; 12. Langley, Virginia; 13. Brazil (2002); 14. The Bronx; 15. Sailors; 16. Christopher Plummer's

QUIZ 298

1. Scarab; 2. 1000; 3. Silver; 4. Sari; 5. Banksy's; 6. Skeleton; 7. Schooner; 8. Roy Lichtenstein; 9. 24; 10. *Green Eggs and Ham*; 11. Richard Adams; 12. North Sea; 13. Richie McCaw; 14. Asparagus; 15. Four; 16. Two

QUIZ 299

1. 'The wipers'; 2. Crossing streets; 3. Lenin; 4. The Buggles'; 5. Pacific Ocean; 6. *A Clockwork Orange* (Anthony Burgess); 7. Bubbles; 8. TNT; 9. TRACTOR; 10. Three; 11. Tin; 12. Golf; 13. Virginia Woolf (*Who's Afraid of Virginia Woolf*); 14. Prague; 15. Copycat; 16. *Coronation Street*

QUIZ 300

1. Mog; 2. 20,736; 3. Arsenal; 4. An albatross; 5. Procol Harum; 6. Rome; 7. Brain; 8. Sofia; 9. San Francisco; 10. Baldrick in *Blackadder*; 11. Chimney sweep; 12. Hercules; 13. Veruca Salt; 14. *Dancing With the Stars*; 15. Knee; 16. George Gershwin

QUIZ 301

1. Farmer Grey; 2. The dark; 3. Basalt; 4. The logarithm; 5. Ferris Bueller in *Ferris Bueller's Day Off*; 6. Rake; 7. Vietnam; 8. John; 9. Venus; 10. Bronze; 11. Chester; 12. Lend money (in Shakespeare's *Merchant of Venice*); 13. *Spectator*; 14. *Doctors*; 15. 29; 16. Scarborough

QUIZ 302

1. Curd; 2. Cordelia; 3. Antifreeze; 4. Michelangelo Caravaggio; 5. Pete Sampras; 6. SCOTLAND; 7. Nightingale; 8. Dave Allen's; 9. Aviatrix; 10. Toga; 11. *The Girl with the Dragon Tattoo*; 12. Scotland; 13. David Copperfield; 14. Fe; 15. Durham; 16. South Africa

QUIZ 303

1. Pippi Longstocking; 2. Carbon dioxide; 3. Anthony Trollope; 4. Meg; 5. Glory; 6. The Orkneys; 7. 1997; 8. Jack Dee; 9. Raith Rovers; 10. Chariot race; 11. Althea Gibson (1957); 12. Wan; 13. San Francisco; 14. The Red Devils; 15. Dover; 16. Joachim von Ribbentrop

QUIZ 304

1. Mr Tickle; 2. Gordon Sumner; 3. Evelyn Waugh; 4. Gilbert and George; 5. Pasty; 6. Athens; 7. Bibulous; 8. Black Abbots; 9. Nintendo; 10. The Red Arrows; 11. *A Beautiful Mind*; 12. Scut; 13. Lerwick; 14. Rugby; 15. Alaska; 16. Flowers

QUIZ 305

1. *Madeline*; 2. Brenda Lee; 3. Yorkshire; 4. *A Streetcar Named Desire*; 5. Denmark and Sweden; 6. Fang; 7. Bowler; 8. Reinhard Heydrich; 9. Teenage Mutant Ninja Turtles; 10. Wild boar; 11. Laudrup; 12. Yitzhak Rabin; 13. Deerstalker; 14. Ewe; 15. Shearer; 16. Score

QUIZ 306

1. Christopher Marlowe; 2. Egypt; 3. Sophocles; 4. Rahul Dravid; 5. Sty;
6. Jack Dee; 7. Pacifier; 8. Roy Kinnear; 9. 100; 10. Quito; 11. 1936;
12. Sicily; 13. Sir Ben Kingsley; 14. Camille Saint-Saëns; 15. Refugees;
16. Jay Leno

QUIZ 307

1. Star; 2. Jim Trott; 3. France; 4. William Wordsworth; 5. 13th; 6. Pingu's;
7. Peter Carey; 8. Imperial Chemical Industries; 9. Two; 10. Ribs; 11. Asp;
12. St Ives; 13. New York; 14. Amelia Bedelia; 15. Mormon; 16. Surrey
(2000)

QUIZ 308

1. Squirrel; 2. Rolf Harris; 3. *Vanity Fair*; 4. Paul Bettany; 5. Camel;
6. Centre; 7. Egyptian pound; 8. Edo; 9. *Sex and the City*; 10. Skiing;
11. Ice hockey; 12. Charles Saatchi; 13. A house; 14. Krakow, Poland;
15. Flippers; 16. Rugby league

QUIZ 309

1. The Red King; 2. Ronald Searle; 3. Stephen Fry's; 4. Albania;
5. Germany (Bavaria); 6. Telephone; 7. Thurso; 8. The sinking of the
Titanic; 9. Doughboy; 10. Skylight; 11. Pat Richards; 12. Reading;
13. Lurch; 14. 'Whatever will be will be'; 15. Undercarriage; 16. 'Elegy
written in a Country Churchyard' (Thomas Gray)

QUIZ 310

1. Baby Bear's; 2. *Trail of the Pink Panther*; 3. Henri de Toulouse-Lautrec;
4. 18; 5. O Henry; 6. 64; 7. The Three Stooges; 8. Paul Newman; 9. Cantor;
10. Once; 11. Chocolate button; 12. 'Land of the Long White Cloud';
13. Jib; 14. *Aurora borealis*; 15. St Mary le Bow church; 16. Edinburgh

QUIZ 311

1. Nancy; 2. Three; 3. Dolly; 4. Jean's; 5. Baboon; 6. Hairdresser; 7. Pieter Bruegel the Elder; 8. Tasmania; 9. Uganda; 10. Temple; 11. France; 12. Sailing; 13. Caroline Aherne; 14. Thomas Chatterton; 15. Blue; 16. Steve McQueen

QUIZ 312

1. TEACHER; 2. John Masefield; 3. Tooth enamel; 4. Anil Kumble; 5. One minute; 6. Alan Bennett; 7. Hearing; 8. 'The Pharaohs'; 9. Stockard Channing; 10. Icicles; 11. India; 12. Antony Gormley; 13. Inhabitants of European stock; 14. Queens Park Rangers; 15. Brown; 16. Shakers

QUIZ 313

1. *Rebecca* (Daphne du Maurier); 2. Rainbow trout; 3. Spleen; 4. South Vietnam; 5. SIREN; 6. Shirley Eaton; 7. Table tennis; 8. Hitler diaries; 9. Susannah Constantine and Trinny Woodall; 10. Venom; 11. Illinois; 12. Colossus; 13. Pinkie; 14. The googly; 15. Studs Terkel's; 16. 'Some broth without any bread'

QUIZ 314

1. Wolf; 2. Gunther Grass; 3. Hobgoblin; 4. Gladys Knight, Elton John, Stevie Wonder; 5. Gymkhana; 6. Antony Worrall Thompson's; 7. Trimontaine; 8. Jean-Jacques Rousseau; 9. 1905; 10. Gemini; 11. Fontanelles; 12. *Animal Farm* (George Orwell); 13. Sir Alan Parker; 14. The purse; 15. Pupil; 16. The end